HOW TO
TRUMP THE ENEMY

Strategies for Trumping Your Leadership Opponents

MICHAEL KOULY

Trump[1] **(verb):** *"to surpass (something) by saying or doing something better."*

Synonyms: outshine, outclass, upstage, eclipse, outdo, outperform, beat, do/be better than.

[1] "Trump | Definition of Trump in English by Oxford Dictionaries." Oxford Dictionaries | English, Oxford Dictionaries, en.oxforddictionaries.com/definition/trump#h70034872932020.

First Edition

ISBN 978-0-9992181-4-3

To my

**Brother Joseph and his wife Rula, sisters
Kima and her husband Daniel, Soughit
and her husband Ibrahim and Sina, the
sacred heart of our family.**

CONTENTS

Part Two: Principles / Strategies Reference 157

ACKNOWLEDGMENTS

I would like to thank the following good people for their contributions to the creation of this book: Rajaa Barbari for being the first writing assistant to work on this book; Roy Sayegh for continuing much of the work with diligence; Dr. Susan Murray, Susan Simons, and Mary Shammas for their feedback on its content; Mary Shammas for designing the cover and formatting the book for publishing; Jo Lavender for editing the book.

Last but not least, I would like to acknowledge all those who resisted and opposed my leadership initiatives throughout my career. Sometimes you were right for resisting, and sometimes I was right for standing firm. In both cases, however, I genuinely learned a lot from you, and for that I am grateful.

WHY THIS BOOK

This book is for all individuals wishing to exercise purposeful leadership and bring about positive, beneficial change. It was written with people from various walks of life in mind, ranging from heads of state who exercise leadership on a national and international scale, to leaders in the corporate sector, to non-governmental organizations, and even to people bringing about purposeful change on a social and personal level. The aim is to help those who wish to exercise leadership, irrespective of the scale, understand and deal with any resistance they may face.

Resistance is an inevitable companion to purposeful change. It is therefore crucial that people who wish to exercise leadership understand who or what they are up against, and how they can go about dealing with resistance in the best possible way. The principles and strategies outlined in this book can be adapted to suit the context in which you are exercising leadership, whether it is governmental, corporate, organizational, social, or personal.

When you decide to exercise leadership and bring about purposeful change, you will face resistance at varying intensities. My hope is that you will turn to this book as your go-to reference when dealing with your opponents and enemies, whatever context you wish to exercise leadership in.

Good luck!

DEFINITIONS

Enemy[2] : "one that is antagonistic to another; especially: one seeking to injure, overthrow, or confound an opponent"

Opponent[3] : "one that takes an opposite position (as in a debate, contest, or conflict)"

---

[2] "Enemy." Merriam-Webster, Merriam-Webster, www.merriam-webster.com/dictionary/enemy.

[3] "Opponent." Merriam-Webster, Merriam-Webster, www.merriam-webster.com/dictionary/opponent

PREFACE

Honorable reader, if you think this book is thick and wordy, you are right. I do not want this fact to discourage you. It has been done intentionally, as I did not wish to compromise its detailed and comprehensive nature for the sake of shortening it. It is intended to be a reference book, much like a dictionary, that you can consult whenever you face any form of resistance discussed within its pages. I highly recommend you read it, take your time, and move at a pace you are comfortable with.

To make it easier to navigate, I have split the book into three parts.

The first part talks about how resistance is an inevitable by-product of exercising leadership and purposeful change (or any change for that matter). This part includes:

- An exploration of a crucial leadership element (purpose), and the key role it plays in understanding why you wish to exercise leadership, and why you tend to face resistance.

- A discussion on the driving forces behind your opponents' and enemies' resistance. This allows you to see the human side of your opponents, and understand the reasons behind their resistance.

- An outline of the various strategies and techniques you may adopt to prepare for and preempt against your opponents' attempts to put an end to your leadership initiative.

- A breakdown of the roles your opponents may play, and the intensity with which they may choose to resist you.

The second part presents you with 104 principles, strategies, and tactics that you may apply to deal with your opponents. You can examine them and adopt them at your own discretion to deal with whatever resistance you are facing.

The third part is a compilation of 36 different scenarios, combining roles and intensities, to offer you a general understanding of the different forms of resistance you will face. In addition to this, I have added a recommended set of principles/strategies that apply to each scenario.

Good luck in your journey and enjoy.

PART ONE

WHO
IS THE
ENEMY

INTRODUCTION

"When we dehumanise and demonise our opponents, we abandon the possibility of peacefully resolving our differences, and seek to justify violence against them"

– Nelson Mandela

When you hear the word **resistance**, does it remind you of any person in particular? Does this individual bring up any feelings?

When you read the word **competitor**, whom do you think of? Do you have any particular feelings about that person?

When you see the word **enemy**, is there someone who springs to mind? What emotions does this word evoke for you? Do you feel it has negative connotations, or do you feel prepared and equipped to deal with it?

Have you ever tried to introduce a change at home, at work, or in the community? And did it ever fail because you experienced resistance?

Can you think of examples of great leadership and/or change initiatives that failed because of resistance, opposition, or sabotage?

Is it likely that in the coming years, you will try to introduce ideas, initiatives, changes, etc., at home, at work, or in the community? If the answer is yes, would it be logical to assume that you might face resistance, whether this comes from your closest family members and friends, from your colleagues and bosses, from your constituents, or from total strangers? If you find yourself answering "yes", then are you ready to successfully deal with such resistance, opposition, competition, enemies, etc. to bring about the desired change? If you are not ready, then your initiative will most likely fail.

The leadership challenge of mobilizing your supporters, although an art in itself, is minuscule compared to the bigger leadership challenge of dealing with the inevitable resistance to an idea that seeks significant change. In other words, most leadership acts don't fail because of the shortage of good intentions, brilliant ideas, or originality. They fail because the people who are driving those ideas forward struggle to navigate the treacherous road of progress, which is littered with barriers of opposition. Just imagine how many great ideas have fallen through because their leaders lacked a proper understanding of how to deal with opposition, resistance, and enemies. More than anything, the mark of good leadership lies in the art of intelligently dealing with the opponents and enemies of progress and change.

Resistance is, unquestionably, found in great densities in the workplace, where tensions rise because of competition or rivalry.

- 85% of all employees, at all levels, experience conflict in the workplace, with 29% of them having to deal with conflict always, or at least frequently.

- Research shows that 60-80% of all difficulties in organizations stem from strained relationships between employees, not from deficits in an individual employee's skill or motivation.

- The typical manager spends 25-40% of his or her time dealing with workplace conflicts. That's 1-2 days of every work week.

- Change initiatives have a 70% failure rate, ending before

they have a chance to reach their goal. The two main causes behind this are employees resisting the change, and management not supporting the proposed change.

Facts, figures, and numbers, though at times daunting, are not just statistics. They are useful tools because they put things into perspective and allow us to see the bigger, global picture of the matter at hand. In the case of resistance, they help us explore and understand the reasons behind it, and allow us to see the impact it has on acts of purposeful leadership. Understanding the impact which resistance can have on our goals lets us better approach it.

Do the above statistics trigger anything in your mind? How do these figures make you feel? Do you find yourself recalling personal or professional instances related to the above statistics? Do they reflect things you recognize in your own life?

Some people may take a look at these statistics and conjure up a long list of incidents they have experienced or heard of, while others may shy away from the concept of conflict altogether. For many people, "enemy" is a loaded word, the mere utterance of which brings up a myriad of unpleasant feelings, thoughts, and memories. This is unsurprising; the word encompasses adversity and conflict, which most people seek to avoid in day-to-day life. If you find yourself uncomfortable with the concept of enmity and conflict, do not stop reading this book. It is geared towards demystifying the topic and presenting it in a constructive light.

Indeed, if your reaction is to step away from conflict, you may find that it's even more important to address both that feeling and the conflict itself. This is particularly true when you consider, as shown by the noted statistics, how many initiatives fail because of the resistance they meet, and the innovators are not equipped to deal with it. Some people spend so much time on trying to create a support network for their innovations and ideas that they forget to adequately consider the other side of the coin: resistance.

Whenever you choose to: 1) make a difference, 2) introduce a new groundbreaking idea or invention, or 3) implement a new policy that will make others' lives in the organization, company, or family better, you will encounter some people who disapprove of what you are doing. They will try to stop your idea from progressing. If you are not prepared to deal with those who oppose what you are trying to do you may find yourself asking "what went wrong?"

Let's reflect for a moment: can you think of a time when you proposed a new idea to your company, only to have your boss shoot down your idea? Or maybe you had a groundbreaking entrepreneurial concept, only to find that no one would fund your project? Did you ever try to introduce a policy only to find that most people decided it was unnecessary? Perhaps you wanted to start a new family routine, but your family just did not see the point of change? In all these instances, you have experienced some form of resistance.

Leadership can breed resistance in two main ways: it may create enemies, or it may create opponents. Although in our everyday vernacular we may use these terms interchangeably, there are major differences between the two.

When we talk about enemies, we refer to those who are seeking to get rid of you. They are aggressors who target you because of opposing views, which may span decades of conflict. Although your interventions are not affecting them — and sometimes they are not even part of the same system — they will still target you simply because they perceive your existence as a threat to their values, beliefs, agendas, interests, etc. For instance, terrorists target the civilians of a country because they view them as the enemy, regardless of what those civilians are doing and how little it may relate to the actions of the terrorist. The same goes for companies using illegal and malicious methods to destroy their competitors. The aggression does not stem from actions of the competitors, but from the attacking company trying to remove threats.

This distinction is important, and you should be wary of referring to anyone as an "enemy" simply because they do not want to get behind you on something. In addition, you should not take the statistics as a carte blanche to start calling people your "enemies" left and right. In this book, we will be touching, briefly, on this kind of relationship. However, we will focus primarily on the types of resistance you may face from your opponents (people who have a different opinion, stance, or point of view on what you are doing) when you exercise leadership and introduce significant change. The difference is that your opponents may no longer be your opponents when you give up on your initiative, while your enemies are not necessarily tied to your actions and, as such, may still target you regardless of what you are doing.

Therefore, in the context of this book, I want to take the term "opponent" and stretch it to its limits. I want to broaden its definition to include any person who resists a positive change. I will expand the term "opponents" from its most passive members all the way to the extreme, active members that we commonly label as enemies. In the end, even your most intense enemy is human, and you should not consider being inhumane with them. Some of them will only choose not to participate; others may decide to voice their concerns and issues with your proposed plans; others still might try to actively stop what you are doing (think protests and sit-ins). Others may even start their own initiatives aimed solely at countering yours and putting an end to it. Whatever the situation may be, forms of resistance will follow when you try to create a change that is not universally accepted: it is only natural.

Therefore, let us consider the word "opponent" as an umbrella term to include people who are competitors, resisters, antagonists, protesters, rivals, among others. Each of these terms has differing nuances spanning a broad spectrum. In no way is a protester to be equated to an antagonist. If someone is targeting you personally (antagonist), they are not the same as someone who simply cannot get behind what you are doing (protester). However, they are both resisting your initiative, and therefore you will need to deal with them accordingly. Each different opponent will require different tactics and techniques.

I feel I should also caution those who think that dealing with "opponents" utilizes a one-size-fits-all solution. This is certainly not the case. It is also important that empathy and compassion are at the core of your dealings with everyone, both supporters and resisters.

Bear in mind, this book does not want to suggest that you are surrounded by "opponents". That is far from the truth. What we are addressing is the fact that you are bound to experience at least some degree of resistance whenever you introduce a change, idea, intervention, or initiative, that challenges the status quo.

> "When we see others as the enemy, we risk becoming what we hate. When we oppress others, we end up oppressing ourselves. All of our humanity is dependent upon recognizing the humanity in others"
>
> – Desmond Tutu

If what you are doing is harming others, then you should stop and consider changing your outlook. When you lead, you must do so with the intention of benefiting others, not crossing legal and ethical boundaries for the sake of seeing your dreams come true. Leadership will breed resistance, but purposeful leadership breeds resistance that can be dealt with compassionately, humanely, and empathetically.

The purpose of this book is to highlight how important it is to understand the resistance that arises in response to purposeful change. The type and strength of resistance you experience will vary depending on how you are affecting the lives of those involved. If they feel that you are threatening their livelihood or future in the system (company, social group, organization, etc.) then they may be more aggressive in their resistance than someone who does not feel threatened.

Leadership Breeds Resistance

"I always felt like you had to be important to have enemies"

– John Green

We are more likely to associate opponents with individuals that are making a major difference, something worthy of the evening news or the morning papers. Opponents become more obvious when individuals exercise leadership. To be sure, anyone in a position of prominence is bound to have supporters and resisters, but have you ever asked yourself why that is the case? Is it because they are in a powerful position? Or could it be something else?

Let us take a look at some of the prominent leaders in history, such as Mahatma Mohandas Gandhi, Martin Luther King Jr., Rosa Parks, and Nelson Mandela. At first, it seems that they had opponents because they were leaders. This may be true on the surface, but it is worth exploring in more depth.

Each one of these famous historical leaders focused on bringing about change and challenged the status quo. Individuals who were comfortable with the status quo, especially those who were benefiting and thriving, were naturally inclined to resist and, even more, to actively work against the leader's change initiatives. At times, this meant resorting to tactics that threatened not only the growth of these leaders, but also their survival.

Mahatma Gandhi challenged an empire and sought independence and fair treatment for his fellow Indian citizens. He contested years of occupancy and helped gain independence for the India we see today. He proposed a change initiative that shook the system and, in turn, brought about significant change, and as soon as he did, the British empire attempted to stop his progress. He and his supporters were imprisoned multiple times, and some of his supporters were victims of violent, sometimes fatal, resistance. However, in the end, they prevailed, and we can see the results of

that lasting change today. Nonetheless, Gandhi's actions constantly bred resistance, later on even from his own kin. His belief in the
equality of all humans regardless of race and religion led others
within his own country to oppose him, ultimately leading to his
assassination.

Now let us consider Reverend Martin Luther King Jr. Almost
everyone who knows of him associates this historical leader with
the civil rights movement and the "I have a dream" speech. It was
the essence of this dream that spurred millions into action to bring
about equality for all citizens, regardless of their race. Although we
can all agree that the segregation which they were challenging was
illogical and inhumane, many of the individuals who were comfortable with the status quo did not see it this way. Naturally, these
opposing views brought about intense resistance, and indeed, Reverend Martin Luther King Jr. was the target of an assassination, and
many of those who supported the movement experienced abuse.

Yet another example can be found in Nelson Mandela. He saw
the injustice that was apartheid, and he decided, after many incidents of seeing the inhumanity of segregation, that enough was
enough. Therefore, he began his campaign to challenge the status
quo, and it bred years of turmoil, resulting in 27 years of imprison-
ment for him. In the end, he and those who followed him prevailed
despite the hardships they faced.

Many of you may be saying, "well, of course they faced resistance; they led a nationwide movement". Let us consider another
individual whose simple action spurred a major change in the civil
rights movement. Rosa Parks famously refused to give up her seat
on an Alabama bus. She decided that it was her right not to move
for another passenger based on the color of that passenger's skin.
This simple 'no' sparked a year-long strike that ended up changing
the laws segregating bus passengers based on race. It was a major
stepping stone towards a national movement that saw civil rights
restored to all citizens, and the end of segregation as a whole. It
started with one woman refusing to give up her seat.

From simple acts to more complex national movements, these historical leaders all had supporters and resisters. They all challenged the systems in the name of beneficial change and progress.

Although these leaders may be seen as special cases, the reality is that whenever an individual, whether in a position of power or not, attempts to make a change, anyone who does not benefit from it, or whose own interests are threatened by it, will do whatever they can to sabotage the change initiative. By extension, this makes this person a force that cannot be ignored.

Many of us favor consistency over the idea of change. Our "comfort zone" is a term often used to describe the familiar routine we have established, and we often dislike being removed from this zone, or having the routine disrupted.

Many people do enjoy and thrive on change, but there is a crucial detail in this; they usually instigate the change themselves.

Can you remember a time when your boss, your parents, or the leader of your political party decided that change needed to happen? Did it at any moment occur to you that they seemed to be making the wrong decision? Did that beneficial change come at your expense? How did you feel about it? You might not have considered yourself as an "opponent" to the change, but you might have expressed dislike for it. If this situation was then repeated, you might become more verbally active, and start to oppose the change. This is the position which many opponents find themselves in.

In this book, we will be exploring how purpose is a crucial first step in leadership and change, not to mention a key component in helping you to overcome your potential opponents. We will also explore and highlight some possible characteristics of the opponent's personality, and the driving forces behind their actions, to help you better understand how you can address their opposition.

In addition, we will explore the many ways in which you can

identify your opponents before they make a move against you. This will allow you to preempt their resistance. You will be prepared to take them on in a way which is constructive, regardless of who they are or why they oppose you.

To further increase your insight on the subject, I will address in detail the intensity with which they may oppose you, and the roles that your opponents may play in your life. I will also lay out some of the different categories which your opponents may fit into. This will give you an understanding of the shape an opponent may take, and will also get you one step closer to dealing with the less obvious ones.

At this stage, you should be more aware of what and who your opponents are. It is also important to contemplate how you can best control the damage they may do. With a detailed inspection and clearer understanding of their driving forces and resistance, dealing with them may be less intimidating than it appears on the surface.

This final insight into the world of opponents may seem less complex than described here. Possible simple approaches include "just cut them out" or "just crush them". There may be moments where this is exactly what you need to do, but most of the time, you will find yourself capable of taking a more constructive route to achieve your goals.

Let us journey together and address all the different aspects of dealing with opponents. It is time to look this topic straight in the "eye" and see it for what it really is. Let us lift the veil and demystify your opponents, so that we may pave the way for purposeful change that is intended to make the world better.

"You have Enemies? Good. That means you've stood up for something, sometime in your life"

– *Winston S. Churchill.*

CHAPTER 1

PURPOSE

Everything in life has a purpose. Nothing can continue to exist if it does not have a guiding principle. The ultimate purpose for all organisms and systems is to survive and grow. They are instinctively driven to ensure their survival, doing whatever is necessary to stay alive. However, humans generally want to find something greater than just surviving, and so we have a constant need to grow. To satisfy our drive towards growth, we each have an individual purpose to help guide our lives towards our greatest potential. After all, we do not want to remain static, but to progress and continue our journey. How do we do it? How do we grow? This is where our purpose is important. Our purpose guides our journey of survival and growth. It helps us to navigate through all the obstacles thrown in our way. But what is purpose?

> **"Where the willingness is great, the difficulties cannot be great"**
>
> – *Niccolò Machiavelli*

What Is Purpose?

We have all heard the word **purpose** before. Many of us have spent a lot of time searching for our purpose. But what does purpose actually mean? Put simply, your purpose is your WHY. It is why you are doing what you are doing. It is the reason behind all your actions.

Think of it as a compass. Purpose helps to guide you through every decision you make, and past every obstacle you meet along the way. It helps to keep you focused on what really matters. It has nothing to do with ambitions, passions, or goals, but having a clear understanding of your core purpose will allow you to set focused goals, have relevant ambitions, and experience passion for what you do, while clearly understanding why you are doing whatever it is that you are doing. As Nietzsche famously said,

"He who has a why to live for can bear almost any how"

Still confused? Well, if it helps, you can think of purpose as something you enjoy doing at the core of your being. Something that lets the stress fade away and, at the end of the day, makes you feel satisfied. Purpose gives you a sense of accomplishment. With a guiding principle for every decision you make, you will feel happier and more confident about what you are doing. Purpose gives meaning to every decision you make.

Elements Of Purpose

Purpose can also be defined as: putting your uniqueness in the service of others. This is the definition we will be focusing on. There are two elements in the definition to focus on that will help you understand purpose a bit better. The first is your **uniqueness.**

Uniqueness

Everything about you, from your DNA to your most recent experience, has led to a blend of qualities that make you unique. I want you to consider that you as an individual will never be repeated ever again. In other words, you are the only 'you' that will ever exist in this world. Whether you believe you are special or not, your genetic makeup, the people you have in your life, and the experiences you have gone through have molded you into the person you are today. As such, you have a unique blend of qualities that nobody else has. This uniqueness is a big part of your purpose. It has helped you figure out what you have to offer the world, and what you enjoy doing. To pinpoint your uniqueness, you will want to consider a few things.

Take some time to reflect on yourself, to think about your talents. This could include something you have been good at for as long as you can remember. For example, some people are naturally funny and have an almost innate talent when it comes to making people laugh. It could also be some talent which you have acquired over the years, one that you have spent countless hours learning and practicing. For instance, many of the world-renowned musicians began learning how to play an instrument at an early age, and with hours and years of practice, we now enjoy the symphonies of their lyrical or instrumental talents. Whether acquired or natural, your talents offer themselves up to your uniqueness.

Then there are those quirks we all have. The peculiarities and "weird" qualities that many people associate with you. These can be harder to pin down. They lie in the things you do that tend to be a bit out of the ordinary, but are a part of how you interact with the world around you. For instance, there are some individuals who have a knack for tidiness and organization. Their homes and office spaces always seem pristine and organized. To others, this may seem like odd or obsessive behavior, but this aspect of the individual adds to their uniqueness.

> "Always remember that you are absolutely unique. Just like everyone else"
>
> – Margaret Mead

There are also your preferences. As you go through your life, you start picking up preferences in all different areas; you form a plethora of things you like and things you dislike. These impact on which activities you enjoy, what types of books you read, which movies you watch, etc. All these add to your uniqueness.

When you mix all these elements together, you end up with what makes you unique. It cannot be expressed in a single phrase, but is dependent on all these things. When you figure your uniqueness out, you will be one step closer to understanding your purpose. However, there is a second element to add alongside your uniqueness to make the picture whole.

Service

> "The best way to find yourself is to lose yourself in the service of others"
>
> – Mahatma Gandhi

You must put your uniqueness in the service of others. Your purpose must add value to others. This ties back to the ultimate purpose of survival and growth. Purpose pushes society and yourself to growth. If what you offer does not help others in your group survive or grow, then you will find that you are wasting your time. Why? Because you will eventually stop growing and thriving.

This means that you will need to consider how you can apply your uniqueness so that it pushes you and those around you forward. We tend to find meaning in what we are doing if others are benefiting from our actions. Many people talk about finding pleasure, joy, and peace of mind when they apply themselves in a way that makes other people's lives better.

As an example of this: you discover that you have an ear for music, so you spend years honing your craft. Once you have established yourself as a musician, you decide to pass on your knowledge and skill by opening a music academy for underprivileged kids who have a knack for music. Their creativity feeds into yours, and everyone involved in the venture is able to learn and grow in a way which would have been impossible had you kept your talents to yourself.

How Your Purpose Complements Survival And Growth

Purpose helps you and the system(s) you are a part of survive and grow. When individuals in a given system offer up their unique contributions, the system will benefit from an array of talents and strengths in many different areas. This in turn will benefit the group as a whole, and the healthiness of the group then benefits the individuals who are contributing to it. Every individual's purpose works in harmony with this grand purpose, and the spread of talents allows continued growth. Ultimately, having a sense of purpose which allows you to contribute leads to a more focused, meaningful, and fulfilled life for all those involved.

Purpose is also important when dealing with obstacles. We have discussed how vehemently some of your opponents will try to ensure that what you are doing does not succeed. With a clear sense of your purpose and direction, you will be able to overcome these obstacles and propel the system, including yourself, forward.

Different Types Of Purpose

Existential Purpose

This is the purpose of your existence, and you can look at this as the core personal purpose in your life — what you choose to devote your life to.

Furthermore, each organization has an existential purpose. For instance, in your company, you may have one unifying purpose that you and others are working towards.

As you may recall, organizations and systems share the same grand purpose all organisms have — survival and growth. Therefore, a system (company, government, etc.) will also need a purpose that will help guide it towards surviving and growing. This purpose is separate from the individual, personal purposes of its constituents. Think about it as a unifying purpose for all involved – the reason behind the existence of the organization — its "WHY". Its constituents are all working in line with this unified organizational purpose. For instance, individuals in a company that builds medical devices may share the following purpose: to prolong and improve life by offering innovative and smart medical devices.

A company with a clear and communicated purpose can motivate its employees to make business-related decisions that are in line with its purpose. Understanding this purpose will give meaning to their decisions and, as such, they are more likely to work in a way which fulfills the purpose. This is particularly true if they believe that what they have to offer is meaningful. The same applies to any organization, whether it is a small shop, a government body, or even a multinational governing group, like the United Nations (UN).

Remember that purpose must add value, or else it needs to change. For example, a company's purpose may be to add value to their society by offering their clients top-notch, innovative products. Alternatively, a government might work towards improving the quality of life for its citizens and residents. Whatever these organizations do, it is intended to help make the lives of those around them easier and better.

To delve deeper into this concept, let us return to the medical device company's purpose. They add value to the society when they provide new and advanced medical devices that help save people's lives. If they lose sight of that purpose, the society will suffer, and it is quite possible that the survival of some individuals will be at stake. This, in turn, will put the company's survival and growth at stake.

We may experience resistance from the opponents of our existential purpose. This is usually because our existence triggers negative feelings in them, possibly because it threatens them or their way of life in some way. They therefore focus on stopping us. To continue the same analogy, the medical company might face opposition from rival companies, since sharing the market affects the survival and growth of competitors.

Purpose On The Role Level

Purpose also exists on a smaller scale, focused on the roles you play in your daily life. There are different roles that you play in life, depending on the system you are working in. For example, you might be a parent, employee, student, citizen, child, or partner. Every role you play will have a specific purpose assigned to it. You bring whatever unique qualities you have and contribute to these roles, benefiting others in the process. For instance, when you play the role of a parent, your purpose is to raise your child in the most functional and beneficial way. Your role as a citizen is to elevate your fellow citizens by giving back to your community. Your role as a soldier might be to protect your country against any threat.

If you lose sight of your purpose, this will affect how the system in which you are playing a role perceives you. If you fail to fulfill your purpose, you may find yourself being shunned by the system. In the end, your survival and growth will also be at stake.

Sometimes opponents target individuals not for their actions, but simply for the roles they play. For example, consider how a thief might view a policeman as their opponent, not for the policeman's actions, but for their role in the social system.

Task-Related Purpose

Finally, each initiative you introduce has a specific purpose that drives it. When you realize that something in the system is missing, you may decide to introduce an initiative that will focus on filling that gap. Whatever the situation is, there must be a reason behind introducing your initiative. Change just for the sake of change might do more harm than good, and constant change can trigger confusion and resistance.

You can think of this purpose as the reason behind the initiative, as the point of introducing it in the first place. It will complement the existential purpose (organizational or personal), and the fundamental purpose of survival and growth. This means that if you do not have a clear reason for doing something, you open yourself up to failure. You cannot introduce a successful initiative if you are guessing and improvising from beginning to end with no clear goal or sense of why your initiative is important.

It is here that your initiatives are most likely to create opponents. This means that the opposition is not personal, since your opponent's issue lies with what you are doing and not with who you are. It is usually because your initiative is affecting someone's life in a negative way, or because someone believes that it will. When you cause pain to, or potentially threaten, the livelihood of someone else, they will probably respond by trying to stop you, and they are unlikely to see that you are attempting to bring about improvements.

Fulfilling Your Purpose Breeds Resistance

Whenever you take a step towards fulfilling your purpose, at any level, you will encounter individuals with different perspectives. Some of them will support you. Some of them will be passive and not act with or against you. Others will be decidedly against you. It all depends on how invested they are in what you are doing. If they feel supported, they will, in turn, support you. On the other hand, if they feel threatened, they will oppose you. It can be a messy business, especially when you are actively introducing change.

As you probably know from personal experience, there are times when we all try to avoid change. Certainly, when we feel positive and enthusiastic, we may feel motivated by change, especially if it benefits us.

However, for many of us, there are moments when someone decides to spice things up, and we respond with: "What is s/he doing? Things are fine the way they are!" Consider how you might feel towards the instigator of change in this scenario. Consider whether your response is a direct result of how you anticipate the change affecting you. It's likely that changes you see as beneficial to your own growth produce positive responses, while changes which could have a negative impact on you provoke a strong, negative answer.

This is usually the case. When someone goes about fulfilling their purpose, it is going to disrupt and influence people's lives, and those people will inevitably respond depending on how they perceive the change. Do not be surprised to find people standing against you. Purposeful action breeds resistance, and it's important to anticipate that.

Understand Purpose, Understand The Opponent's Presence

Have you ever had a sudden moment when everything seemed so clear? Perhaps a time when your friends were upset with you and you had no idea why, until you looked back and had a "Eureka!" moment. Well, it is probably because you suddenly understood what you had done, and why they were upset. Perhaps you did something which had an ambiguous meaning. For example, you might have told everyone at the office that they should start exercising. You probably said that because you believed in the importance of exercise to maintain a healthy lifestyle. However, you still found some of your employees giving you some dirty looks or cold stares. Initially, you might feel shocked or confused – "Why are they acting this way?" Then you ask an employee and s/he tells you that some people thought you were commenting on their weight. "Eureka!"

"Eureka!" moments are a given when you have clarity of purpose. A clear purpose allows you to understand from the beginning how you are shaking the system. This will give you an idea of where you are going and how some people might be negatively affected by your interventions. You can therefore spend less time in conflict or trying to fathom the actions of those around you. Remember that a clear purpose is like a compass. It is always there to provide a heading, and helps you deal with the obstacles that lie in your path. Therefore, when the opponent comes knocking on your door, it will already be open, awaiting their arrival; you are expecting them.

Take this example: you are the founder of an eco-friendly construction company. You are able to persuade major companies to buy your environment-friendly materials. Adopting this initiative will affect the older, more traditional suppliers and they will most likely attempt to stop your company's growth. Having a clear purpose allows you to understand the system you are shaking. This will help you to recognize why you are making opponents, and will give you a better understanding of how ignoring them might be the end of your company.

Are You The Opponent?

Taking this theory a step further, we can see how a clear purpose will also help you to accurately predict who will be with your initiative and who will be against it. Whatever your purpose may be, understanding it helps you anticipate who will come knocking on your door. You can begin to prepare yourself to deal with them in the best and most compassionate way possible.

This has an obvious benefit: you know your supporters and your opponents. You have taken the first step by splitting them up. This lets you move forward and deal with your opposition in the best way possible.

Let us return to the example of suggesting exercise to the office. You now understand that some individuals will protest the exercise initiative. This allows you to identify who is with it and who is against it, and in turn allows you to tailor your strategy to fit your opponents. You might do this by explaining yourself to them individually, letting them know you care about their well-being and that your initiative is not a judgment of their weight. Their initial hostility may be dissolved by your approach, and your initiative will succeed with less opposition than if you had not anticipated their reaction.

In the example of the eco-friendly construction company, you will know who is likely to stand in your way. You can keep an eye on them, watch their attempts to oppose you, and respond swiftly and effectively to their opposition. Knowing in advance who is likely to resist you allows you to prepare yourself for their imminent protest and rebuttal of your initiative.

Petty Fights Are Just Distractions

Shaking the system will affect some people negatively, creating opponents, who will do what they can to stop you from furthering your initiative. At times, however, their battles will be nothing but a distraction. It is important, when considering your strategies, not to let these fights distract you. In the end, if you spend all your time caught up in endless battles, you may lose sight of what you set out to do in the first place.

Again, a clear purpose will act as your compass. It will point out to you when you are straying from your original course. Unfortunately, many people end up constantly trying to defend themselves. As such, they come to a standstill and forget what the purpose of their initiative was, focusing on defending it instead of pushing it forward. Make sure you fully understand your purpose, so that you can anticipate the opponent and constantly keep in mind why you set out to change the system in the first place. You do not want to spend all your time in conflict with your opponents; they should not be the focus of your initiative. Your goal is to move towards growth, not to clash with others. Keep your compass pointed north towards growth.

For instance, as the founder of this eco-friendly company, your purpose might be to make all our infrastructure safer for the environment. This should remain your primary concern. You should not engage in countless campaigns attempting to discredit your competing suppliers, even if that is what they are doing to you. Do not let such petty conflicts distract you. A coherent purpose makes sure you do not get lost and distracted.

Purpose Grants Me Courage

I know it can be difficult to imagine sitting on the sidelines and watching your opponents bring your progress to a halt. After all, experiencing obstacles can be quite discouraging. However, remember that purpose keeps you on course. It grants you the patience and courage to weather any storm. There will be times when an obstacle is too large, an opponent is too strong, or the first round ends in your defeat – it is just part of the process. Failure will happen. Do not let this discourage you. Instead, prepare yourself for such events. It helps to keep in mind your reasons for starting your initiative in the first place. This way you are less likely to be discouraged by anything your opponents throw at you.

With a clear purpose, you can constantly tell yourself: they may have won this round, but that does not mean the end of my initiative. When you are being pushed down, sometimes you will fall, and it may seem like you will never get back up. This is when you need to focus on your purpose even more. The certainty it grants you will open the door and give your discouragement the boot.

I Cannot Give Up!

Once you are back on your feet, you may realize that you have been taking one step forward and two steps back. Progress is not happening – indeed, you might actually be moving backwards. Instilled with the courage and patience provided by your purpose, you can stand firmly on the ground and push forward with all your might. As you heave and huff, you do not give up, no matter how tough it might seem. Why? Because you have a clear direction provided by your purpose, and the motivation to achieve your goals. You are certain that your initiative is to the benefit of the system's survival and growth.

Clarity of purpose inspires persistence. You will not only want to move forward, but you will persevere even if your opponents are setting you back a few steps in the process. After all, you need to be ready to weather the storm, and you already knew it was coming.

You saw the clouds from far away and have been preparing yourself to deal with it.

Remember to not get distracted. Remain courageous and patient, and, most importantly, stand your ground. This all starts with a clear purpose. Do not give up on your purpose. Keep pushing forward.

Are We Going Northwest Or Northeast?

"Change can be beautiful when we are brave enough to evolve with it, and change can be brutal if we fearfully resist"

– Bryant H. McGill

Your journey is likely to be riddled with detours. The path's trajectory will be more like a zig-zag than a straight line, meaning you are going to have to constantly rethink your strategies and implementations. The good news is that when you understand your purpose fully, you will become more flexible on how to go about fulfilling it. When you understand what really matters, you will have little difficulty adjusting the way in which you carry out your purpose. Bear in mind that there isn't just one correct way to fulfill your purpose.

Spend some time coming up with ways to fulfill your purpose. You will not get stuck if you have different options to choose from. If you find a couple of ways that are less bumpy than the rest, or you find that others have more twists and turns, you can pick and choose the best way to start. Of course, it is possible that after you start you may have to change trajectories, going Northeast instead of North.

Do not worry about steering off course. When you understand why you are moving forward, no obstacle will keep you from fulfilling your purpose. You may be forced to change course for a little while, but if you stay focused and don't give up on what really matters, you will find your way.

Purpose Leads To Choosing The Right Strategy

You are going to have to find ways to deal with your opponents. Ignoring them and pretending they are not there will rarely lead to a positive outcome. This means that you will need to make sure you choose the right strategy to deal with them. Having a clear understanding of your purpose will help you do that. Why is that the case? It is likely that when dealing with an opponent, you will have a multitude of options to choose from, but not every choice will benefit your purpose and/or the system. Fully understanding your purpose and the system you are working within allows you to assess which options do not interfere with them.

Even if you are committed to your purpose, choosing the wrong strategy may mean that you become distracted by petty conflicts and waste valuable time. As you set out to shake the system towards growth, you do not want to create stagnation or allow a faulty status quo to flourish. Purpose helps you choose the best strategies which will put a stop to your opponent's resistance, while allowing your initiative to progress.

For example: you find out that the organization standing in your way is a multinational construction company. Since you are supplying eco-friendly construction material, you know that they are losing clients to you. You have anticipated this resistance, but you find yourself unable to fight them. There is simply too much at risk, and dealing with them has an expensive price tag attached to it.

Instead of going to "war" with them, you will need to consider what alternative routes you could adopt to fulfill your purpose. You might try and find a way to align them with your purpose. You might propose that they allow you to supply them with some materials, and you will persuade your clients to hire their firm to take control of the project. This will have ensured that your purpose (making eco-friendly buildings) is fulfilled, while you have avoided outright conflict with this stronger, wealthier, and better-connected company.

There Seems To Be A Misunderstanding

You may have heard people say that they can explain a concept more easily if they understand it fully. The same applies to purpose. When you have an understanding of your purpose, it will allow you to clearly explain to others what it is that you intend to do and why. This includes the ability to explain it to your potential or existing opponents. Many pointless conflicts start because one or both sides have no comprehension of what the other side intends to do. You will need to have a well-thought out and clear understanding of your purpose before you try to explain it to anyone else.

Let's return to the office example from earlier in the chapter. When you decided to enact the rule that all employees must exercise, you will have anticipated that some of your employees would protest about it. Having a clear purpose will have helped you to identify who is for it and who is against it. This then allows you to address potential opponents and explain your reasoning before they get a chance to react. This will help clear the air and put some, if not all, of the potential protesters at ease, allowing you to avoid conflict before it has even begun.

It is quite possible that the reason others are against your initiative is because they do not really understand the purpose behind it. When you carefully explain it, the end result may surprise you. Potential opponents may stop frowning and being defensive. They may even smile and say something along the lines of, "Oh! That is actually a really good idea; thank you for clearing things up".

You need to think carefully about the best way to introduce your initiative; it is as important for the system and its constituents to understand the WHY behind your initiatives as it is for you.

They Can Have It

Of course, you cannot always win opponents over with an explanation of your purpose. You will still face resistance. So, what do you do next? Well, as always, a

"Give way to your opponent; thus will you gain the crown of victory"

– Ovid

coherent purpose makes things easier, allowing you to have lined up, in advance, all the best options to bring your purposeful change to life. Clarity about your purpose will let you know when you can bend and when you cannot bend to meet your opponents' demands.

If the opponent had their way, they might ask you to give up the whole initiative, but of course that is not what you want. The change you are introducing is not only necessary, but purposeful. There are bound to be certain things you cannot give up, no matter the resistance.

A clear purpose gives you the ability to negotiate and compromise, if necessary. It will guide you on whether a proposed compromise is either: 1) something you are able to let go of without any real impediment to your purpose, or 2) a situation in which you need to stand your ground and push forward in order for your initiative to remain purposeful. In addition, you will have a better understanding of your opponent and will have some sense of their version of 1 and 2 – what they will concede on, and what they cannot give up.

A clear purpose will offer you better comprehension of the whole situation and will give you an idea of what is negotiable and what is non-negotiable for all parties.

RECAP

With a clear purpose, your opponent will be less likely to win, because your purpose allows you to:

1. Understand the game from every angle.

2. Anticipate potential opponents and understand why they oppose you.

3. Identify who supports you and who is against you.

4. Remain focused and not fall victim to distractions.

5. Remain persistent in the face of any obstacle, setback, or opponent.

6. Adapt your plan and think of the strategy that is best suited to fulfilling your purpose.

7. Explain to others in detail what your plans are and avoid misunderstandings.

8. Know when to compromise.

9. Know what is negotiable and what is not.

Do Not Take It Personally!

Finally, purpose helps you to understand that, most of the time, it is not personal. This might sound odd; if you are passionate about something, how can someone opposing it not be personal? When you are fulfilling your purpose, you need to keep two things in mind.

"Don't take the wrong side of an argument just because your opponent has taken the right side"

– Baltasar Gracián

Firstly, you should not be focusing on conquering, overcoming, crushing, or defeating your opponent. Fulfilling your purpose really is just about your purpose and not about your opponent. It is not personal.

Secondly, it is rare for your opponent to have anything against you. Most of the time, their issues lie with your initiative and the disruption it is causing in their lives. If someone else was heading the initiative, they would have the same issues with him/her as they do with you. Their objections lie with what you are trying to do, not who you are. It is not personal.

In the end, a coherent purpose helps you understand that (most of the time) the source of the resistance — your opponent — has no ill-feelings towards you as a person. In addition, it helps to make sure that you are not personally focusing on your opponent. Instead, you are bringing your purposeful initiative to fruition. A business which is prepared to help it competitors benefit is far more likely to succeed than one which wastes its resources trying to fight all competition.

As we move forward, keep in mind the importance of purpose. Reap the benefits it offers you, use it to get a clear understanding of the system, and get ready to face some resistance. Do not be too quick to patronize or judge your opponent, but remember that they are another human being who happens to be at odds with your purposeful initiative. Remember that the issues are not personal. Be a wise leader, preempt, and understand the game from all angles. How do you do that? It starts with a coherent, all-inclusive, and cohesive purpose.

CHAPTER 2

UNDERSTANDING YOUR OPPONENT

"There is some good in the worst of us and some evil in the best of us. When we discover this, we are less prone to hate our enemies"

– Rev. Martin Luther King Jr.

Consider this situation. You decide to undertake a purposeful initiative: you want to increase customer care in all the restaurant chains under your supervision. You spend many months attempting to keep the company as it is while still fulfilling your purpose.

Alas, there is no solution that will maintain the status quo without compromising on your purpose. It seems that you have to shut down one of your smaller departments; it simply is not relevant to what you are trying to do and has nothing to offer, becoming more of a liability than an asset. The problem is that this small department houses 20 employees.

You go ahead and give your employees the required month's notice, and they respond by protesting. Of course, you anticipated this — people are not going to react favorably to losing their jobs. You have disrupted the system, and some people in your vicinity are drawing the short straw. Some may go on to organize protests, sit-ins, and other demonstrations that will slow down your progress, and could prove quite a nuisance to the company. You then ask yourself, "why are they wasting their time on protests, instead of taking my offer to help them find another job?"

Before you attempt to deal with your opponents, you must consider the root cause of their resistance.

Your strategies may not be working, and the reason for this could be that you do not have all the information you need. When you get to know your opponents, you will discover their perspectives, thoughts, and the driving forces that lead them to resist. As you gather more information, you will be better equipped to deal with their resistance.

You have already taken the first step towards answering that pesky question: "Why are they doing this to me?" The "me" in this case refers to your leadership initiative. With a clear understanding of your purpose, you were able to guess why you might have opponents – they are losing their jobs. However, getting a real understanding of what drives your opponent will give you the whole picture. You will be able to answer with almost 100% certainty why they wish to resist your initiative.

In the last chapter, we compared purpose to a compass. Now, think of understanding your opponents as representations of the landmarks you need to navigate. If you add these landmarks to a map, the map better represents the difficulties which your compass needs to guide you through. A blank map makes a compass of minimal use, but once it has been filled in, you will be able to work out how to navigate the obstacles you face.

Your opponent is another human being, and like you, they have their own life. They too face stresses, have worries, and have people in their lives that depend on them. You may be surprised to know that what drives them in life is not so different from what drives you. To start off, you at least share one main purpose in life.

We Share The Same Grand Purpose

The opponent, like us all, has the same grand purpose: to survive and grow. They are not some evil entity, but human beings who also strive to ensure their own survival and growth. Everything they do must be in line with this purpose.

If something does not benefit their survival and growth, they are likely to consider better options, even if to you it may seem selfish at times. Securing your own well-being is only natural. We each have our own obligations, responsibilities, and commitments to uphold; it is part of our survival and growth. Your opponent, like everyone else, is driven to find what benefits them. If they are faced with a threat, they may start to look for opportunities elsewhere. If they cannot do that (e.g. leave a paying job), they will stand their ground and defend what is theirs.

In either case, your initiative is not only disrupting the system, but it is also disrupting lives. Someone may be losing everything, while you are gaining everything. Are you still surprised when they become your opponent?

Let us reverse the situation: you are one of the 20 employees that will lose their jobs, and the proposed initiative is negatively affecting you. You face uncertainty, and the good which is being proposed does not seem to outweigh the negatives in front of you. It is quite likely that, put in this situation, you would reject the change too. Initiatives are almost always disruptive, and the individuals who face this disruption may reject it.

Why do they not see the bigger picture? Well, what we as individuals stand to gain out of a system-shaking initiative is not equally beneficial. What benefits one person does not necessarily benefit another. This means that when you are changing things around, some people are likely to be impacted negatively, and they will object to this. In the end, if you are threatening the survival of an organism, they will fight back. Similarly, if you stop another person's growth, they will fight back. It is only natural.

How hard they fight depends on how much you are affecting their lives. The more the change is harming their interests, responsibilities, etc., the more passionate they are about stopping your progress.

To see clearly how their lives may be affected, let us take a closer look at the other driving forces in their lives.

Oh! So That Is What Is Bothering You?

As you look deeper into what drives a person's reactions, you will get a better sense of why someone might oppose you. To begin with, you will need to ask yourself what it is that your initiative is robbing them of. The obvious answer is that you are negatively affecting their lives, but to get the full picture, you need to widen your view and see what exactly is at stake for these individuals. You will have to look beyond their protests to find the root cause of their resistance. In addition, you will need to stop viewing them as the opponent before you try and take an in-depth look at what is driving them, what is at the root of their resistance.

You may be surprised at what you uncover when you take the time to get to know the opponent. It will probably be one of those "Eureka!" moments we talked about in the previous chapter.

Are You Talking To Me?

We all have voices in our minds, we all have influencing thoughts that drive our decisions. We are often unaware of these, to the point that the idea of "voices" may seem ridiculous. We do not always realize that they are pushing and pulling us, influencing our decisions subconsciously.

However, these voices play such an important role in our decision-making process that we ought to be aware of them. If you want to truly understand the opponent, you will need to take into account the voices in his/her life.

Within this category, we have multiple dimensions. These all combine to give us an idea of the construct of a person's character. Voices influence a wide range, from our fears to our hopes and dreams. There are 9 total dimensions and we will be referring to them as the 9-Ds. Let us take a closer look at each one.

1-D: Hungers

We all have hungers. When our stomach gurgles, it sends us a signal that it is time to open the fridge and get something delicious to eat. However, this is not the type of hunger that concerns us here. Our use of the term refers to hunger of the psychological variety.

As you may already know, each individual has a number of basic psychological needs. A famous illustration of this comes from Maslow's "hierarchy of needs." In this hierarchy, he discusses how we have a need to survive (e.g. food, drink, shelter, safety), and then needs to belong, to feel loved and appreciated by others, and to be the best that we can be: to grow to our best potential.

Unfortunately, in this imperfect world, we are bound to have some unfulfilled needs. For instance, individuals have an innate need to belong. Even at a young age, many people face difficulties with becoming part of a group: they may not be social enough, they may be picked on for their quirks and uniqueness, they may not have clicked with anyone yet, etc. Therefore, they have been unable to fulfill their innate need to belong, and so this need takes precedence in later interactions.

Whenever our needs are unmet, we strive harder to try and fulfill them. However, if for some time we do not find what we need, the desire develops into a hunger. To compensate, we may seek to satisfy it in dysfunctional ways. For instance, someone who has a deficiency in the need to belong may join a gang and get involved in gang activities, simply because they are afraid of being kicked out of the group and finding themselves isolated again.

It is possible for any of us to have an unmet need, and it does not have to be fulfilled in an extreme or immoral way. Some people may simply maintain shallow relationships, afraid to show their uniqueness for fear of being rejected. Can you think of a moment in your life when you felt an unsatisfied yearning? What did you do in that situation?

As this theory applies to you, it also applies to your opponent. S/he may have some unmet needs that have developed into hungers. It does not matter if the choices they are making are just offering temporary relief. As soon as you introduce an initiative that somehow robs them of this relief, you can be certain they are not going to sit there and "starve". They are going to do all they can to reverse the situation. They were comfortable, even if only temporarily. This is not hard to relate to; we all strive to avoid the pain of constantly experiencing yearnings which we cannot satisfy.

Ask yourself:

1.   What is my opponent's comfort zone? How am I pushing them out of it?

2.   What possible unmet needs do they have? How am I robbing them of fulfilling these needs?

2-D: Insecurities

Fear can be a strong motivator. Many of us will go to great lengths to ensure the feeling goes away. We have an instinct to survive, and we are wired to run away or freeze when we are confronted with our fears. We dislike dealing with them, despite being advised countless times to "face your fears." We cling to our comfort zones because they are fear-free. We all have things we are afraid of, but we do not worry too much about them as soon as we are comfortable.

Our fears present themselves in our insecurities. If your opponent's insecurities begin to surface because of something you are doing, they are bound to stand in your way. They want their comfort zone back, and they want the status quo to remain. Any change, no matter how positive, is unwelcome at this point. If their greatest fears are about to come true, they will do anything in their power to stop this from happening. All they will think about is, "I need to end this initiative". This is why fear can be such a strong motivator.

It is important that you understand what your opponent's insecurities are. This is not only because you will better understand why they are resisting you, but also because we tend to magnify issues when it comes to our fears. If you understand your opponent, you can make sure you explain your initiative while addressing their insecurities. The last thing you want is an opponent who invents scenarios that are simply not true, which is exactly what they may do if you make them insecure.

3-D: World Views

We all have different beliefs about how the world works. There are certain rules and laws that we believe in, and we use these to guide us through different scenarios. These rules may be passed down from our parents, guardians, or cultures, or established from our own experiences on this earth. Each time we are faced with a situation that relates to our world views, we consult our "rule books" and make decisions accordingly.

Our world views are difficult to change. A belief system becomes deeply ingrained because it has either proven to be of use, or because the person who passed it down is very important to the believer. Either way, it is difficult to change one's belief system.

Your opponents will have world views that go against what you are doing. This means that you may want to take some time to figure out what their world views are. This will help clarify why they are opposing you. It may be that your initiative is not disrupting their lives, but is forcing them to go against their belief system, which may be reason enough for them to try and stop you.

For instance, some people believe manager positions are masculine roles. You come along and propose an initiative which will diversify the company roles, and as a result many women will occupy managerial roles. If one of your male employees holds a world view that managers should be men, they will be less willing to accept your initiative; they may even refuse to work for a woman. In this day and age, many people believe that this should no longer be an issue. Nonetheless, your employee may not do his work, and might attempt to stop your initiative from succeeding.

Whatever your opponent's belief system is, it is of paramount importance that you understand it, or else you will spend hours wondering why they are opposing an initiative, especially if their world views are not commonly held ones.

4-D: Values

Values categorize what we hold in high regard. The term might refer to objects, relationships, people, or systems. Whenever we value something, we give it importance. Our values also help us establish our moral compass, guiding us on what is right and what is wrong. As with our world views, our values may be passed down by our societies, cultures, guardians, or parents. They are hard to change, and they become part of who we are. When we want to make decisions, our value system is right there, suggesting options and giving us directions.

For example, "stealing is wrong" is an almost universal value that we all share; "friendship", on the other hand, is a more individualized value. To some people, the importance of friendship might not be so high up the list. "Love your opponents" is definitely not a universal value. Some people think it is important to love everyone, including one's opponents, while others think it is an impossible and ridiculous suggestion.

Your opponents will have an issue with you the moment you threaten their values. It is possible that what you are choosing to do is wrong in their eyes. Since we do not all hold universal values, it is important that you understand what your opponent's individual values are. Subsequently, you will be better able to see how your initiative(s) may be threatening their values.

For example, in the United States, given the recent shootings, many people have been calling for stricter gun control. On one side of the fence, individuals feel that you cannot stop American citizens from purchasing firearms, especially since the "right to bear arms" is part of the Constitution. On the protesters' side, an initiative that maintains relaxed gun control threatens their values — to prevent unnecessary killings — and also threatens the survival of the protesters, their families, and many others. The value systems are clashing, and initiatives that support one side threaten the value system of the other.

5-D: Hopes and Dreams

We all have dreams. Many of us have dreamed of pursuing a specific career or making extraordinary achievements since we were children. These dreams become such an integral part of our lives that, whatever they may be, we tend to structure our lives around them. We focus on trying to fulfill what has, for a long time, been a key life goal (e.g. to be president, to increase economic status, to offer the upcoming generation better education, etc.).

For example, we hear a lot of stories about children who want to become astronauts, presidents, teachers, artists, doctors, and so on. In general, their parents and guardians encourage their dreams, so much so that "you can do anything you put your mind to" is the common mantra.

However, as many people come to realize, life and unexpected circumstances tend to change things around. We may either discover that we are unable to reach our dreams, or we lose interest and come up with new dreams. In either case, dreams will come and go.

What if you had settled on a specific dream and were only a few steps away from achieving it? How would you feel as you drew nearer? Hopeful? Excited? Encouraged? It is likely you would feel positive.

Now imagine if someone came along and shattered your dream like glass, taking away any possibility of achieving it. How would you feel then? Angry? Sad? Spiteful? You probably would not be feeling positive if your dream suddenly seemed impossible. Your opponent, like any of us, has dreams and hopes for the future. If your initiative threatens their dreams, they are unlikely to brush it off as another disappointment and move on with their lives.

Consider your opponent, as you would yourself, and think about their dreams and hopes. This is such an important dimension. You cannot understand why your opponent is resisting you if you do not take this into account. When you take the time to consider this dimension, you will realize that you are standing in the way of something that is bigger than the both of you. In addition, you will not be able to come up with a way to appease your opponent unless you can think of ways which allow them to maintain their hopes and dreams.

For instance, let's imagine a person who had a dream of studying in the top medical school in the world. She received her acceptance letter and she was over the moon; she could finally fulfill her lifelong dream. Given her socioeconomic status, she could only attend this expensive medical school if offered a full scholarship. However, a new initiative to cut scholarship funding for international students meant that she could not attend. She was furious, feeling that her hopes and dreams for a better future had been washed down the drain. She then decided to use her widely-followed vlog to start an online protest campaign. It quickly gained traction and the medical school faced backlash. Apologizing, it promised to look into ways to gather funding for future scholarships.

A bleak future is one that no one wants. Do not be surprised if your opponent gives it all they have got to get their dreams back on track.

6-D: Experiences

Our experiences play a considerable role in our lives. They are part of what makes us who we are. Each individual will go through different experiences in life and will come out of them differently, depending on how they look at the experience and how they fared during it.

Most of us use our experiences as reference points: we learn what we like and what we dislike from trying things out. We learn what mistakes to avoid repeating, we learn how to act around different people based on our experiences, and we learn what to expect from life.

Your opponent is bound to oppose you if what you are doing has led to a bad result in the past. No matter what you say or how hard you try, if your initiative is related to any of their previous bad experiences, they are most likely going to say: "No, thank you!" and do all they can to make sure you fail. This is tricky; you cannot possibly pick the right strategy to deal with this individual if you have no clue what they have gone through. In other words, you must understand what the person has experienced to get an understanding of why they are opposing you.

For instance, imagine that when you inform your subordinates about your initiative, you promise that it will benefit them as much as it will benefit you. You use charts, projections, and statistics to back up your claims. After you have finished speaking, you ask for their support.

Most of them agree, but one of your department managers stands up and tells you that you are offering them nothing but a "sales pitch", and that you will not deliver on your promises. If you were to ask him why he thinks that (trying to understand his perspective and thoughts on the matter), he might say that all his bosses in the past have done the same thing. They have made guarantees and asked for support and commitment, only to fall through on their promises, leaving their managers and others to struggle without the promised benefits.

It is also possible to learn from the others' experiences. This is one of our human strengths: we only need to witness or hear about an experience to learn from it. Bear in mind that your opponent may not use his/her own experiences as a reference point, but rather the experiences of someone they know or have heard about.

For instance, if your colleague's sister-in-law was recently fired from her marketing job after a new cost-effective initiative was passed, then your colleague will most likely be first in line to oppose a similar initiative you are planning to introduce. She may have learned from her relative's situation that such initiatives run the older generation out, making way for the younger generation to take over.

You really need to take the time to understand what your opponents have been through if you want to be able to deal with them, especially if their experiences dictate their decisions. Remember, you cannot just ignore people who are passionate about ending your progress. You must treat them like fellow humans if you want to find the best strategy for everyone.

You may need to ask them about their experiences:

1. What similar scenario are you referring to?

2. What did other people promise you and fail to follow through on?

This way you will be better prepared to address their concerns by outlining the ways in which your initiative is different. However, do not expect them to agree with you even after you have understood their story. There may be other dimensions at work.

7-D: Loyalties

We thrive in groups. It is a part of our evolution. Our survival and growth are best ensured when we are part of a group. As such, people have others who they depend on, and those who depend on them — they have people who they are loyal to. Every time they act, they make sure that it not only benefits them, but also the others in their extended network. For example, a manager may be responsible for a dozen employees. Whenever they decide to act, they make sure that their actions benefit not only them, but their employees as well.

We all have individuals who we are loyal to. Unless they give us a reason to doubt them, we are unlikely to replace and abandon them for others. They expect us to take care of them, and vice versa. We have certain obligations towards them. Most of the time, we strive to fulfill these responsibilities. For example, a parent is expected to care for their child. They have a responsibility towards them, and so they will do all they can to make sure they are provided for.

Once we decide to understand our opponents, we must also be willing to understand where their loyalties lie. It seems obvious that if you want them to support you, you should not go about questioning their loyalties, or, worse, asking them to abandon them.

This is a vital yet tricky concept that you need to pay attention to if you are introducing a change, as this dimension involves more than one person. There is a larger network behind them that you need to think about. If you want to get to know your opponent, you will also need to consider their extended network, since your initiative will affect them indirectly. If your initiative asks your opponent to side with you, while foregoing others, they are more likely to oppose you. Most people do not easily give up their loyalties, and you do not want to be involved with someone who does.

You would not want someone on your team if they could easily jump to the other side. Having to constantly keep an eye on them and repeatedly ask yourself if you trust them is a drain on your resources and energies.

So, look at where their loyalties lie: do they have many people that depend on them? If so, how does your initiative affect those people? This will give you a general idea of what your initiative is doing to this person's life, which will bring you one step closer to understanding why they are resisting you.

You must also investigate how easily they give up their loyalties. If someone is overly excited to join you, you may need to ask yourself: did they have any loyalties? If yes, why did they abandon them so quickly? Here are a few potential reasons:

- They may have thought it through and found that your initiative is really the one they want to side with.

- They may have attempted to talk their network into getting behind you, but the others were not interested.

- It is possible that this person's idea of loyalty is weak, and they jump from one opportunity to another.

- Worst of all, they may still be loyal to others and working to ruin your initiative from within.

You will need to consider this dimension if you want to fully understand your opponent.

8-D: Commitments

In addition to loyalties, we have promises that we have made to others. We all have commitments we want to keep. These can range from simple promises, like buying your child the newest action figure, to complex promises, like always putting food on the table for your family no matter what happens. The concept of commitments is one which you may be familiar with from your own life. Most of us hate breaking promises. The feeling of guilt and possibly shame for not delivering what we promised is horrible.

Of course, if we do not care about something, we are less likely to have negative feelings when we do not deliver. The opposite is also true: if we care deeply about upholding a promise, our failure to do so will probably ruin our day, week, or even month. The importance we place on a commitment will determine the magnitude of our feelings.

Now imagine that the reason you could not follow through with a commitment was because someone stood in your way. You might not feel guilt or shame, but you would probably experience anger towards the person who stopped you from fulfilling your promise. This is exactly how your opponent could react if your initiative prevents them from following through with their commitments.

Ask yourself: Whose life is my initiative disrupting? What commitments do they have?

It is important that you gauge how significant commitments might be to your opponents. If they do not give their commitments any importance, or if they do not have any major commitments, then they are probably not going to be your opponents (of course, if another dimension is being transgressed, they might still be).

However, it is equally important that you see how they deal with their commitments.

Ask yourself:

1. Do they make and break commitments easily?

2. Do they shy away from commitments?

As these individuals may side with your initiative, you need to make sure that if they commit to something, they will follow through. They will still be your opponents if they make major commitments and do not follow through. In the end, you do not want someone on your side who hinders the progress of your initiative. This can ruin your plans.

9-D: Agendas

"What is on the agenda today?" We all have our priorities and we have lists of goals we wish to address and achieve. Whether it relates to government, a company, a family, or our personal lives, every action plan we make addresses specific priorities. Even your initiative has an agenda — there is something you wish to achieve.

The moment you decide to go ahead with your initiative, you must realize that your agenda will not suit all the people involved. Regardless of why they have set their particular agendas, your opponents will not let you trivialize their goals. Just as the decisions you make must be in accordance with your priorities, your opponent will seek to follow their agenda.

For example, imagine you are at corporate meeting, and you are setting down the plan for next quarter. One of the first questions someone will ask is "What is on the agenda for today?" Naturally, some people will believe that one item is more important than the other. This is where the quiet conference room turns into a chaos of incoherent suggestions. Every person, or group, is addressing whatever is on their own agenda. If you succeed in introducing whatever items you want, the others in the conference room who had a different agenda could become your opponents.

It is important not only to understand that there are experiences, lessons, and internal driving forces that make up every individual (including yourself). It is essential to realize how these forces help individuals to prioritize their lives and initiatives. Consider your opponent from all angles, understanding that you and they are the same, that you each have your own driving forces, and that you are each unique human beings. Keep this in mind, and you will be less surprised and upset by their resistance – you will be better prepared to deal with it.

Now that you have a clearer understanding of what drives your opponent,

Ask yourself:

1. Why is my opponent opposing my initiative?

2. Which of your opponent's dimensions is your initiative affecting?

It Is Just A Matter Of Perspective

We have covered the driving forces behind your opponents' lives. Now it is time to step away from this perspective and take a look at yourself through their eyes. It is time to try and understand how the opponents see you and your

"Everyone sees what you appear to be, few experience what you really are"

– Niccolò Machiavelli

initiative. It is difficult to imagine everything your opponent is going through, but at least you can consider all of the above 9-Ds to understand how the opponent might view the situation.

This will help you to better understand your opponent's resistance. It has the added advantage that you will feel less inclined to blame them for not understanding the benefit behind your initiative.

I Can Only See You Through My Eyes

It seems almost too obvious to say that your opponent sees you through their eyes. It is not an opinion, but a fact. This points to how natural it is for them not to view you the way you view yourself. As soon as your opponent is introduced to your initiative, they will see it in a different light to the one you see it in. They will not necessarily see it for the wonderful opportunity it is. Instead, it may seem like their worst nightmare.

As such, they will label you as the opponent, the person who is disrupting their lives. It is not their fault: anyone in their position would look at your initiative with negative feelings. They only see what you are doing to them, and not how your initiative opens up the system to continue its survival and growth. In other words, they are focused on their own lives and 9-Ds.

Intentions... Suuure.

Unfortunately, your opponent will judge you: it is inevitable. The question is, how will they judge you? Your opponents do not have access to your thoughts, which means they cannot gauge what your true intentions are. Instead, they will focus on your actions. They will judge you based on how your initiative is affecting them. In the event that what you are doing, or plan to do, is turning their lives upside down, unfortunately, they are likely to reach a negative verdict. Even if your intention is to help everyone, they will not see that. They are solely focused on how you are negatively affecting their lives.

When you want to understand your opponent, it is important that you bear this in mind. You should not be too quick to defend your intentions, if in reality the issue lies with their lack of information. After all, you have probably heard the famous proverb, "the road to hell is paved with good intentions." That is how they see it. Regardless of what you intend to do, they feel that they are not benefiting, and that they have drawn the short straw.

In Another Life, We Could Have Been Friends

It is not personal. Remember that confusing statement? Let us take a look at it again. Your opponent may be judging you, and may be harboring an intense dislike for you, but the truth is that they have an issue with your initiative. It is not a personal attack on you. If for some reason you decide to stop, they might actually become your friends.

Your opponent does not care about you. This statement is not to suggest that they are heartless, but to remind you that their eyes are on your initiative and how it is changing their life. The more you seem to rob them of their current lifestyle, the more passionate they become about putting an end to your initiative. However, even at this point, it is not personal.

For example:

- John promised to pay for his daughter's wedding, but with the recent pay cuts to his department, he will have to reconsider.

- Jenny was the only working member of the family and a cost-cutting initiative has led to her losing her job. The company currently pays for her children's education at the top school in the country. Now she is struggling to figure out which school to move her kids to.

- Sarah had her eyes on the VP position in a start-up. With the reassignment, she became manager at an international branch. Although this was a promotion, the new initiative has crushed her dreams and limited her rise in the company.

Focus on understanding how your initiative is impacting others. When you try to take their side, you may realize that a person has actually lost so much more than you might have originally thought.

I Have No Clue What You Are Doing

It is hard to adopt another person's perspective, especially if you do not see eye to eye. Even if you share similar views, it can be challenging to understand how they see the world without asking them. After all, you are not them, and you do not see life the same way. You do not have the exact same values, beliefs, dreams, insecurities, etc., as anyone else. Your uniqueness limits how much you can really see things from another person's perspective.

Now your opponent, who is not on the same page, will be affected by your initiative differently. Once it seems to them that you are winning, and they are losing, it can become difficult for them to put everything aside and take some time to see things from your perspective: they are not you.

I Do Not Feel Your Pain

You have been working tirelessly to get a flawed system back on its feet. You have a clear purpose in mind, and have crafted many ways to introduce your initiative(s). You realize that it is a risky business, but you know that what will come to pass will be wonderful. Everyone involved will thrive and lead an elevated life.

On the other hand, you also see the approaching waves of resistance. You have been able to identify who will side with you, who will side against you, and who will be a spectator. You are now ready to take on the opponent, but you cannot help wondering: Can they not see that I am working hard to make the system better? Why are they so oblivious to my pains? Why can they not be patient and share in what is to come?

As we have already mentioned, it is difficult for anyone, let alone your opponent, to understand your perspective. One reason for this is that they cannot feel your pains, and they do not have your hopes and dreams. You may have the same dimensions, but that does not mean that they are focused on the same thing, or that they are pushing in the same direction. They do not have a backstage pass to your life and your mind, just as you do not have one to theirs. Therefore, do not be so surprised if all your sacrifices remain unseen and unappreciated by your opponent.

It is important for you to know that it is not that they are relishing in your pain, but that they simply do not see and feel the same way as you do. Again, they are not you and cannot possibly understand you if you do not explain yourself, just as you cannot not understand them unless you invite them to explain themselves.

RECAP

All this emphasizes how important it is that you remember that you and your opponents have different perspectives. They are being pushed and pulled by different forces, which are unique to them. They have their own 9-Ds (hungers, insecurities, world views, values, hopes and dreams, experiences, loyalties, commitments, and agendas).

They do not have anything against you, but rather what you are doing. It would not be far-fetched to say that they do not know who you really are, and you do not know who they really are. Avoid making assumptions about them, but instead ask and listen to the answers. This will allow you to better understand your opponents' forces, and give you specifics about how they see you and your initiative.

When you are leading, bear in mind that your opponent is the same as you. Each one of you sees through a different lens. Sometimes the wisest and simplest thing to do is ask.

You and I Are The Same, Really

"When you begin to see that the enemy is suffering, that is the beginning of insight"

– Thich Nhat Hanh

You have been reading this chapter to try to get a better grasp of what drives the opponent, and to get a better understanding of the real cause behind their resistance. This complements what you learned from having a clear purpose. Let us briefly go over why.

- A clear purpose helps you gain insight into the system, so that you understand the whole game. You know who your initiative affects, who will support you, and who will oppose you.

- Then you take it a step further and investigate the opponent.

   o   You understand what drives your opponent and why they are resisting you.

   o   You take a "big picture" view and understand that everyone has a unique perspective on life.

   o   You ask them about their opinions to get a better understanding of how they see the world.

Hello, My Fellow Human

This understanding allows you to see the person on the other side of the battlefield not as an entity to destroy, but a person who you need to deal with. The point is that if you start looking at the driving forces behind people's decisions, you will be able to humanize them. They will not have horns and red tails. Instead, they will be another average Joe or Jane, who simply does not benefit from what you are doing.

Therefore, as soon as you take steps to understand your opponents, you realize that you are all the same. You each have your own driving forces, but do not see eye to eye on your initiatives.

You and your opponent both have commitments to uphold. However, with your new initiative, you are able to follow through with them, while your opponent is stripped of the resources needed to follow through with his/hers.

These understandings will help you to appreciate the difficulties that events and situations present to people occupying the same system. You will no longer see the current battle as with or against. Instead, you will begin to see it as a natural part of life. You will realize that each individual is not out to get the other, but rather is fighting to survive and grow, the main driving forces we all share.

You will see that everyone is holding on to the system that most benefits their dimensions (including at times their survival and growth). It may be that neither of you want to be on the battlefield, but have been brought there by circumstance. You may want to consider ways to deal with this conflict off the battlefield. "Understanding your opponent" will give you a chance to see if, at least, you have that in common.

Let's Not Fight

Almost no one likes to fight. It is a waste of time, and people end up losing more than they gain. At the very least, people lose precious time that they could have spent elsewhere (e.g. with family, clients, or friends). When you grasp this concept, you may second-guess your opponent's intentions. You may realize, after spending some time understanding them, that neither of you want to take this to the battlefield.

Your opponent also stands to lose time and energy in "battling". The good news is that you have taken the first step and understood what drives us all, which leaves you in a better position to understand whether the fight is necessary.

Bear in mind, your initiative is still negatively affecting the opponent. Therefore, they may be less likely to admit that they want to avoid conflict, and you should make sure that it is not a battle of the wills. They are already on the defensive, and may find it harder to look for common ground.

Let's Win Together

In the previous chapter, we discussed the power of a clear purpose and how it can help us understand what really matters. This will then let us know what we can negotiate and where we can compromise. If they can, your opponents will want to reach a win-win situation. After all, if you can both get out of the situation as victors, that would be ideal. In fact, is your initiative not geared towards benefiting the system and its constituents?

If there is a situation where you and your opponent can both ensure your 9-Ds are met, and you each get what you want, then it's probably the best option. When you see your opponent for the person s/he is, you may be able to spend time collaborating and finding creative solutions to avoid conflict, with the end goal of keeping both your opponent's and your survival and growth intact.

Help Me Help You

Pick the Right Strategy

Your opponent can be your greatest source of information. Let your opponent help you help them. Taking some time to understand your opponent will allow you to choose the right strategies for dealing with them. This may be by fighting, or you may be able to find ways to negotiate instead.

Here is a possible scenario: both of you want to resolve the issue, and you will probably both want to save face, so you choose to go down the negotiation route. However, you cannot possibly offer up a deal if you have no idea who your opponent is. Maybe they want something you cannot give, or maybe you are offering them something (other than your initiative) that they simply do not want. It will be hard to come to an agreement. To change this, you must understand your opponent. When all the options are clear, it becomes easier to find a compromise and negotiate a mutually acceptable deal.

If you choose the battlefield, understanding who you are dealing with is essential to coming up with an effective strategy, tailored to their needs. As you can imagine, there is no one-size-fits-all solution to dealing with the opponent. The good news is that you have already got two secret weapons at your disposal: 1) your purpose, and 2) knowing what drives people's decisions.

Fill in the Gaps

Imagine you spent many nights coming up with a system-shaking initiative, only to find that there are gaps you have not addressed. Not the ideal situation you were hoping for? Your opponent is your go-to person for such an event.

"Love your enemies, for they tell you your faults"

– *Benjamin Franklin*

Why? It's likely that your supporters and friends are not going to be the best advisers. This is because, sharing your excitement or seeking to be supportive, they may have the same blind spots you have. Your opponents, on the other hand, will be so focused on ending your initiative that they will make it their mission to look for the weak spots.

Sometimes, your initiative might be nearly perfect, in which case your opponent is just "barking up the wrong tree". At other times, your initiative may indeed have some gaps that you have been blind to. When this happens, you will want to consider taking some extra time with the opponent to address all the gaps they point out to you.

How? Well, as soon as you get to know the core issues your opponent has with you, you can prod a bit deeper and see what exactly they think is wrong with your initiative. This could be some aspect of your initiative, its delivery, or how it is executed. If it is a weak spot, something you can address, then let your opponent express themselves and listen carefully.

You cannot know if there is an actual threat to the structure of your foundations unless you take the time to know your opponents and see things from their perspectives.

Find Creative Solutions

It is wise to try and ensure that you go for the route which causes the least destruction. As we mentioned earlier, you and your opponent would both like a win-win situation to minimize conflicts. However, neither of you can bend completely to the will of the other, otherwise you are not negotiating – you are yielding. This is where having a coherent purpose and an understanding of your opponent must be combined.

- Without the clarity of your purpose, your initiative is lost and chaotic. You do not have a sense of direction, and your initiative will have no strong foundation to stand on. Eventually, when you set out to implement it, it will not come to pass.

- Without understanding your opponents and their driving forces, you cannot negotiate with them. You will be unable to tailor a strategy if you do not understand their core issues. This will threaten your initiative, and ultimately it will probably lead to failure.

Once you bring these two concepts together, you are more likely to look beyond a win-lose situation. You will know what you want to achieve, and what core issues your opponent has with your initiative. You can sit down with the opponent and consider what solution(s) would work for both of you.

Give You A Warning

What if you could stop some of your opponents from becoming your opponents? This is obviously ideal, rather than having to waste hours trying to put an end to their resistance. The information you have gathered about your opponent may help you figure out how to make sure they do not rise up against you. Preemptive strategies are dependent on the individuals you are dealing with, their positions, allies, and the impact your initiative is creating. These things are all important to consider, and will help you figure out how to be one step ahead of your opponents.

There are many strategies you can use to preempt and prepare for your opponents. In the next chapter, we will take an in-depth look at some of these preemptive strategies.

CHAPTER 3

GETTING READY

Welcome To Reality

Did you know that the rate of fatal accidents in the aviation industry is now at an all-time low? Indeed, in 2017, the rate of fatal accidents was around 1 accident per every 16.67 million flights! Did you also know that in the healthcare industry, more than 200,000 avoidable deaths happen in hospitals every year? That is the equivalent of more than 1 jumbo jet crashing every day! So, what is the difference between the two? According to Matthew Syed in his book, *Black Box Thinking*, it lies in how these two industries deal with failure. The aviation industry invests time and money in learning from their mistakes, while the medical industry chalks these failures up to a by-product of the industry, without investigating the reasons behind them.

Mistakes, miscalculations, and poor preparation lead to failures and incur costs, costs which might have been avoided. Sometimes, the cost of making a mistake can be harmful or even fatal, especially when you consider that if a pilot makes a mistake, s/he risks the lives of everyone on the plane. The same applies to medical professionals. If a doctor makes a mistake or miscalculation, there are times when s/he risks the patient losing their life.

You might be wondering what all this has to do with leadership. When you exercise leadership, you are disrupting people's lives, and changing the fates of organizations or countries. A mistake or miscalculation on your end can lead to some irreversible consequences. Indeed, given the wide spectrum of fields in which leadership can take place, people may suffer anything from financial loss (e.g. losing their jobs, getting demoted, losing their funding) all the way to losing their lives (e.g. assassinations, revolutions, wars).

If the leader of an initiative goes ahead with it without making the necessary preparations, mistakes will be made and people, including the leader, may pay costs they could have avoided.

In his book *The Checklist Manifesto*, Atul Gawande talked about how the healthcare industry, specifically surgery departments, introduced one simple protocol that decreased the mortality rate by 47%. What was the simple protocol? Checklists. Just by having a checklist to actually go through the necessary and key steps in the surgical procedures, they were able to avoid 47% of unnecessary deaths — almost half. There are other places where checklists can play a paramount role. If you look at the aviation industry, for example, you will find that all pilots have a physical checklist that they go through before, during, and after takeoff.

What else contributes to aviation's strikingly high safety rate? Going back to Matthew Syed, he talks about the "black box" that is available on every aircraft. This box records all the flight data, including the conversations. When something happens, the *National Transportation Safety Board* (NTSB) and similar organizations retrieve and carefully examine this data. They see exactly what the mistake was and learn from it, preventing it from being repeated in the future. This type of thinking is not reserved solely for the aviation industry. You can use what Matthew Syed calls *"Black Box Thinking"* as a way of understanding any mistakes and miscalculations you make in your initiative, allowing you to avoid similar ones in the future.

There will certainly be some mistakes or miscalculations that you can avoid altogether, and all it takes is some preparation. You need to be willing to spend time and resources to make sure you have covered your bases. You don't want to rush into a leadership initiative without being well-prepared. It would be reckless on your part, not only because you would put yourself in harm's way, but also because you risk unnecessarily disrupting the lives of others in the system.

To avoid failure, you must think about how you are going to handle having opponents. The first step is to consider strategies that will help you prepare for, preempt, and deal with your opponents both before and after you introduce the initiative. Many individuals have started initiatives unprepared to deal with the resistance. This generally leads to them being unable to take the pressure of resistance and the initiative failing. Take a moment to imagine how many groundbreaking and life-changing creations and leadership acts we may have missed out on because the instigator was ill-prepared.

If you really believe that what you are doing is going to benefit the system, do not let lack of preparation be your downfall. Figure out how you are going to prepare for your opponent's arrival before you jump into the ring. This way, you will be able to continue doing what you intended to do. Be creative and flexible, but be prepared so that your creativity has time to engage.

Take a lesson from the books of the healthcare and aviation industries. Do what you must to prepare for future obstacles and prevent avoidable mistakes or miscalculations. With people pressuring you to give up what you are doing, you are bound to make mistakes but ensure you prevent as many as possible by looking at and learning from previous mistakes *("Black Box Thinking");* considering the logistics and necessary analyses *(Checklist thinking);* and accounting for what obstacles will stand in your way *(WOOP[4]).*

You should also take measures to preempt against having opponents if you can. These preparatory and preemptive measures will increase the chances of success for your initiative. Let us dive right in and talk about the many ways you can prepare and preempt against your opponents' arrival.

Checklist Thinking

One method of preparing for what is to come is to create a checklist. With your clarified purpose, you know what your initiative is intended to do and who it will affect. With a clear understanding of your opponents, you know how your initiative will affect them and why they are resisting you. It is time to incorporate all this information and use it to prepare for the resistance you are going to face.

As part of your checklist, you should carry out some analyses, including a stakeholders analysis, a resistance analysis, an authority analysis, and a casualties analysis.

Stakeholders Analysis

This type of analysis is about the people who have a stake in your initiative. For you to understand where everyone involved stands in respect to your initiative, you need to consider who is involved in the first place. When you carry this step out, ask yourself these questions:

---

[4] WOOP: Stands for Wish, Outcome, Obstacle, Plan. It is a concept created by Danielle Oettingen to explain how you can work towards overcoming the obstacles in your path and making your wishes a reality by following this procedure (explained below).

- In what system are you planning to introduce the initiative?

  - Is it a personal system? A family, a neighborhood, a club, etc.?

  - Is it a professional system? A company or a non-profit organization?

  - Is it a government, county, or country?

- What is the scale of the initiative? Is it organization-wide? Or is it more specific?

- Who will be affected by it?

At this point, your purpose will lend a hand. Since you know how your initiative will affect the system, you can figure out broadly who will be involved. You can then use the information you have on the 9-Ds of these individuals to figure out how they will be affected.

Resistance Analysis

The next step is to figure out who among the "stakeholders" will be your opponents or your supporters, and who will sit on the sidelines. This will help you get a better understanding of the system's constituents and where they are leaning in terms of your initiative. You can also use this information to assess if it is the right time to introduce your initiative. You can see how many potential supporters and opponents you have. If the opponents are strong in numbers, or are more powerful and influential, then you have two choices. You can either make them your supporters, or you can rethink the idea of introducing your initiative. To help with this analysis, consider adding these questions to your checklist:

- Who are your supporters?

  - What do they stand to gain if you succeed?

- Who are your opponents?

  - Why are they your opponents?

  - What do they stand to lose if you succeed?

  - What can you do to get them to relinquish their opposition and come over to your side?

- Who will be neutral towards the initiative?

  - Why are they neutral?

  - What can you do to sway them to your side?

With this analysis, you can see whether your initiative will be welcome. You will also have a chance to look for ways to change the breakdown and try to increase the number of supporters and decrease the number of opponents.

Authority Analysis

Most of the time, authority can make or break the initiative. The power they have over the system puts them in a crucial position, and you would be wise to ensure that they are not against your initiative. You should carry out an analysis of the authority, who they are, and where they stand in terms of your initiative.

- Who are the relevant authorities?

  - What stake do they have in your initiative?

  - Who has formal authority[5]?

  - Who has informal authority[6]?

---

[5] A person or entity has formal authority when they hold a position of power that they were hired or elected into.

[6] A person or entity is considered to have informal authority if they do not hold a formal position but still hold power and/or sway over the system and its resources.

- Why are they important?
    - Do they hold resources that you need?
    - Does your initiative positively or negatively affect them?
- What are they communicating directly, or indirectly, about their position towards your initiative?
    - How do they feel about your initiative?
    - What are their thoughts?
- What can you do to win their support?

This analysis is essential. Your authority could shut down your initiative in an instant, and it is vital that you know where they stand. They are like a litmus test. If they are not convinced about your plans, they will put a strain on the system, and possibly end the initiative, or at least magnify the difficulty of your journey. They will affect the views of others, and also reflect these views to a degree; if the initiative is popular, your authority is more likely to be behind it. You should monitor their position throughout the initiative and also, perhaps more importantly, before its introduction.

Casualties Analysis

It is unfortunate but, as with every battle, there will be casualties on both sides. You cannot hope to disrupt a system without experiencing some losses. It is important that you prepare as best you can. Try to conduct an analysis before you introduce the initiative. For instance, the costs might be others losing their jobs, money, relationships, etc. Of course, you should minimize these costs, and the best way you can do that is by trying to predict who is vulnerable and why.

- Who are the likely casualties of your initiative? Why?

    ◦ What makes them vulnerable?

- What will they lose?

    ◦ What is your initiative asking of them?

- What can you do to help them? What can you do to compensate for their losses?

    ◦ Is there a way to introduce the initiative which minimizes the cost?

With this analysis, you can get a clearer picture of who might oppose you, especially if the costs are high. This will not only help you and your supporters (or your opponents, depending on who the casualty is) mentally and physically prepare for the loss, but it will let you look for ways to prevent it from happening in the first place.

Logistics

Whenever you introduce an initiative, you need to consider the logistics of the whole process. The main thing to consider is what resources you will need to increase its chances of success. It could be that you need time, money, or people, depending on what you are planning to do. Logically, you cannot move forward with the initiative if you don't have the means to do so. Just as a pilot does before takeoff, you should ensure that everything is in place and functioning before you introduce your initiative. Take the time necessary to list all the assets and resources that you will need.

- Will you need funding?

- Will you need people?

- Do you have access to those resources?

- How can you get those resources?

- Who should you talk to? Who has access?

WOOP

"WOOP" is a concept created by Gabrielle Oettingen, mentioned in her book *Rethinking Positive Thinking*. It is an acronym that is intended to help you think about what you want in life, imagine it, and move forward to realize your goals. In the case of this book, I want to take the same idea but apply it to acts of leadership.

The "W" in the acronym stands for *wish* — that which you want to make happen. In the case of leadership, this would be your initiative. It is what you intend to do. Therefore, your first step should always be to carefully consider your initiative.

The first "O" is about *outcome*. In this case, it is about what your initiative is going to achieve. This includes your purpose, why you want to do it, and the benefits that your initiative is expected to bring to the system and its constituents.

The first two steps are crucial in any act of leadership. With a clear purpose and expected benefits, you can present your initiative to the system. However, we have already covered this in a previous chapter. What is important to consider is the next two steps, which deal with resistance.

The second "O" is about *obstacles*. In the case of leadership acts, this translates to the resistance you are going to face, and as we have seen in the chapter "Understanding Your Opponent", we each have a combination of dimensions that will affect how we react to change. Therefore, the resistance you will face varies from opponent to opponent, not only in the way they choose to resist you, but in the intensity of their resistance and its effectiveness. As we will see in the next chapter, there are roles that your resisters will play in your life, and as such, there are relationships and dynamics that will affect how they resist you. The obstacles you will face will vary enormously, and you will need to consider to the best of your ability what possible hiccups you might experience along the way. Make a list of these obstacles, so you can use them in the next step.

Finally, the "P" in the acronym is about *plans*. This refers to the plans that you should make to deal with your obstacles, whatever shape they take. These are "if-then" scenarios, and you will need to prepare yourself to deal with obstacles from the previous step should they become a reality.

The last two steps are crucial in dealing with resistance. If you can predict what type of resistance you will face, you can work on a strategy for dealing with it. This means that you are less likely to be ambushed or surprised because you will have anticipated the situation, and you will have a plan in place to effectively deal with the obstacle. With leadership initiatives, you cannot "wing it". Lack of preparation can be the downfall of the initiative, and will also affect you, your supporters, and quite possibly the system as a whole.

Black Box Thinking

Remember that *Black Box Thinking* is about analyzing failures and mistakes so that you can learn from them and improve your future strategies.

Of course, you don't have to wait for your initiative to fail before you can learn from the past. If you are introducing an initiative and there is a similar precedent, you can use that to learn from. Look at its weaknesses or failures. See where it went wrong and how the people involved fixed it. If they didn't succeed in fixing it, try and come up with strategies that you might be able to employ if you end up in a comparable situation. Consider how you can avoid making similar mistakes.

In terms of your own initiative, you should constantly be learning. Consider breaking your initiative into steps, and focus on addressing any failures that arise in each step. This will allow you to accept these failures, learn from the mistakes, and improve the future steps. This way, the final product — your initiative — will be free from any avoidable failings. Of course, there are bound to be circumstances that you haven't predicted, and so you may need to make some changes when these arise.

Time to Preempt

All the above measures are geared towards preparing you to deal with future obstacles when they arise. However, it might be possible for you to stop some of your opponents from becoming your opponents in the first place. This is obviously ideal, saving hours that you would otherwise spend trying to put an end to their resistance.

Use all the information you have gathered about your opponents and their driving forces to stay one step ahead of them and prevent their opposition. Remember, preemptive strategies are dependent on the individuals you are dealing with, their 9-Ds, how your initiative is impacting them and the system, etc.

Let us take an in-depth look at some of the preemptive measures you can take. Remember to incorporate strategies of your own that you feel will fit the situation.

Aim High, Resist More

There are moments where your initiative only involves a few individuals in the system, while at other times, it involves the whole system. Obviously,

"I ask you to judge me by the enemies I have made"

– Franklin D. Roosevelt

the more people it targets, the greater the potential number of opponents. However, the number of people involved is not the main factor: it is usually more related to the impact your initiative could have. The greater the impact of your initiative, the greater the resistance you are likely to face.

We can see how the number of people involved may affect the number of opponents. If you have an organization-wide intervention, you may face many opponents, since your intervention may disrupt the lives of many people. However, if the impact this intervention has involves more people, but does not uproot their lives, you may have a smaller number of opponents that you originally imagined.

The same applies to a narrower initiative. If you are introducing change to a small department, it is possible that you will not face any opponents. It will barely make an impact, only lightly nudging the system.

However, if your initiative creates a more noticeable change, almost reversing the direction the department has been going in, you are likely to have many people opposing you. It is possible that the majority would be against it, protesting the decision before it even has a chance to show results. A big change, affecting a small number of people, can still lead to multiple opponents.

When you are considering your initiative, you must always take into account the impact it will have. The greater the impact of your interventions, the more likely it becomes that other people will draw the short straw. Do not focus solely on who will be affected, but also on how they will be affected. You already have the tools to make this calculation, by considering your purpose, your opponent's driving forces, and your general understanding of their perspective.

Know Yourself

Resistance will bring varying amounts of stress. At times, the pressure may be minuscule, but at other times, resistance can bring about what seems like insurmount-

"If ignorant of both your enemy and yourself, you are certain to be in peril"

– Sun Tzu

able pressure. Stressful resistance will test your resilience and your values; it will instill self-doubts in you, and make you question what you are doing. Therefore, the first preemptive measure should be knowing yourself.

You need to consider your own 9-Ds (hungers, insecurities, world views, values, etc.). You will need to know your own strengths and weaknesses. Your opponents and enemies will probably discover and exploit your weaknesses, and if you are unable to preempt against this, the stress may build and take a toll on you emotionally, and possibly physically.

"When you fear a foe, fear crushes your strength; and this weakness gives strength to your opponents"

– William Shakespeare

One way to prepare for and preempt your opponent's resistance is to know yourself well, and this includes knowing how you react to conflict. Some individuals tend to shy away from conflict, others panic and cower in fear, while others seem to hold steadfast and are undeterred. You need to reflect on how you personally deal with conflict.

Consider past events of conflict and resistance:

1. How did you react to conflict? Were you able to deal with it effectively?

2. Did your opponents take advantage of your weaknesses (e.g. fear, hesitation, doubt)?

Before you move forward, you need to examine yourself from all angles. The rest of the preemptive measures fit in from this point onward. Understanding yourself is the beginning of ensuring you can deal with and win against your opponent's resistance.

Interact To Provoke Or Pacify

Some of your opponents will work or live in your vicinity. As such, you may meet them, interact with them, say "hello" to them in the hall. How you interact with them helps to determine how they will feel about you. Consider this carefully.

Before you move forward with shaking the system, plan how you will treat your future opponents, keeping in mind that your actions will help determine their responses. If your first reaction to their resistance is to provoke or attack them, expect them to repay you in kind. The more you attack your future opponents, the more likely it is that they will try to make your life difficult. If they are mistreated or provoked, they will intensify their resistance, and when that happens, it may be too late for you to remedy the situation.

Remember, you are the only person who has access to your thoughts and feelings. If you feel that an aggressive response is the way you prefer to react, then you must take that path, though it is usually inadvisable. Remember these people will interact with you often, if not daily, and it would be better to avoid complicating your life further; you already have a lot on your plate.

Your other option is, of course, to act in a way that does not provoke them. If your interactions with the opponent gives them reasons to respect and admire you, they may end up letting go of their resistance, though this will depend on how much impact your initiative is making on their lives.

Once you understand that your interactions have major impacts on how your initiative unfolds, you are another step ahead of your opponent. Aim to pacify, not to provoke, as your leadership act is already doing the provoking.

Everything You Do Can Be Used Against You

The moment your initiative is in effect, all eyes will be on you, particularly your opponents' eyes. Those who support you are looking to you as their role model, while those who oppose you are waiting for you to do something wrong. You will need to be prepared to have your every move watched. You will become the most important person in the room, "the person who saved the system" and "the person who ruined my life" simultaneously.

You need to preempt what is to come. You cannot afford to slip. If you want to create an impact, you do not want to supply your opponents with information they can use against you.

The resistance has no mercy. The minute your tongue slips, you lose your temper, or flop a minor deal, they will be there before you can say "oops". Your opponents will magnify your mistakes and minimize your accomplishments. This is one of the best ways they can damage your initiative.

As such, you will need to be careful. Constantly keep watch over yourself and your actions. Train yourself to be patient. You need to be self-aware as well as aware of your surroundings. It is a tiring and messy business, but a clear purpose (good planning, being flexible, adaptive, persistent, resilient) will get you through it.

To Respond, Not React

"In the practice of tolerance, one's enemy is the best teacher"

– Dalai Lama XIV

Our behavior can take two forms: we can either be reactive or we can be responsive.

- If you base your behavior on your emotions and you follow your first impulse, you are reacting.

- If you take in all the information, address your feelings in your mind and not verbally, and you think about how best to act — ways that are in line with your purpose — you are responding. You allow yourself a little time and space to consider the situation before deciding how you will deal with it.

As you may have guessed, you will want to opt for the second form of behavior. You need to train yourself to act in a responsive way; you simply cannot afford to react. If you step out of line, fierce opponents will take your reactions and retaliate in kind, or try to use them against you. Do not give them a seemingly justifiable reason to do this.

Since you will be in the spotlight, your actions must mirror your purposeful initiative. You should not give others, especially your opponents, the impression that you are hot-headed, inconsiderate, careless, selfish, or anything along those lines. This will only provoke them further, and they will increase their opposition in response to your reactions. They may try to persuade others that your initiative has poor leadership and will not succeed.

Instead, you will want to exhibit behaviors that are in line with your purpose. When you respond in such a way, you will disarm your opponents, since they will not have any damaging information to use against you. In addition, responding well will give the people on your side an idea of how to behave. Your responsive behaviors will set an example of how to deal with opponents. This should mitigate the chance of your supporters reacting and escalating the conflict.

I recall Gandhi in this scenario. When his fellow Indians were beaten, imprisoned, and killed, I am sure many individuals in his group wanted to react in kind to the British oppression. However, Gandhi responded in line with his purpose, and he was able to convince his supporters that they could gain their independence by presenting non-violent resistance. In fact, non-violence was such a core value of his that his family protested the hanging of his murderers. They claimed that it was not what Gandhi would have wanted. His extraordinary achievements are a prime example of responsive, purposeful behavior and the impact it can have.

Protect Yourself; Do Not Personalize It

One of your greatest strengths will be not taking things personally. Think back to what we talked about earlier in this book: your opponent has nothing against you personally, and anyone in your position would experience the same resistance.

> "I learned that to humiliate another person is to make him suffer an unnecessarily cruel fate. Even as a boy, I defeated my opponents without dishonoring them"
>
> – Nelson Mandela

Use this knowledge to your benefit. If you keep it in mind, you are less likely to react to your opponent's provocations. They will resist you, and in doing so, they will push and prod you — they want you to react. Do not give them the pleasure of seeing you irritated. Try to understand their resistance and respond to it with empathy.

Remember also that it is not personal in terms of them either. This means that you should never make the disagreement about them. Do not attack your opponent on a personal level. This is likely to happen when you behave reactively: you are bound to target your opponent's character, not their behavior. This will get you nowhere. You will end up battling it out, and the conflict will escalate unnecessarily. Instead, focus on your purposeful initiative.

Consider this example: two of the largest television news stations in the country are battling over ratings. Station A is attacking Station B for the type of "in your face" content they are broadcasting. Station B can follow suit and attack Station A as having a conservative and outdated approach to journalism.

However, if Station B's owners are responsive, they will instead focus on increasing their ratings. They will do nothing but focus on their programs, offering their clients what they see as honest journalism. If their purpose is good, they do not need to twist facts to suit a select clientele. By not taking the attacks personally, Station B are behaving responsively. It would be irresponsible to retaliate and lose sight of the bigger picture, which is offering their clients honest and unbiased news.

Scream Purpose From The Top Of The Hill

Let the system know the WHY behind your leadership acts. Before you embark on your purposeful, disruptive journey, you must make sure you clearly communicate your purpose to the system and its constituents. You may be surprised to see that many who oppose you do so simply because they have no idea why you are doing what you are doing.

Remember that your opponents cannot know what you are thinking, so you must make your reasons absolutely clear. Your opponents will want to know how they will benefit. For the sake of your initiative and the system, explain your purpose in a clear, simple fashion. Opponents and supporters alike will then be able to see the bigger picture and get an understanding of the details behind the change.

In addition, you can garner more support if you explain your purpose clearly. If you leave people to make assumptions about what you intend to do, many individuals may feel unmotivated and disinterested. However, if they understand the purpose behind your initiative and the benefits it might bring about, they may be more likely to join you.

With this in mind, make sure you take the preemptive measure of letting the system know the purpose behind your initiative. Clarity in your explanation will indicate a considered plan and good leadership, and will let people know exactly what they (and the system) could gain by supporting you.

Know The System

Consider this scenario: it is your first day at a new company. As soon as you get out of the elevator, you hear a loud buzz in the office. When you enter the common workspace, you find people sitting on the floor. There are beanbags and it looks like the stereotypical modern tech office. Instantly, your suit and tie look out of place.

Let us now imagine another scenario. It is your first day at the corporate office, and the moment you step out of the elevator, you hear the clicking of keyboard keys. The common area is comprised of cubicles, and your coworkers sit quietly working. Your suit and tie fit right in. Now imagine that you are going to introduce a company-wide intervention. Would you introduce the subject irrespective of the workspace atmosphere? Or would you tailor your introduction based on the system's environment?

If you choose the second option, you are on your way to successfully shifting the system. It is nearly impossible for you to change something you do not understand.

This is a major preemptive step. You must comprehend the

inner workings and culture of the system. This means getting to know the norms, the expectations, and how to deal with its constituents. If you don't do this, your initiative is almost certain to fail. Being clueless about the environment where change is happening is self-sabotage. It is like walking into a minefield blindfolded, with no clue where you are going.

Think about it. Would you be capable of introducing change to a system you knew nothing about? How could you differentiate between the opponent and the supporter? How could you choose the best delivery system to introduce your intervention? How could you even be sure that what you were planning to introduce would benefit the system? With every act of ignorance and ill-preparation, your chances of success would decrease.

You might say you surely know the system if you know what needs changing. You are right. However, it is one thing to know the system from an objective point of view; it is another to understand how the gears are turning.

For example, it is possible that someone who has no formal position is the most popular person there (they have informal authority). If you do not understand the system dynamics, you would miss out on this crucial aspect. Why should you care? Let us assume that this person opposes your initiative. With a snap of their fingers, they have most of the system siding with them. Your leadership acts will be rejected by the system, because you failed to realize how best to broach the subject and who might be a key supporter or opponent.

It is necessary to familiarize yourself with the system's culture. You will gain insight into the following questions:

- Who is involved in the system?

- Who has the informal power within the system? Who has everyone's ear?

- What are the system's norms? What is acceptable and what is unacceptable?

- Who should you watch out for, and who do you need to get on your side?

- How should you introduce the initiative? What are your options?

This will help you tailor your purposeful initiative to the system.

It is of paramount importance that you do not slack off. Ignorance is not "bliss" in this situation. You cannot go about creating rules that the system cannot accept, or you may face resistance from the whole system. Breaching the norms of a system will upset people regardless of why you have breached them, so familiarize yourself with what people will expect and adhere to these expectations as much as possible. Otherwise, everyone will be the opponent, and your leadership acts will not have a chance to move past a concept.

It is like playing a game of chess. You cannot move the pieces however you please. There are rules. The queen moves in almost all directions, but cannot move like the knight. The bishop moves diagonally, but the pawn can only move forward. You cannot change the fundamental rules of the game or you will cause chaos, confusing your opponents and your supporters alike, to the degree that nobody wants to join in, and everyone wants to stop you. If you do not understand the system, you cannot play the game, let alone influence it.

Remember Their Cultures

Part of knowing the system is understanding that you may deal with individuals who come from different cultural backgrounds. The way these individuals conduct themselves, in situations of opposition, depends on the accepted cultural protocols for expressing their opinions, concerns, emotions, support and/or opposition, as well as their overall attitude towards authority, opponents, and conflict.

Some cultures have great respect for authority, some value individuality, some believe in competition, and others appreciate teamwork. These views may differ between members of the same system. If you want to know the best way to introduce your initiative, ensure you have a good understanding of your opponent's cultural background — in addition to the system's culture — before you try and introduce change.

If you don't take the time to do this, then you risk offending them and turning them into your opponents. You may also alienate the neutrals and your potential, and existing, supporters if you disregard their cultural practices. Especially, if they feel like you violated their principles, values, and ways of life.

Presenting the Initiative

I Am Not You

You want to introduce your initiative to the system. You think you know how, but you are not sure. What should you do? You need to remember that not everyone involved shares your perspective, and that each individual will have a different view on your ideas. Therefore, you will want to start by understanding their perspective. Lay out multiple options and try to step out of your own mind and into theirs.

Everyone is individual, with different thoughts, feelings, and unique takes on their driving forces. Consider not only your opponent, but everyone within the system, even if you do not think they are involved. Use your knowledge of the driving forces to map out possible viewpoints. Finally, go back to your list and eliminate the executions which are unlikely to succeed.

Use this information, coupled with your understanding of the system as a whole, to consider how you want to present your initiative to those involved, including your opponents.

Go For The Wider Frame

To save yourself from some of your potential opponents' resistance, no matter how small, it might be wise to change how you frame your initiative.

Personal Frame

If the change you are introducing comes off as a personal goal for your own benefit only, most people will not stand behind you. They may support you from afar, possibly give you a gentle tap on the shoulder, but they will not take the risk with you. People do not want to get involved in a situation that reaps no benefits for them.

Your opponents, on the other hand, will have a field day. It will be an easy task for them to just end your initiative. Without any support, your initiative may not be strong enough to withstand the constant pressure from your opponents. You need to make sure people have your back because otherwise you will be an easy target.

Wider Frame

If you opt for a wider frame, coming from the angle that it is a win-win situation for all involved, you will relay to others in the system that change is not a personal achievement, but a systemic necessity. People will be jumping up to help you, making sure you get where you need to go. They will no longer tap you on your shoulder, but push you forward. Your opponents will now face their own resistance: the battlefield just got larger. It will be harder for them to push you down when you have a large support group pushing you back up.

In addition to this, the chances of your opponents decreasing their animosity towards you and your initiative will improve. When you introduce your initiative as a systemic benefit, your opponents may not be so quick to stand in your way. It is possible that they may even change their thoughts and feelings on the matter, since they now see that what you are doing is for their benefit as well. They are no longer expecting to reap no reward. If the impact does not ruin their lives, they may become neutral on the topic, or they may actually support it. Either way, having a wider frame allows you to increase support and decrease resistance.

Tailor The Frame

You may consider tailoring the frame of the initiative for each type of opponent. You will need to take some time and consider how you can customize it to suit the individuals involved. If you are able to show your opponents the benefits they will receive, while explaining that the consequences are necessary, they might reconsider their position and support you. If the change is presented as pure risk, they will probably not want to go along with what you are doing; they need to see the benefits.

Often, their opposition may stem from the fear that you are taking away too much. If any of their dimensions are threatened, you will need to make sure you specifically address them and put them at ease. Your framing must consider their insecurities, hungers, dreams, hopes, and agendas. This way, you can both avoid conflict and end up with a win-win situation.

RECAP

Remember, if you can prepare and preempt for resistance, it will increase the chances of your initiative succeeding:

- Make a checklist and go through it before and after you introduce the initiative.

- Consider using WOOP to envision your initiative and its best outcome, and to pinpoint the obstacles you will face so that you can come up with an action plan.

- Use Black Box Thinking to approach your failures, mistakes, and miscalculations and learn from them so you don't find yourself repeating them.

- Reflect on your own strengths and weaknesses. You need to make sure your weaknesses aren't used against you.

- Think about how you react or respond to conflict.

- Try not to provoke people, and instead approach individuals in a calm and collected manner.

- Make sure you don't give your opponents information they can use against you.

- Always respond thoughtfully and purposefully to conflicts or provocations. You don't want to instinctively react.

- Don't make it personal.

- Focus on, examine, and explain your purpose. It is the reason you are exercising leadership in the first place.

- Study and understand the system you are working in.

- Take the time to understand your enemies so you can form strategies on how best to introduce your initiatives.

- Always tailor the frame to the system. Your intervention is not about how it benefits you, but how it benefits the system and its constituents, so make sure you frame your intervention this way.

Dipping Your Toes In The Water

A weak initiative will get you nowhere. Your opponents will take advantage of any opening they see to bring it down. That is why it is important that you consider any major gaps in your initiative. You will need to see how people will react to what you are trying to do, but also ensure that you do not have a faulty project on your hands.

Pre-mortems

One method of "testing the waters" is a concept mentioned in Matthew Syed's *Black Box Thinking*: the idea of a "pre-mortem". The point is that you and your supporters assume, before you introduce your initiative, that it has failed. Instead of trying to see what weaknesses your initiative has, you will start with the premise that it has failed, and work on figuring out why that is the case. This will hopefully free your initiative of blind spots and miscalculations that you might otherwise have missed.

If possible, try to get your potential resisters to contribute. They may be less hesitant to point out the mistakes. You need to try to involve as many people as you can, allowing you to almost dissect the initiative, learn from the potential mistakes, and patch them up so that you can come as close as possible to make the initiative foolproof.

In other words, propose the hypothetical failure so that you may preempt against experiencing this failure.

Red Teams

Depending on how high the stakes are, you may want to consider hiring an outside, objective party to take a look at your initiative. One such type of investigator is what is called a Red Team. This group of qualified and competent individuals are hired by your organization to test out specific issues. They do that by temporarily taking the side of your opponent. Their sole focus becomes looking to exploit the gaps in your change initiative.

Since they are not part of your organization, they have no vested interest in making you happy. Instead, they focus on all the possible ways in which your initiative could go wrong. They look for gaps which your opponents might exploit and highlight the problems these gaps could cause. Depending on how much is at stake (e.g. governmental body intelligence, international organization, personal customer info), these gaps might put your constituents' survival and growth at stake, not just their interests.

Different forms of organizations procure the services of Red Teams. These range from the military, to national security agencies, to cybersecurity companies, to airports, to international corporate organizations, to name a few. The Red Teams can think like hackers, enemy troops, bank robbers, foreign intelligence operatives, etc. Basically, Red Teams can take on the role of any opponent or enemy. Hacking and spying happen at the corporate level, and you need to make sure you safeguard yourself by preempting the ways your opponents or enemies may bring your initiative to an end. Consider hiring a Red Team if your change is important and may possibly restructure the system for the better. It is of paramount importance to consider using this resource when dealing with enemies, since they will probably aim to "destroy" you. Red Teams will allow you to polish your initiative and remove weaknesses which might otherwise bring it down.

The same concept can be applied preemptively on a smaller scale, or a more personal level. Your friends, family members, colleagues, lawyers, former opponents, etc., can provide valuable insights into blind spots in your initiatives, and the possible reactions that your initiative might trigger in the system you are trying to impact.

Gauge Their Feedback And Reaction

Before launching a new product, most companies release a prototype or demo as a way of gauging their clients' reactions to the upcoming product before releasing it for mass sales. In the gaming industry, they release a Beta version a little while before the official release date. This will allow their clients to experience the game and give some reviews. In the movie and television industry, they release trailers to increase people's interest and to see their comments. In all these cases, if the product, game, or movie is negatively received then the people who released it will consider making changes. In other words, they listen to the system and their clients.

Consider doing the same. As we mentioned in the previous chapter, you may understand the forces at play, but you will never really know what is driving your opponent unless you ask them.

> **"Instead of trying to prove your opponent wrong, try to see in what sense he might be right"**
>
> *– Robert Nozick*

The same goes for your supporters. Therefore, when you have a clear understanding of your purpose and your initiative, it is a good idea to run it by others, possibly brief them on the specifics, and ask for their advice.

For this tactic to have the optimal effect, you will want to practice active listening. I have outlined below some key points of active listening to help you get an idea or recap on what active listening is. Read each subsection carefully. It is important that you take the time to address each point. This will help you grasp your opponents' or supporters' ideas, thoughts, and advice better. Think of it as beta testing, giving you information that will allow you to evaluate how your initiative will be received.

Strategies For Listening More Effectively

Leave Your Biases At The Door. When you make the decision to listen to what others have to say, make sure you get as much as you can out of it. When you meet up with or talk to others (colleagues, competitors, family members, etc.), leave all your prejudices, judgments, and subjectivity at the door. Keep an open mind and focus on what the person is saying. Do not spend the time cross-referencing all the information they are conveying with your subjective database. Instead, take an objective stance. This will allow you to get the most out of the experience. Do not just hear the words and judge, but listen, learn, and grow.

> "Learn to control ego. Humans hold their dogmas and biases too tightly, and we only think that our opponents are dogmatic! But we all need criticism. Criticism is the only antidote to error"
>
> – *David Brin*

When They Speak, You Just Listen. A core requirement to effective listening is the listening part. When the person opposite you is talking, do not interrupt them. Let them finish their thoughts, and avoid jumping to conclusions prematurely. This will allow you to get all the facts before moving forward. You are asking for their advice on what you should do. It would be counterproductive not to listen to their perspective.

Don't Plot, Listen. As you have made the decision to listen, do not spend your time mentally preparing your rebuttal. Even if what the other person is saying is completely out of proportion, you will miss out on crucial information if you spend most of the conversation plotting your next dispute. Prepare your next question only when they have finished talking; this is not an argument, but a discussion.

See It From Their Perspective. In addition to leaving your prejudices at the door, you need to make sure you are not filtering the information. Do not spend your time picking and choosing interpretations so that they fit with your point of view. The entire point of listening to others is to gain an understanding of their perspective. After all, it is easier for you to correct either your approach or their take on it once you understand how they have formed their conclusions.

In addition, make sure that you are crystal clear about what they are trying to say. If you feel that something is vague, do not hesitate to ask them to elaborate or repeat. One tactic that is proposed for active listening is to double-check what they have said by rephrasing and repeating it. This ensures that if there are misunderstandings, they come to light, and this is particularly important if what they said did not make sense to you. If they have made a mistake, repeating it back to them will help them see it.

I Feel You. Another element of active listening is paying attention to what is unsaid. It is important that you also focus on body language, tones, gestures, etc. There will be times when the person sitting across from you will verbalize something, but their body is saying something else. When you actively listen, you are able to discern any dissonance between their words and their body language, tones etc. The unsaid is an important element of the conversation as it may point to their true feelings.

Furthermore, the unsaid can help you interpret how your words are being received. There may be tension at the beginning of the conversation, especially if you know the person in front of you could be a future opponent. However, if you find that you are both beginning to relax, this indicates that you are starting to see eye to eye on some parts, or all parts, of the issue. You can then infer that you are finding your way towards a win-win situation.

> **"One of the most sincere forms of respect is actually listening to what another has to say"**
>
> – *Bryant H. McGill*

Map Out Your Supporters and Opponents, The Neutrals, and Authority

It is wise to have an idea of where everyone in the system stands. As you may recall from the previous chapter, your opponents (among others involved) are the landmarks on your map. Mapping out who stands where will give you a clearer idea of who will support you, who will oppose you, who is going to remain neutral, and who holds a postion of authority.

You can take this a step further. Look more carefully at how much support or resistance each person will put up. This will give you a clearer understanding of how passionate your supporters and opponents are.

Some of your supporters will be fans of your leadership act, but may not do much to actually drive you forward. For instance, many of your colleagues may verbally agree with what you are doing, but when push comes to shove, they will not act on their support. Other supporters will be more reliable when the going gets tough. They will not only agree with your leadership act, but they will do whatever they can to make sure you succeed. These individuals may sign petitions, spread the word, or even stand with you in protest.

The same goes for your opponents. You may not have to worry so much about some of them. They will verbally disagree with you, but will not take it further than that. They will not actively try and stop what you are doing. On the other end of this spectrum, you have opponents who will be spirited in their opposition. They will do everything in their power to put an end to your initiative. The moment you introduce it, they will jump on any opportunity to bring you down. They may try to discredit you, spy on you, use your weaknesses against you, or even break the law to end what you are doing.

Trying to prepare ways to deal with all these individuals can be mind-boggling. Mapping them out before you start will give you the general picture of what to expect. In addition, you may be able to target specific individuals and change where they stand. For instance, you can:

- Make your passive supporters more active, this will increase the impact of your intervention, and give you the support needed to back it up.

- Speak to your future opponents, explain your purpose, and frame it in such a way that they see the benefit. This may get them to support you, meaning you face less resistance and have more support.

- Target the neutral parties and try to get them to join your side. This way, you can make sure that they do not resist you in the future. If the impact of your initiative increases, it is likely that the neutral parties will become more involved with what you are doing, so preempt their involvement by ensuring their support.

- Consider who is the authority in the system and see where they stand. You can then try your best to gain their support. Authority plays a key role in deciding the fate of your initiative; with them in your corner you increase the chance of the initiative's success.

- Finally, you can check in with your active supporters. You may have wrongly assumed that past allies will support you. They may decide that what you are doing now is not worth the risk, so you need to know where they stand.

This is where you can use your checklist analyses to get a breakdown of the positions. You will then need to use this to preempt against your opponents and try to rectify any misunderstandings or losses that your opponents are worried about.

Say Hello To My Many Friends

Your Colleagues' Support

To cushion the blows of your future opponents, you will want to have people who are ready to catch you. Before you introduce your initiative to the system, take some time to find supporters.

Whenever you interact with your colleagues, make sure that you treat them with respect and dignity. You are bound to build good relationships along the way. When the time comes, you may introduce them to your purpose. Thoroughly explain your plan and how you intend to implement it. If they choose to support you, it is because what you represent and what you are doing resonates with them.

Surround yourself with as many allies as possible. This will allow you to strengthen your position and credibility, and heightens the chance of your initiative succeeding. Should it come to a fight, it would be dangerous to take to the battlefield without a great army. You will also have more individuals to watch your back and keep an eye on the movements of your opponents.

I Have Power On My Side

"There is strength in numbers", as the old idiom goes. But what about actual power on your side? When you undertake a risky venture, you want to have people who can add to your credibility and whose voices carry weight. You are far more likely to increase your impact if you have authority on your side.

For that reason, you will want to take some time convincing people in positions of authority to give you their blessing. Your opponents will have a harder time trying to bring you down if their bosses are putting pressure on them. Additionally, the people who were originally hesitant to lend you their support may reconsider. The risk level goes down, so those who wanted to join (passive supporters) have nothing to fear.

Do Me A Solid And I Will Think About It

Building relationships is not easy. One sure way to do it is to be supportive of other people and their ideas. If they come to you with a proposal, consider giving them your support, and if it is for the system's benefit, do not hesitate. Actively participate and push them forward. In the end, it will be to your benefit too. You will have played a part in improving the system and you will also have built a good, solid relationship. When the time comes, and the tables have turned, you are more likely to gain their support if you have supported them in the past.

Another way to build good relationships is to do favors for your fellow system cohorts. These could take any form, such as covering their shift so they can attend their child's football game, staying late at the office to help them hand in the report on time, signing a petition for a cause that you have no interest in, or even offering a small loan to your neighbor to buy his fiancée a ring. Whatever form it takes, if it is not against the law or against your purpose, consider agreeing. They will owe you, even if you never cash in that chip.

Help people out, do them favors, and support them. Do the same for those you consider your opponents. Remember that your opponent has nothing against you personally, and before you introduce your initiative, they are just another one of your cohorts. If you have established a good relationship with them by doing them favors and building a rapport, they are more likely to listen to your ideas and reserve their judgment until they have heard you out. Even if they do not particularly like what you are doing, they are more likely to support you, or at least stay neutral, if they feel you are respectful and helpful.

Stay Close To The Neutrals

As you build good relationships, do not forget to explain your purpose and what you are representing to everyone. This includes those who have no specific viewpoint on the change you are creating. They may remain neutral because they are unaffected by the change, or they may be actively choosing to stay out of it. However, do not forget about them. If your initiative intensifies in the future, they may become more invested and end up choosing a side.

You will want to make sure that side is yours. You need to court them, but never mislead them, otherwise you are giving your opponents a pretext to mobilize the neutrals against you. Do not try to falsely seduce them to your side. Instead, focus on being clear and accurate about what you are doing. You will ensure that there is no misunderstanding that could sway them away from your initiative in the future. Ultimately, you will have helped your purpose and leadership initiative by avoiding another opponent.

You may want to consider tailoring your frame to show them how they could benefit from your initiative, but remember to stick to hard facts. This way they will have heard everything you have to say, and when the time comes for them to make their choice, they will choose the side that best suits them.

I Can Be Emotional Too

I Have A Certificate In Emotional Intelligence

We are emotional beings. One of the key elements to understanding your opponent is to understand their emotions. You cannot hope to preempt and prepare yourself for your opponent's resistance if you do not understand emotions.

Emotional Intelligence is a term we have been hearing about for at least the past two decades. It is a popular concept that truly is important if we want to lead and deal with people in the best way possible.

Having emotional intelligence means that you are able to understand what emotions are, what expressions they take, and how to differentiate between them. Utilizing this expertise will allow you to pinpoint and dissect your own emotions with great accuracy, as well as the emotions of those around you.

As you can imagine, emotions run high in tense situations. We have all had many conflicts in our lives, and most of the time we just want to get them over with. People rarely enjoy fighting. We may love watching it on TV or in the movies, but we rarely enjoy experiencing conflict firsthand. The key to avoiding such situations is to become an expert at defining emotions and differentiating between them.

When you understand how you are feeling at a given moment, you can identify and hopefully deal internally with any rising emotion. This will help you achieve a degree of self-control that other individuals, who are less adept at understanding their emotions, may not achieve in their lifetimes. This self-control will help you avoid reactive behaviors, and will strengthen your resolve when dealing with attacks. In addition, being able to understand your emotions allows you to better control your body language and facial expressions, so that your opponents do not know when they have succeeded in upsetting or angering you.

Furthermore, when you understand and are able to pinpoint how others are feeling, you know when you have hit a nerve, when they are feigning emotional reactions, or when they are trying to mask their emotions. Every one of these responses is crucial. You will be able to gauge their responses and how effectively you are shaking them. Remember, your intention is not to get a rise out of your opponents, but understanding when you have done, and gauging the strength of their feelings, will help you decide how to act afterwards.

For instance, if you are proposing a new intervention, and no one verbally opposes you, you may assume that all are in favor. However, if you understand emotions and expressions, you will see when their face or body betrays them. They may be trying to suppress an outburst, but their face and body will display their anger, fear, disdain, or disgust more clearly than their words could. Then and there, you can ascertain who will oppose you, who will support you, and who is disinterested.

Remember to bear in mind the cultural aspect we discussed earlier. The accepted protocols behind emotional expressions can make it difficult for you to read your opponent. When working with an individual from a different cultural background, you will have to adapt your emotional intelligence skills to their specific culture, or else you risk misinterpreting situations. In turn, you may fail to understand whether they are with or against you, risking the initiative and complicating your relationship with the individual.

Finally, to show you care, you will need to pinpoint and address the emotion your opponent is feeling. If you want to try to get them on your side, you will want to let them know you understand not only their pain, but their other emotions. If you can show this, you may catch them off-guard. They are more likely to assume that you know what you are talking about, and that you do actually understand them. The result might be less resistance on their end, and in the best-case scenario you will gain another supporter.

Beware The Shock Wave Of Emotion

When their lives are disrupted, or even turned upside down, your opponents will experience a spectrum of negative emotions. They may feel guilty and ashamed of being unable to uphold their commitments, failing to meet their agendas, and losing the chance to pursue their dreams. They may feel anger towards you for being the source of this disruption. They may grow to despise you if you have ruined their lives or experience sadness at the idea of losing a part of their identity. Anticipate this spectrum of emotions. Understanding your opponents solely from an objective viewpoint will not prepare you for the impact of their emotions.

Intense emotions can make you doubt what you are doing. If the change you are proposing is causing people to lose opportunities or jobs, thus affecting their survival and growth, it can lead to anger and confrontation. Imagine that your opponent confronts you and says something along the lines of, "How should I pay for my children's college tuition?", "What do expect me to tell my wife?", "You have ruined my family's life!"

If you are not ready to take this, if you do not mentally prepare yourself for this shock wave of emotions, then you may find it hard to keep moving forward. It is messy and difficult. Emotions take over our minds and bodies. We empathize with people's suffering, but our opponents might not want to hear that.

Therefore, prepare yourself for curse words, intense reactions, and many more emotional displays that could wear you down.

You Must Know I Care

Empathy is an important part of what makes us human. It may be difficult to show your empathy after the damage is done, so instead try to show your opponents you care beforehand. You already know that your purposeful act of leadership will cause a rift in some people's lives. Sadly, some may thrive in a broken system, and when you fix it, they will not make the cut. You do not intend to harm them, of course, but they do not know that. After the damage is done, you cannot apologize to the opponent and say you care. They are unlikely to see any value in the apology.

Expect your initiative to bring pain. Before you introduce it, preempt the emotional recoil. Communicate to the system as a whole that you care, and that you understand how some people may experience pain from what you are doing, but explain that it is unavoidable.

Using your map, target the individuals who will probably experience some pain — use your casualty analysis. It will mainly consist of your passionate and active opponents. Take some time to sit down with them and listen to their concerns. You may be surprised by what they tell you. They may point out something you have missed, and you might have an opportunity to correct it. Alternatively, you may be able to come up with a solution that suits them, or you may be able to explain the necessity of it.

When you take the time to listen to your opponents, you convey to the person seated across from you that you respect him/her. This instantly sends them the message that it is not personal — you are not out to get them — and that you intend to resolve whatever misunderstanding they have with you. Because of this, they will be more likely to keep an open mind and lower their defenses. At best, this will lead to a win-win situation. At worst, you will have shown them respect and that you do care for their well-being, despite what your initiative may do to their lives.

This may sound strange: if you do not offer your opponent concrete benefits, why would they care about respect? Of course, not all of them will; you may still come across people who will flood you with waves of emotions. However, you will have done your job, acknowledged their concerns, and attempted to explain your position. You may have even tried to find a solution to their issues, but sometimes there is nothing you can do. Even if you compromise on some aspects, you will find that their lives are not going to be the same.

Patience Is A Virtue

Are you a patient person? It is extremely important that you know the answer. Be honest with yourself. Leadership needs you to be patient, especially if you want to deal with the emotional tidal waves and the resistance you will experience. Purposeful patience grants you the ability to consider all the information before you respond. You will avoid getting caught in the moment and reacting negatively. However, purposeful patience means that you will be patient up to a point — not to the degree that you lose sight of your initiative. In the end, you do not want to sit idly and allow others to throw away everything you and your supporters have been working for.

Patience also grants you endurance. As one of Aesop's fables demonstrates, you need to be like the reeds in the field, moving with the winds, but never uprooted. Focus on your purpose, know that it will take time, and do not give up. Let the wind blow. The storm will pass.

Silent Treatment

Patience, understanding emotions, and having the ability to control your own emotions are vital skills, especially when you are in conflict with the opponent. It isn't always easy to know how to respond to a sudden attack.

"When you have nothing to say, say nothing; a weak defense strengthens your opponent, and silence is less injurious than a bad reply"

– *Charles Caleb Colton*

One of the strongest preemptive skills you can learn is silence. Being silent is not about doing nothing. It is not freezing in fear. It takes enormous self-discipline to stay silent amid the havoc and tension caused by conflict. Many situations have gone awry because the person being questioned succumbed to the pressure of conflict. Many trials were lost, causes crumbled, and inventions failed, simply because the individuals could not keep their mouths shut when they needed to. Silence is a powerful tool, but it requires patience, courage, clarity of purpose, an immense understanding of emotion, and control over your own emotions.

Can you recall a time when you had a fight with a close friend or family member? How intense was that encounter? Take that feeling and intensity, consider the discomfort and mass of emotions. Now, multiply it many-fold. Your opponent is out to get you and so they will not go easy on you.

They will push and prod, waiting for you to react. The moment you slip is the moment you have handed them their victory.

Silence helps you counter this: you cannot say something you regret if you say nothing. It is a powerful yet difficult skill to hone. We are emotional beings. We struggle to sit idly as our opponents spit words of poison at us. They may bring up personal issues and surprise us with below-the-belt comments and questions. However, if you can master silence, despite all this emotional tension, you will throw them off-guard and defeat the attack.

Silence can be used in two ways: Strategically and Tactically. Both are equally important skills.

Strategic Silence

When you intentionally choose to stay silent despite what your opponent is saying, this can be considered strategic silence. This skill requires immense powers of self-discipline. As you are being battered by the opponent, you sit there listening carefully to what they are saying.

As you listen, you will begin to uncover your opponent's true intentions, plans, and strategies. If you spend time worrying about what to say next, or you let your emotions get the better of you, you will lose. However, if you let them do the talking, you can think about their hidden agendas. Why are they saying what they are saying? What is the purpose behind their words? Is it because they want to stop your initiative? Do they want to provoke you? You cannot find this out if you rush to defend yourself.

Your opponent will win as soon as you react impulsively rather than responding purposefully. The moment you let a word slip is the moment they smile and say, "I have nothing to add". However, you will win once you have grasped an understanding of what they want from you, what their hidden agenda is. You will also give them the impression that you are not to be trifled with. When they have finished saying whatever they have to say, you move on. With strategic silence, you take the high road and show them that you will not respond.

Tactical Silence

There is another type of silence that will also require all the skills we talked about previously (self-discipline, emotional aware-ness, patience, etc.). When you exercise tactical silence, you will still need to stay calm and collected. You will need to pay attention, listening carefully to your opponent's arguments. Avoid reacting at all costs, no matter the urge to retort. Wait for them to finish, and when the ball is back in your court, you may speak and/or act.

This is the main difference between strategic and tactical silence. In the former, you act as if what just happened was of no consequence to you. In the latter, you will respond, not react, in the appropriate time and manner, to what your opponent has said. You will respond using all the information you have gathered from what they have said, and what you have deduced their hidden agenda to be. You will then offer a calm and collected retort to their argument.

In either case, silence can be a powerful tool. However, as you can imagine, it is a difficult skill to master. If you are able to hone this self-discipline, you will almost always have the upper-hand, although it is not foolproof. Sometimes, you will lose and the arguments they will throw at you will be too much. Be ready.

Silence is an essential tool for shaking the system.

Get Ready For The Heat

"Never let us do wrong, because our opponents did so. Let us, rather, by doing right, show them what they ought to have done, and establish a rule the dictates of reason and conscience, rather than of the angry passions"

– James Joyce

All of this chapter has been preparing you for one thing — the heat of your opponent's resistance. You will also need to prepare the rest of your team for what is to come. It is time to take out your map and put it to work. Gather up all your supporters, even the passive ones, and talk to them about your opponents. Make sure you let them know what to expect. You may consider outlining different strategies, and explaining what to do and what not to do.

You will have to make sure that your team adopts all the strategies you have become familiar with. The last thing you want is for your team member to go screaming and yelling, as this will escalate conflicts when you are trying to avoid them. Make sure that your team does not treat your opponents with unnecessary animosity, make sure that they do not forget that these are people they deal with on a regular basis. They are fellow human beings that are standing in your way only because of the disruption to their lives.

You could tell your team members that if they find themselves in a heated situation, they should consult you before acting. Of course, you may have a lot on your plate already, but imagine how much harder your life would be if you had to worry about resolving conflicts between your team members and your opponents.

If possible, you might consider holding a meeting or two to explain your position and how you intend to deal with opponents. This will help avoid internal misunderstandings, and you will ensure that everyone is on the same page.

Et Tu, Ally?

Your allies need not be your strongest supporters. In fact, when you approach them to ask for their support on your new initiative, you may find that they refuse. Do not be surprised if this is the case. Just because they have supported you in the past does not mean that they will have your back every time. If they believe that what you are doing will cause too much disruption, they may become your fiercest opponents. They may advise you to stop what you are doing, spouting facts and statistics, or they may just give you a long list of reasons why you should not go ahead with your initiative.

Expect this to happen. It will lessen the blow and your surprise will not betray you. Instead, sit down with your ally and try to get to the root of their reluctance. They will explain to you why they are not interested. Reframe your initiative to this individual, and see if you can change their mind. If not, then expect that they will vigilantly observe what you are doing. In cases where their lives are disrupted, do not be surprised in the future to find them on the other side of the battlefield. Remember, your ally may one day be your opponent, just as your opponent may one day be your ally.

You Win Some, You Lose Some

Your opponents would not be a "thorn in your side" if they did not put up a tough fight. Indeed, there might be times when it seems like you have no hope against such overwhelming forces. Their metaphorical army may seem to stretch for miles. Do not fret;

you are not expected to win every fight. In fact, you are going to lose some battles along the way, especially when your impact gains momentum. I am reminded of a quote by Gandhi,

"First they ignore you, then they laugh at you, then they fight you, then you win"

Your experience is likely to echo this. Even after you have given them fair warning, your opponents may not take your actions seriously. As your momentum increases, they may mock you or laugh at you. However, when everything is in place and you start shaking the system, you will find that they have gained momentum themselves, and their passion for ending your intervention has magnified. If you have a clear purpose, an understanding of who you are facing, and a rock-solid support system, you will be able to persevere and emerge victorious in the end.

Therefore, do not fret when you lose. It is part of the "war". You will lose some, and you will win some. It is important for you and your team members to know this.

Finally, while you should not give up, there will be times when you might need to lose the "war". If you find that you must abandon the initiative, even if temporarily, don't refuse to consider it. Don't be stubborn when continuing will only bring harm to you, your supporters, and the system.

We Knew The Risks

As on the real battlefield, some battles will end with casualties on both sides. It is a risky and messy business, not just because you will experience resistance, but because you are bound to get hurt as well. You cannot shake a system and hope to remain unscathed.

You have two options when you go head-to-head with the opponent. You can either choose the negotiating table, if that is the route both sides agree on, or you may have to go for the head-on collision. Both options come with underlying costs.

Negotiations

When you negotiate, you are trying to find a mutually beneficial solution. Assuming that you have the upper-hand, you may end up tipping the scale towards your end, and you may get more than your opponent wants to give up. However, even in this best-case scenario, you will still have to make some compromises along the way. Whenever you compromise, what you are really doing is conceding on a specific part of your agenda. Although your purpose may remain intact, you are still giving something away.

This is a cost that you would usually prefer not to have incurred. In a more likely scenario, you will have to give away much more than you had hoped for — as will your opponent — to reach a situation where you are both satisfied.

Head-On Collisions

If you opt to go to "war" with your opponents, you will pay a price. No side ever emerges unscathed. Even the victorious side will have casualties. No matter what the situation, when you lead, expect that you will pay a price. What the price is will depend on the situation and your opponent's "weapon of choice", but here are some possibilities:

- You pay the price physically, as did the African American civil rights activists, who were brutally beaten by the police officers as they marched from Selma to Montgomery. There were many losses due to the horrible injuries they sustained.

- You pay the price professionally, when your opponents attack your credibility and reputation. For instance, in many election campaigns, we see candidates attack each other based on character, trying to point to the flaws and personal issues of their opponents.

- You pay the price emotionally. It is not easy to be constantly battered, and it is bound to take an emotional toll, not only on yourself, but also on your supporters. Some of them may decide to pull out if they feel it has become too much.

- You pay the price financially. In many sit-ins and protests, individuals decide to concede because they cannot afford to carry on. They find themselves at the negotiating table because they need the business to go on or because they need money for their families.

In all of the above cases, there are costs on both sides. You will inflict damage on your opponents, and they will inflict damage on you and your supporters. It is important that you consider this and inform your team members of it as well. They need to know and understand what is at stake. You do not want to create opponents among your supporters simply because you did not warn them of the possible dangers ahead. That may be a cost you cannot afford to pay.

<u>RECAP</u>

Remember, you don't need to wait until after you experience resistance to act. Instead, take the wiser step and prepare for and preempt your opponent's arrival. This will help you minimize the future resistance. Remember to:

- Consider hiring Red Teams to pinpoint the weaknesses of your interventions.

- Ask for people's feedback and thoughts on your intervention before you introduce it.

- LISTEN. People can only voice their thoughts, concerns, and opinions if you let them. Apply the strategies of effective listening to help you do this.

- Make a map of who may be with you, who may be against you, and who may be indifferent. It will help you get a general overview of the landscape before you jump in.

- Ask your colleagues and authority figures for their support.

- Do favors for others.

- Keep an eye on neutral parties. The more intense your intervention becomes, the more likely they are to join a side. Make sure it is yours if possible.

- Hone your understanding of your own and others' emotions.

- Prepare yourself emotionally for intense setbacks. You don't want to get caught up in a wave of emotions and lose sight of what you are trying to do.

- Be empathetic. You need to show people you care, and empathy is essential in achieving this goal.

- Learn to be a patient person and avoid acting irrationally.

- Learn to use both strategic and tactical silence to your advantage.

- Prepare your supporters for the intense resistance they will be facing. Consider teaching them some of the preemptive strategies so they will be better prepared.

- Always check if your old allies are with you on this new initiative. It might just be too risky for them to offer their help.

- Expect some losses. You cannot win every battle, even if you win the "war".

- Aim to negotiate and compromise before opting for a head-on collision.

- If you must go for the head-on collision, make sure you prepare yourself and your supporters for the wave of resistance and its consequences.

Are You Ready?

Now is the time to go back to your checklist for the final, most important check.

Ask yourself:

1.   Am I ready for this?

2.   Am I fully equipped to take on the challenge?

3.   Is what I am doing worth it?

If your answer to any of the questions above is no, then you may need to reconsider introducing an initiative. You need to think long and hard about whether you are up to the task. There is no shame in admitting that now might not be the right time. However, do not lie to yourself and take the easy road out. If what you have is worth it, and you are ready to risk it, do not hesitate.

Be prepared and preempt the opponent's inevitable arrival, because they will put up a fight. If they end up winning, do not fret – you may need to adapt and possibly compromise on certain aspects of your plan now, in order to eventually get where you want to be, pushing the system and yourself towards survival and growth.

Constantly ask yourself what your purpose is and how you can gain support, so that you can maintain the momentum and succeed in your initiative.

From this point onward, we are going to consider and discuss some of the shapes which your opponents might take. This will give you an understanding of what to look out for and who your most ferocious opponent might be.

CHAPTER 4

WHO IS THE OPPONENT?

When we face up to the fact that we have opponents, there is one question which must be answered before we can try and deal with them. Who is the opponent?

"People are like dirt. They can either nourish you and help you grow as a person or they can stunt your growth and make you wilt and die"

– Plato

There is no one type of opponent. People who resist your initiative are part of a large spectrum of opposition, which ranges from the passive resister to the archenemy. Their position will depend on how much of an impact your initiative is making.

As we mentioned earlier, if your impact on the system is minor then you will have less opponents. It is also more likely that they will be predominantly passive, in the sense that their opposition will not significantly affect your initiative. They are more likely to give you cold stares, talk behind your back, or publicly air their views. However, they will probably not actually do anything damaging to your endeavor.

If your impact on the system increases, you will probably encounter more opponents, or at least more active opponents than if your leadership is just a simple nudge to the system. These people may take their opposition up a level, and they may try to slow you down or stop you entirely.

Understanding the differences between passive and active opponents will allow you to better identify who will be standing in your way, and to gauge their level of resistance. You will also be better equipped when it comes to choosing the right strategy for dealing with them.

Now, let us take a look at the different degrees of opposition your opponents may incorporate into their resistance. Each level of resistance and every type of opponent requires a specific, custom-tailored strategy. To make it easier to choose the proper strategy, we will be splitting the types of opposition into two categories: 1) Intensity and 2) Roles.

How Intense Are They?

This first category is the one you will utilize when you are trying to size-up your opponent. You will want to gauge how passionate they are about putting an end to what you are doing. Check where they fall on the intensity spectrum. Where they appear on this spectrum will depend on the context and the impact you are making in the system.

You may encounter individuals who passionately attack your initiatives. They will not only verbally oppose you, but will also do whatever is in their power to stop you. Sometimes, they may go to extreme lengths, such as breaking the law, to get what they want. In such cases, your opponents become your enemies.

At other times, your opponents may be less aggressive, and might simply refuse to use their power and resources to help you achieve your goals. Going a step further, you may encounter individuals who are not passionate at all about stopping what you are doing. These individuals may sit back and resent your initiative without taking action, and at times without even voicing their opinions. The resistance you meet will depend on how you are affecting the lives of those around you: the more threatened they feel, the more intense their counter-initiatives will become.

As you can see from the diagram below, within this category we have six main subcategories. Let us take a closer look at them and understand the differences between them. The categories are: Passive, Passive-Aggressive, Active, Active-Aggressive, Malevolent, and Archenemy .

Intensity Spectrum:

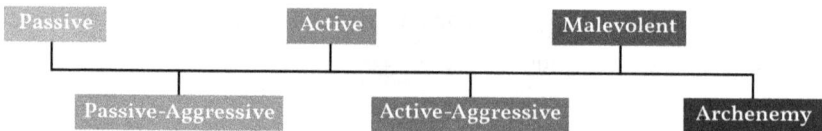

Passive		Active		Malevolent	
	Passive-Aggressive		Active-Aggressive		Archenemy

Passive

As you have spent many hours considering who your initiative will affect and how, you will have a general idea of which side most people will sway towards (support, opposition, or neutral party). On the lowest end of the spectrum we have the least passionate form of resistance: passive.

Individuals in this subcategory tend to be inactive, indecisive, or unmotivated regarding your initiative. This summary of them may give you the impression that they are not actually your opponents. After all, they are not doing anything directly or indirectly to stop or slow you down. However, it is important to differentiate between a neutral party and a passive opponent. A neutral party is unaffected by what you are doing, and as such may choose to stay and watch from the sidelines. A passive opponent, on the other hand, is usually affected by your initiative, but in a minor way, and they are hesitant and not motivated enough to put energy into opposing you.

However, it is important that you do not mistake their indecisiveness and lack of motivation as a signal to ignore them. If your change gives them more motivation in the future, these individuals may increase their resistance, and you want to avoid making more active opponents if you can. Therefore, do not spend excessive time on passive opponents, but do not forget about them, especially as your initiative progresses. If they suddenly choose to actively oppose you, you may be surprised and unprepared, so keep them on your map and bear their position in mind.

Passive-Aggressive

Moving further up the spectrum, as we increase the intensity of opposition, we come to our next subcategory: passive-aggressive. Individuals that fall into this category are resisting you, but are still not willing to act on their resistance directly. This means that they will not voice their concerns, they will not side with you, and yet they will hinder your progress through inaction. Why is inaction something you should be concerned about?

These individuals may never give you the impression that they are opposing you, but they may choose to slow down your interventions simply by failing to follow through with their commitments, giving you the cold shoulder, retorting in subtle ways, etc. Their resistance is subtle, and this makes it quite difficult to discern.

This is not an issue if their role in your plan is not essential. Even if they are inactive or opposing you behind your back, as long as what they are doing does not threaten your growth, even slightly, then they are less of a "thorn in your side". On the other hand, if their support or cooperation is necessary to implement what you are planning to do, you will encounter bigger problems. Although they do not outright oppose you, their subtle resistance can become quite a nuisance, inevitably hindering your progress.

Most of the time, these individuals will give you the impression that they are not against you. However, they may decide to not lend you their support and through subtle inaction, they pose a threat to your initiative. Give them some attention and keep an eye on them, but do not spend more time than you need to deal with them, especially if you are also trying to handle more intense and passionate resisters.

Here is an example of the passive-aggressive resister: you want to introduce a new policy and you need some legal documents signed. You hand the document over to a person from the legal department. What you do not know is that this person is not on your side. Because they oppose you, they might take their time in getting the documents to the right person, pass the task on to someone else, claim that they gave it in when they did not, or similarly hinder your progress. They will prolong the process, hoping to slow it down, or make you lose motivation. However, they will probably not let you know they oppose what you are doing, instead opting for subtle hints and inaction.

Active

Now we move further up the spectrum towards the more obvious and intense individuals. People in this subcategory are what we shall call the pleasant and honest opponent. Pleasant, because they are not intent on harming you, but want to stop what you are doing. Honest, because they are straightforward and forthright about where they stand.

An active opponent takes action to bring an end to what you are trying to do. They have heard what you have to say, but they are not convinced that what you are proposing will benefit them. Their interests or agendas are at stake. They will express their opposition loud and clear, and they will do what they can to stop you by lobbying against your initiative. They will attempt to get people on their side by pointing out the flaws in your initiative. You know from the beginning what to expect: they do not like what you are doing and they are not on your side. There are no hidden agendas or subtle attempts to stop you.

Given their straightforward approach, active opponents may provide you with a valuable wealth of information about your initiative and their perspectives. In fact, they may actually help to improve your initiative; as discussed, opponents can be useful when it comes to pointing out your mistakes or shortcomings. This will help you get a clearer understanding of anything your initiative may be missing, and how you can fix it. In other words, active opponents provide you with free advice, which helps you and your initiative.

As with other opposing forces, you should lend them not only your time but your ear. Listen to what they have to say, discuss, and negotiate. Their concerns may be legitimate and, as such, you may need to change a few things. If they have the wrong idea about what you are doing then you can explain in detail your plan, the risks involved, and the benefits your initiative entails. You never know what the outcome may be.

Active-Aggressive

There are times when trying to tell you what is wrong with your initiative or discussing how you are disrupting lives may not do the trick. It may be because: 1) you are unwilling to hear them out; 2) you have heard what they have to say but do not feel convinced by it, or 3) you cannot possibly give them what they want because of limited resources, the purpose of the initiative being irreconcilable with their desires, etc.

Whatever the reason, when this happens, do not be surprised to find some individuals turning up the intensity of their resistance. If they believe that the risks far outweigh the benefits for them and their dependents, they may become aggressive in their counter-initiatives (though this rarely refers to physical aggression).

It is also possible that some individuals may be too affected to consider taking the negotiation route first. If your initiative touches on their dimensions and robs them of any element in their life (hungers, dreams, loyalties, etc.), they may opt immediately for the active-aggressive route, telling you that they have a problem with what you are doing and actively trying to stop you. Individuals in the active-aggressive subcategory may stage protests, rally troops against your initiative, and organize sit-ins, among other strategies. In the end, their actions lean more towards personalizing the conflict, and creating chaos for the sole purpose of hindering your progress. Although they are hesitant to attack anyone physically, they are not afraid to create a scene and use a little verbal aggression where they see fit.

They will not opt to break the law, but they may be ferocious in their rebuttal when you first introduce your initiative or the reasoning behind it. They may choose to verbally attack others and lower the team's morale. For instance, they might constantly criticize others for not seeing how much harm your initiative is bringing, or they might publicly pinpoint the faults in your initiative — of course, their perception is based solely on how they see your initiative and how it is affecting them and their dimensions (9-Ds).

Think of it this way: individuals in this subcategory express their opposition in the form of non-violent resistance.

Malevolent

As your opposition's intensity increases, they become potentially more harmful. They may still play within the rules of the game, but they will bend and distort those rules to their own advantage. They will not only try to put an end to your initiative, but may even target you personally in an attempt to stop what you are doing. People in this category will attack your credibility, integrity, and personality. It will seem like it is no longer just about the initiative. They will use manipulation, espionage, and personal attacks to try and stop what you are doing. We often end up viewing these opponents in a negative light, and, depending on the tactics they employ, they may cross from opponents to enemies.

They may attempt to disturb you and threaten you by targeting elements of your life that are unrelated to the organization. They may try to complicate your personal relationships and life. They may even go to the news to sully your reputation, regardless of whether or not their claims hold any merit. They are not only aggressive, but also hurtful, and they will make things personal. While the active-aggressive type of opponent may be hurtful at times, that is not their primary intention; it is just in the heat of the moment. The malevolent type, however, may be calm and collected, but spend their time plotting your end. They will frame your initiative as existing for your sole benefit, and will try to sully your character to get to what they want, maintaining the status quo and putting an end to the change you are trying to implement.

Individuals in this subcategory may also backstab you. They may attempt to get close to you, fooling you into believing that they are on your side, and then when the time is right, they will use all the inside information they have to bring you and your initiative to an end. They may spend all their time with you, scheming and hindering your progress from within. This subcategory is not only harmful, but their presence in your life increases the urgency with which you need to deal with them. Offering them more leeway increases the chance of your initiative failing.

If they feel that you and your changes are somehow threatening their survival and growth, malevolent opponents may transgress both moral and legal boundaries. They may decide to take an illegal route to get the information they need in order to end what you are proposing. They might spy on you, or pass on classified information to other competitors. They might vandalize your workplace, home, or property. If they are set on revenge, you will need to make sure you pay as much attention to them as you can; they are no longer your opponents, but your enemies.

Schemers, manipulators, backstabbers, or spies should be included in this subcategory.

To distinguish between malevolent and active-aggressive, let's imagine a soccer game: an active-aggressive soccer player might foul his competitor, but only in a direct attempt to stop his advancement

> **"Don't act surprised when your friend with the ear becomes your enemy with the mouth"**
>
> – *Unknown*

towards the goal. Conversely, a malevolent player might target his competitor not with the intention of stealing the ball, but to prevent him from playing the rest of the tournament (e.g. elbowing his nose, attempting to twist his knee).

Archenemy

This is the epitome of intense, active, and aggressive resistance, and anyone in this subcategory will blatantly try to bring you down, no matter the cost. There is no question that they are now enemies, not opponents. For them, it is no longer about maintaining the status quo, but has become decidedly personal. They will feel that one of you cannot continue to exist without the downfall of the other party. In other words, their survival and growth can only continue at the expense of yours. They want to "destroy" you.

Their playbook includes anything and everything you can think of. They will sully your reputation, transgress lawful and moral boundaries, even rob you of your basic rights (i.e. the right to freedom or life). Their existence actually threatens your survival, not only your growth.

Luckily, many of us can say that we have not experienced anyone who wants to see us not only fail, but fall to ruin. Indeed, reading this category may make us think more of villains straight from the big screen or the pages of a book than anyone we encounter in our lives. However, although it is upsetting to even think about, such individuals do exist and need to be acknowledged. The examples that come to mind are the assassins of leaders such as Abraham Lincoln, Mahatma Mohandas Gandhi, Martin Luther King Jr., and John F. Kennedy.

What Role Do They Play?

Moving on to the second category or dimension, let us consider the roles that your opponents may play in the system. Leadership acts do not only happen in the workplace, but also in society and in your own home.

Personal relationships tend to complicate how you deal with others. As such, there is no one way to go about navigating interactions. Everything will depend on who the individual is and what relationship they share with you. This is even more important when we talk about dealing with your opponents: you cannot hope to treat every individual based solely on how intensely they oppose you. It is necessary to widen your scope and consider your relationship with your opponent, not just the intensity of their opposition.

As we have discussed, we are all part of systems. This might be:

- **Socially:** We are part of different groups and cultures, each with its own set of rules. These groups include our families, friends, acquaintances, religious or spiritual groups, and social gatherings.

- **Professionally:** Throughout our lives, most of us will have worked or pursued an education. During that time, we played our respective roles and were part of a group or culture that followed the same rules (e.g. office or university).

- **Naturally:** Even if we spend our days alone in a cabin, we are still part of a system — nature.

Consider how any change that shakes a particular system will be met with resistance. Opponents to your initiative will play different roles in different systems. This, in turn, will affect the ways in which you deal with them. You will want to incorporate what you know about the opponent's intensity into the structure of the system. You need to consider where your opponent lies in the hierarchy of that system, and what your relationship with them is. After all, dealing with your superior at work is not like dealing with your family at home.

The categories are: Personal, Constituents, Competition, Colleagues, Subordinates, Authority, and The First Opponent.

Personal

You are part of a family, you have friends and acquaintances, and you may be part of a community (e.g. a club, a committee, a religious or spiritual group). Any role that is based on a social or personal relationship falls into this subcategory (e.g. neighbors, friends).

Decisions you make that affect people in this subcategory may not be met with support, and indeed sometimes those around you may resist the change. They may be concerned about the consequences of your actions. Their resistance may mean a change in your relationship. Sometimes you may give up relationships entirely, and at other times you will form new ones. How you deal with opponents in this category depends on how close you are to them, and what is at stake if you insist upon an initiative that they dislike.

There are times when your closest companions and family members may turn against you because you are threatening their dimensions (dreams, insecurities, hungers, etc.). Although we do not like to think of scenarios where we might hurt our loved ones, there will be situations where you propose a change that will have them drawing the short stick. There will be instances where their resistance is so intense that you may even want to consider changing the nature of your relationship.

This is when things can get a bit more complicated. After all, you expect your friends, family, and community members to side with you on anything that ultimately helps the system you belong to. However, this may not always be the case, and we may find that we lose friends along the way, complicate things with our family members, and/or get shunned from a community solely for acting in a way that challenges the status quo.

It is quite possible that you will find yourself redefining your relationships and their importance. At times, you may decide to turn the other cheek and be patient with them for the sake of your past and current relationship. At other times, turning your back on these individuals, who cannot see how you are pushing them towards surviving and growing, may be the only viable option.

When dealing with someone who plays a personal role in your life, there is a huge amount you need to consider. You will have to think about what you are planning to do, how it will affect their lives in both the short and long term, and how intensely will they resist, but you will also need to ask yourself what their relationship means to you, and what the possible consequences for your relationship are if you move forward with your initiative.

Subordinates

Most organizations will have a hierarchy. As such, there will also be people in the organization who you have authority over – your subordinates. In general, they will tend to fall in line and support you with whatever you are planning to do, since they will not want to get on your bad side. However, it is possible that your planned, purposeful intervention may affect some of their dimensions (9-Ds).

At times when your intervention shakes the system hard, the first people to be affected will usually be your subordinates. Although this analogy may seem harsh, in a game of chess, the pawns are almost always the first to go, and are sacrificed to win the game. However, you want to make sure you do not sacrifice your subordinates. Apart from the morality of supporting those weaker than you, there is strength in numbers and they will probably need less convincing than anyone else within the hierarchy. In other words, they are the support you have in the upcoming battle.

Colleagues

Unless you are working in a startup where you are the only member of staff, you are bound to have people working alongside you, people who have the same status as you do in an organization. They will have the same power that you do, and may be the main force you have to convince and recruit to help you with your change.

Remember when we discussed mapping out your supporters, opponents, neutral individuals, and authority? Well, as you will realize with time, some of your fiercest opponents are going to be the people you work with. This makes sense when you consider that they are likely going to be among the first to experience the change, and if they find themselves on the losing side, they will be quick to let you know their feelings on the initiative.

Authority

Moving up the hierarchy, there is a possibility that you may not be the top brass, and, as such, you will have to report to others. Authority within a system generally holds power over your fate, and you do not usually want to find yourself on authority's bad side. If you want your interventions to go as smoothly as possible, you do not want to jeopardize authority's dimensions, or worse, their survival and growth.

If authority does not like your initiative, it is not difficult for them to hinder or even end it by closing channels or firing you. All in all, the ball is almost always in their court, and if you want to play, you need to make sure you are ready. You do not want to challenge a whale if you are but a small fish.

Unfortunately, sometimes you will have to go head to head with authority. You need only think about the protests for apartheid in South Africa, or the fight for independence in India, or even more recently, the many women speaking up who were sexually assaulted by the entertainment mogul Harvey Weinstein and other authority figures. Authority is difficult to challenge, but there are times when the change is important and risks must be taken.

Sometimes, you will propose similarly significant initiatives that will shake the system, and it's possible that authority will be the first people to "feel the earthshaking vibrations". Anytime you propose something that challenges the authority's status quo, the aftermath of the shock will be huge, due to the power they have.

Competition

You are probably not surprised to see this as a subcategory. Indeed, in our definition of the opponent, we include competitors. As you can imagine, your competition is unlikely to be on your side. However, the fact that they are competing with you does not necessarily mean that they will be opposing you. They may be working solely on improving their presence and their product or service. They may not do anything to hinder your progress, and their existence may even drive you towards growth.

However, if your presence and your innovations and interventions in the market are threatening their dimensions (9-Ds), this is unlikely to be the case. As with others, if your competition feel they are losing the game, they will up their ante and try to restore their position. If they feel they have fallen behind you, they will start targeting you. This means that you need to bear in mind where your competitor lies on the intensity spectrum. They may be passive, doing their own thing, or they may be your archenemy. It all depends on how you are affecting them.

Constituents

As part of an organization, whether it is corporate, a government, or a non-profit organization, you will have people whom you serve — constituents (clients, customers, citizens, etc.). In general, your existence is contingent on their support. It would be unusual for a company not to have paying customers, or a non-profit organization not to have people it is offering its services to.

When you introduce an initiative, the purpose is usually to serve your constituents' interests. However, there will be times when you introduce a change that some of your constituents do not understand or like. They will meet this with resistance and, depending on the percentage of resisting constituents, you may be in for a difficult journey.

In general, you will want to avoid creating unnecessary tensions with your constituents, especially since your future and the future of the organization is dependent on their support and overall attitude towards the organization. This can make introducing initiatives difficult.

For instance, if you work in the customer service industry, your sole focus is on providing your customers with the best service your organization can offer. If you introduce a new initiative which customers don't like, you may find your constituents rapidly decrease in number. You might face boycotts, account closures, withdrawals of support or funding, petitions, or other difficulties if you do something which makes your constituents unhappy.

The First Opponent

> "And God said 'Love Your Enemy,' and I obeyed Him and loved myself"
>
> – Gibran Khalil Gibran

What if you are your own opponent? How is that possible? Take this moment to consider a time when you looked in the mirror and thought to yourself, "What am I doing with my life?" or something similar. Also consider a time when you felt hesitant or lacking in motivation. Did you promise yourself to commit to something, only to find yourself breaking that promise? A new year's resolution, for instance?

Before we move on, it is important to remember that you as a person are NOT YOUR OPPONENT. The opponent is the resistance you face, which stems from your bad habits, negative loyalties, faulty commitments, etc. As such, when you are faced with any type of resistance that reflects the above, you need to be one step ahead and get to the root of that resistance. You need to remind yourself of who you were before all the dimensions got jumbled into the mix.

The reality is that acts of leadership must start with self-leadership. After all, you cannot hope to get others moving forward if you cannot lead yourself. If you find yourself hesitating, fearing commitment, breaking promises you made to yourself, or simply giving up on opportunities, then at that moment, you may be your own worst opponent.

If an opportunity arises which will shake your internal system (mind), and you find yourself postponing it or even declining it, you need to stop and understand that at that moment, you are

"Self-pity is our worst enemy and if we yield to it, we can never do anything wise in the world"

- Helen Keller

standing in the way of your own progress, and quite possibly the progress of the larger system (family, organization, community, company, etc.). It is important that you question what dimensions this opportunity for growth is affecting. In other words: what in the world is stopping me? Only when you take the time to truly understand your own self will you be able to grab that opportunity and turn it into something that will push your life and the lives of those around you forward.

Furthermore, as with any other role, this form of resistance will come with varying degrees, and sometimes you will find yourself needing help from others. As you intend to help those around you thrive, you must accept that sometimes you will need others, not only to help you advance your initiatives, but to push you personally forward towards growth.

Whatever role and intensity the opponent may fit into, you can only deal with them by considering these two categories. After all, you cannot deal with an active opponent the same way you deal with a passive opponent, and nor can you deal with an active colleague the same way you deal with an active authority figure. Take this information and consider the numerous types of opponents based on the combination of their roles and their intensities. In the end, you can choose the best strategy only if you know exactly who you are dealing with.

PART TWO

PRINCIPLES/ STRATEGIES REFERENCE

PRINCIPLES/STRATEGIES

"You will never reach your destination if you stop and throw stones at every dog that barks"

– Winston Churchill

The underlying philosophy for the strategies[7] below is to make sure that the "caravan" reaches its destination, without focusing on winning side battles against the "wolves" and "barking dogs". We want to get the people who joined the caravan to where they need to be, to where we promised to take them.

Why? It is not about vanity, ego, pride, proving who was right or wrong, winning or losing, or an "us versus them" mentality. It is solely about fulfilling the purpose of your leadership initiative and helping others create a better reality for themselves.

Below is a list of 104 strategies that you may use at your discretion to fulfill the purpose of your initiative. You may choose to use an individual strategy or a combination of strategies, tailored to the specific requirements of the case you are dealing with.

---

[7] I have thought time and again about what the right word to describe the points in the section below would be. I considered the words strategy, principle, technique, and tactic, but found that none of these words alone technically capture the nature of these points. Call them what you like, but make sure you understand and apply them

When applying the strategies, they must fall within the following parameters, being:

- Empathetic
- Graceful
- Compassionate
- Adaptive
- Elegant
- Firm
- Assertive
- Flexible
- Confrontational (when necessary)

The aim is to study the case you are tackling and strike a balance between the above parameters. You should emphasize certain parameters depending on what the case calls for. There will be situations where you will need to be firm rather than flexible. There will be other situations where you need to be compassionate rather than confrontational. It all depends on your analysis of the situation and its requirements, which will help you choose the right balance of the above parameters. This way you can identify the most appropriate strategy, or combination of strategies, to deal with the situation and fulfill the purpose of your initiative.

I am providing you with the fundamental ingredients. It is up to you to choose which recipes you need to follow based on the requirements of the case you are tackling.

1 Ensure any negativity doesn't become contagious

When you encounter resistance, at any intensity, you want to make sure that the negativity doesn't spread from one person to another. The word negativity here implies any form of resistance, ranging from hesitation and indecision all the way up to feelings of hatred and animosity. It is important that you don't allow this to spread. Even the passive opponent might indirectly pass on their indecisiveness to others. People around them will be observant, and if you are picking up on resistance, others are likely to do the same. Some of these people may be loyal to you, but others will be less so, and if you don't do something about it, you may find more people opposing you.

Therefore, to contain the negativity, you will want to try to address it and its source. The lower your opposition is on the intensity spectrum, the better your chances of containing the situation will be. However, this doesn't mean that you should avoid people on the more intense side. On the contrary, the more intense the situation, the more important it becomes to nip the negativity in the bud, or at least to contain and isolate it.

Try to talk to the individuals who have a problem with your initiative, listen to their concerns, and compromise, if possible. You will want to go into the conversation with the aim of minimizing the impact of their resistance. Of course, the more intense their resistance, the less likely it is that you will want to talk to the individuals. Instead, you may focus more on securing your supporters, getting the neutrals to see the whole picture, and getting the more passive resisters to either lessen their resistance or at least not intensify it.

It is important to mention that the complexity of the situation will depend on the role the person plays in your life. Dealing with your spouse, even at a passive level, is different from dealing with your colleagues or subordinates. Each role has specific nuances that mean you will need to tailor your strategies to fit the situation.

---

2 Respect the history of the relationship

Whether it is a professional, personal, or social relationship, you cannot in good conscience forget about it. One way to get people to lessen their resistance is to consider and communicate the history of the relationship. If, for instance, you have a history of following through with your promises, people who know that will probably give you the benefit of doubt before they start resisting you.

However, in the heat of the moment, many people will forget the good times and focus on the bad. Let people know that you acknowledge and respect their relationship and previous experiences. This may help to buy you enough time to show them that you are doing the right thing, or it might encourage them to sit down with you and try to find a solution to the problem.

The closer the relationship, the more urgent it becomes to communicate how much you value it. Some of your resisters will feel like you are personally betraying them, so remember to sit them down and tell them that you have not forgotten about the relationship you share. Stress how much you value it, bringing up some of the crucial, good moments you have both experienced. This will also help soften their resistance, and you can then use other strategies to further mitigate it.

3   Limit the conflict to the relevant issues

It is easy for things to get out of control. Suddenly, one issue "opens the floodgates" and raises other unrelated issues. For instance, conflict over school fees could bring up an unrelated conflict about a lack of intimacy between spouses. Alternatively, a disagreement over longer working hours might turn into an argument about the outdated equipment in the office.

Whatever the situation, people may begin to raise other issues that they have kept tucked away. When you uproot their lives, they will lose their "inhibition" and mention things that have nothing to do with the conflict at hand. You must make sure that you table those unrelated issues, and instead try to get your opponents to focus on conflicts that your leadership initiative is creating. If there are too many issues on the table, you will not be able to move forward.

So, when discussing the initiative and the issues it may cause, make sure to keep the conversation centered on those issues. Tell your resisters that you are glad they are addressing other problems that annoy or upset them, but that you need to move one step at a time, starting with those that are already on the table — issues with the initiative.

Address the issues that the initiative is creating so you can move forward, and when you have the chance, go back and deal with the other issues that you put aside. Don't ignore the other issues, not only because you need to take care of them (if you can), but also because they may provide you with bargaining chips. It might be that replacing the old equipment in the office increases team morale, and they will be more willing to consider working longer hours. Addressing other issues can allow you to move forward and strengthen your relationship.

In the end, keep the main focus on the initiative and the issues related to it. Put a pin on unrelated issues so you can come back and deal with them at a later time, when the initiative is up and rolling.

---

4   Always be kind and courteous

Whatever the intensity of the resistance and no matter how unpleasant the situation becomes, you will want to remain kind and courteous. It makes it harder for your opponents to stay angry with you. If you maintain your composure, repeating time and time again that you care about their well-being, while politely explaining your reasoning, your opponents may at least take their resistance down a notch. Remember that leadership is not about you or your feelings, but about benefiting others, and if you spend your time cursing, yelling, or counter-resisting, you will not get anywhere. Even if your opponent is aggressive and offensive, you need to remain respectful.

For example, if you are in a meeting and your opponents start yelling, thrashing their hands, calling you names, and/or creating a scene, excuse yourself politely and say that you came with the intention of addressing their concerns and resolving any issues. Do not resort to saying hurtful things, looking down on them, or showing them negative emotions.

When you are always polite and courteous, more people will believe that you mean them well. Your supporters will intensify their support, and will hopefully take your behavior as an example of how they themselves must act. In addition, neutrals and passive resisters may change their mind and join your side, especially if you are the caring and polite one, and your opponent is the reason the situation is getting out of control.

Finally, this strategy is key if you wish to sit down with your opponents and discuss their issues. Your demeanor will give them the message that you are willing to listen and try to find solutions.

---

5   Always be compassionate and empathetic

Compassion and empathy are at the heart of true leadership. You cannot hope to resolve most issues if you do not try to put yourself in your opponent's shoes. It is true that you may resolve a few technical issues, but the major issues stem from how the initiative is affecting people's lives, and you cannot hope to gain an understanding of this without being empathetic. You cannot genuinely help without being compassionate.

Therefore, take the time to sit down and understand what is troubling your opponents. This will offer you an inside view into the root of their issues. In other words, it is through empathy, in addition to listening, that you will be able to understand your opponents' 9-Ds.

For instance, if you understand that longer working hours are taking away from precious family time, you may be able to find a solution that helps get the initiative done without robbing the other person of something s/he holds dear.

In addition, compassion and empathy are essential if you wish to benefit the system. You are undertaking your initiative because you genuinely wish to help others. This is at the heart of leadership.

6 Over-communicate

Communication is key. You cannot hope to say, do, or understand anything without keeping the lines of communication open. Let the system and its constituents know that you are open to their suggestions, opinions, solutions, etc. This will help you get a clearer picture of the resistance, and leave you better equipped to deal with it.

It is important that you don't only say things once, but repeatedly. Put simply: over-communicate. There will be times when you think that you have explained yourself, your reasons for introducing the initiative, its benefits, and purpose, but in reality there might be some people who just don't know about it, or people who have misunderstood what you plan to do. If left unchecked, misunderstandings could breed intense resistance that might significantly harm the initiative. Try to avoid them by over-communicating. It is better to have people telling you that you have already given them that information than to have them making incorrect assumptions about what you are proposing.

Sometimes it helps to make a list of these individuals, approach each one, and repeat yourself time and again. Ask them questions to make sure they have understood you, fact-check to see if they can remember everything you said, and do whatever else you feel is necessary to make sure that everyone involved has all the information they need. This will help reduce some of the resistance you face.

For instance, there are times when your spouse, partner, or friend might resist the initiative, not because they have a problem with it, but because you didn't give them sufficient time to make adjustments. They may ask you why you didn't let them know, even though you felt that you had.

Unfortunately, some people will still oppose you even after you have "bored" them with your detailed repetitions. It is inevitable, and you will need to resort to other strategies to deal with it. However, you will know at least that you have excluded resistance borne of misunderstandings.

Remember, don't just communicate... over-communicate!

---

7   Over-communicate your interest in listening to their point of view

---

Let your opponents know repeatedly, and on many occasions, that you are interested in hearing what they have to say, and what their point of view on the initiative is. You need to understand their perspective in detail. Offering to communicate could be used as a gesture of good faith, showing that you genuinely want to sit down with them and hear them out.

Even if this gesture does not quell or lessen their resistance, if they do decide to voice their point of view and concerns, it will still offer you valuable information. You will understand what issues they have, and this information will help you unlock techniques for dealing with them. You can come up with adaptive and creative solutions that allow you to continue with the initiative while simultaneously addressing their concerns and decreasing, or ending, their resistance.

More importantly, as already mentioned, their concerns and perspectives may raise some legitimate flaws in the initiative, which you can then work on fixing, ultimately bettering the initiative and dealing with their resistance.

8   Consider some "quid pro quo"

Some situations call for some "quid pro quo". You may need to take some time to do something for your opponents, unrelated to the initiative, in return for their support. They are, after all, giving up certain things for you, so you need to be prepared to return this.

You need to weigh the costs of doing them a favor. If they make a request that doesn't interfere with the initiative, but will incur some outlay (e.g. time, money, support), weigh up that cost. If it is not too much, consider fulfilling their request. If the costs are too great, or you cannot ethically or morally do what they are asking you, then try to find another way.

For example, you want an influential colleague to use their influence to get people on board with your initiative to introduce environment-friendly practices at the office. Your colleague might ask you to use your sway over authority to increase their chances of getting a promotion. If you think that this colleague deserves the promotion, accept their deal and move forward. If you feel that you cannot do that, then apologize and tell them that you feel you cannot ask that of your boss (you want to remain truthful, genuine, and ethical).

In another scenario, in return for the school board's vote on your intervention to increase scholarship funding, the members ask you to consider teaching an extra course. This may mean that you need to sacrifice time and money since it is an unpaid position. If you feel that the benefits of their suggestion outweigh the costs, you should probably accept.

9 Objectively diagnose the root of their resistance

You need to get to the root of people's resistance if you wish to neutralize it, and not just temporarily postpone it. To do this, you need to take a step back and look at the situation objectively. Let go of any perception you may have about the initiative, and try to see what might be causing your opponents to resist. Remember that not everyone will see the benefits just because you do.

With this frame of mind, you can better understand what issues your opponents may have. This allows you to approach them to discuss it further and confirm your suspicions. After all, if you don't know exactly what is troubling your opponents, you cannot fully understand the root of their resistance.

Remaining objective will allow you to get a general idea before you confront them, as well as making you better able to understand their situation when you do talk to them. There are situations where you might be off-base about what their issues are. To avoid that, you will need to ask them objectively, politely, considerately, and compassionately.

In the end, if you go into a conversation with preconceived notions, biases, and a closed mind, then you will not get anywhere and could possibly make matters worse. Having ideas about what might be bothering them helps you to plan strategies, but remember you should always listen and be prepared to change in accordance with the new information you get from conversations.

10 Be conscious of the cultural codes of conduct and protocols

There may be situations when you are dealing with individuals from different cultural backgrounds. Remember, not everyone will deal with conflict the same way, and so you need to understand their cultural protocols if you wish to successfully deal with their resistance. Don't enforce your cultural codes of conduct on to them, this will backfire and create misunderstandings.

Furthermore, accounting for culture will allow you to accurately identify the intensity of their resistance. For example, if you are dealing with individuals from a less competitive culture, their passive approach to conflict may be misinterpreted as unimportant and you may dismiss their resistance. If you are unaware you would continue with your initiative without giving them much thought. Only to find yourself ambushed later on and facing more resistance than you anticipated.

Therefore, make sure to consider your opponent, the context, and their cultural background. They may be resisting you because you failed to follow their accepted code of conduct, not because they feel your initiative itself is the issue. Avoid these unnecessary issues and give yourself the chance to accurate identify and deal with their resistance. Respect your opponents' cultures and don't risk your initiative over something you can avoid.

11   Keep the fire contained

Work to keep the situation under control, making sure that nothing intensifies your opponent's resistance, and de-escalating it if you can. You cannot control the tension caused by your initiative, but you can ensure you don't add to that tension. Even if you cannot deal with their resistance for the time being, try to contain it, keeping it at the same level.

For instance, you could: show them you care, tell them that you are working on finding a solution, offer to include them in the initiative, ask for their advice, listen to their concerns, take some time off your regular duties to sit down with them. This may not quell their resistance, but it will help show them that you are interested in resolving the problems, and it may keep their resistance at the same level of intensity (if it doesn't actually decrease it).

Containing the fire may buy you enough time for some results to show. This way, your resisters (along with others in the system) may reap the benefits of the initiative. In the process, they may either decrease or give up on their resistance. It depends on how the initiative is affecting their lives, and the intensity they are at.

In the end, make sure that their resistance doesn't get more intense, which will just complicate matters further for most of the people involved.

12 Don't provoke them

Don't make matters worse for yourself, the initiative, your supporters, and the system overall. Don't make matters worse for your opponents either. Make sure that you don't do anything that will provoke them. Even those who are on the fence about resisting you might jump off on the opposing side and start climbing the intensity spectrum if you start acting provocatively.

If you go around bragging about your victories, claiming that you know best, ordering people around, or even moving forward with the initiative without addressing your resisters' concerns, you open yourself up to more intense resistance from your opponents, or initial resistance from neutrals and even your supporters. If your supporters find your actions less than ideal, they will withdraw their support not because of the initiative, but because of you.

You will need to think about your actions before you go ahead with them. Make sure you consider how others might interpret your behavior. You may want to run strategies by your supporters or trusted advisers so that they can give you fresh perspectives on an idea or behavior before you initiate it.

13 Consider involving mediators

There are certain situations where you will need outside help. These might include (among others) situations where: the relationship is important to you, your work is contingent on support from key players, you work or live with your "opponent", you cannot come to a compromise with your opponent, your opponent will not discuss the issues, or other situations where you don't want to lose a person or group. If you are facing these issues, you may want to consider involving a neutral third party to help mediate your conversations.

Mediators will help calm the situation, getting you both to the table to talk. They will also help to control emotions, and will promote a rational discussion. Make sure you fully utilize this opportunity. Express your care and concern for your opponent, highlight your interest in listening, remain polite, patient, etc. Try to understand what the issue is and look for creative solutions together. The mediator might even be able to help you find solutions, or s/he might come up with one themselves.

There are times when mediation might be a good first step in mending broken fences and understanding your resisters and their issues better. After that, you can both make some gestures of confidence and hopefully work things out on your own. If that is not possible then you could listen to the mediator's suggestions, which should be aimed at helping you both get the maximum benefit from the discussion.

Added to this, it's possible that proposing mediation may be seen as a gesture of good faith, implying you are willing to compromise. After all, in your opponents' eyes, you are the source of the upheaval and chaos in their lives, so they may see it as your responsibility to find solutions.

14 Stay focused on your purpose

The purpose is the guiding light, the driving force, and the WHY behind the initiative. Focus on your purpose. If you keep your purpose in mind, you can overcome the pressures of resistance, but you will also become more adaptive and flexible, which is necessary with the inevitable changing circumstances (e.g. people changing sides, supporters withdrawing support, gaining new supporters, unexpected losses). If you focus on your purpose, you can see the many options at your disposal for continuing with the initiative, and you can go ahead with the best plan. You will better understand what is open to negotiation and compromise, and what is not.

In short, if you focus on purpose, you will not lose focus of the initiative, so you will do what you must for the system without compromising on the integrity of the initiative.

Constantly ask yourself:

- What is it that I set out to do?

- WHY am I doing it?

15 Maintain the momentum of your progress

If you are on a roll, and the initiative is moving at a satisfactory pace, the last thing you want is to stop or, worse, move backward. As you are going forward with the initiative, keep up the momentum. Even when you experience resistance, most of the time, you should not stop the initiative just to deal with it. Instead, work on the initiative at the same time as handling the resistance. If that means you need help then don't hesitate to ask for it; your support network is there not only to support the initiative, but to help you overcome resistance. If you feel you need to use mediators, do so. Do whatever you feel will help lessen resistance, but don't stop the momentum of the initiative.

The moment you allow the initiative's momentum to diminish is the moment you open it up to vulnerabilities. Remember that your opponents are resisting you because of the initiative. They are working to slow it down or end it. If you do their work for them, they will win, and the system will be worse off.

Keep the momentum up and keep moving forward. The purpose is to benefit the system, and you will not be able to do that if you stop the initiative.

16 Create and nourish your support network

Support. Support. Support. You cannot introduce an initiative on your own. You will face too many challenges from too many people. Even if you are able to take your opponents on alone, which can be nearly impossible, it will take up too much of your time and energy, and the initiative will suffer. Focus on building your support network. The larger it is, the better off the initiative will be.

Firstly, try going to your previous allies and supporters. Although it is not guaranteed that they will join you, they are still a good place to start. Additionally, look at your current supporters and try to mobilize the passive supporters into more active supporters. This will reduce the pressure on you and the other active supporters.

Next, consider approaching the neutrals again (following from the preemptive stage) and try to convince them about the initiative and its benefits. Now that you have introduced the initiative, some of the neutrals' views and/or their sense of involvement may have changed, so scoop them up before they join the other side.

Thirdly, if you find yourself in a pinch, consider calling in any favors you may have under your belt. If there are people who owe you a solid, ask them to back you up and help you. Although you should not force or coerce them, it doesn't hurt to ask for help, especially considering you have a higher chance of success with them on your side. If any of your opponents owe you a favor, reminding them of this may decrease their resistance or turn them into neutral parties.

Remember also that circumstances change, so it is worth trying to get your more passive resisters to switch sides. Although they may not be active supporters, it will still help to have more people on your side, and fewer people on the opposition's side.

---

17   Stay close to your support network

Keep your supporters informed of all the new developments and relevant information, and involve them in the initiative. The more distant you are from your supporters, the more likely it becomes that they will withdraw their support.

Your opponents may attempt to feed them false information or spread rumors about your initiative. Although your more loyal and active supporters may not believe them, your passive supporters are susceptible to these attempts. To avoid losing them, keep your supporters close. The moment your opponents attempt to spread rumors, your supporters will let you know and you can quickly deny them. In addition, if you keep your support network in the loop at all times, they will know what is going on and may not have to double-check with you to deny the rumors.

There may be times when your opponents win a battle or two, and the initiative takes a hit. At these moments, staying close to your supporters will help ensure they don't abandon ship at the first loss.

Therefore, make sure your support network is:

- A tight-knit group.

- Communicating at all times.

- Informed of all relevant developments and new information.

- Involved in the process and therefore holding a personal stake in the matter.

- Warned of upcoming threats and the intensities of the initiative's opponents.

- A reflection of the initiative, for the initiative is only as strong as its advocates.

18 Don't make it personal or take it personally

Most of the time, it is not personal for either side. It is about the initiative for both you and your opponents. It is not about you, your ambitions, or any of your 9-Ds. It is not a personal endeavor. This means that you should never take it personally or make it personal, even if your opponents try to.

Keep your focus on what you are doing, no matter how intense the situation becomes. It helps to think about your purpose and how the initiative will benefit the system, as well as to understand that your opponents' issues are with the initiative (not with you).

It is also important that you not make it personal by humiliating, provoking, or pressuring your opponents. Don't make it about them when it is not, even if they are liars, cheaters, saboteurs, backstabbers, etc. You will not gain anything by making it about personal conflicts, ones that will not help the initiative.

Remember to always be kind, courteous, compassionate, and empathetic towards all people involved, and remain focused on the initiative.

19 Think creatively

As circumstances change, you need to make sure the initiative is adapting. Always self-reflect and see how you might adjust the initiative to benefit the maximum number of individuals without compromising on the quality and purpose of the initiative.

Keep your mind open and consider different ways in which you could approach a situation. There may be a way that satisfies you, your supporters, and your opponents, while dealing with your resistance and achieving the purpose of your initiative. All it takes, at times, is to think creatively.

Try to get your opponents in on the action. Go to them and ask them to sit down with you and brainstorm creative ways to carry out the initiative. Let them know you are flexible and are willing to find a way forward that suits you both. Although you may not be able to escape hurting some people by introducing the initiative, you can still try to minimize the damage. After all, the initiative is there to benefit, not hurt others.

Always think creatively and remember to utilize the creativity of both your supporters and your opponents.

For example, let us assume you want to introduce round-the-clock electricity in a poor country. While you are introducing the initiative, you announce that you have begun building overhead electrical lines. The country is densely populated, and, despite your best efforts, some of the high voltage electrical lines will run over houses.

In response to this announcement, people begin to protest because they fear for their lives and the lives of their children. After some discussion with a representative for the opposition, s/he proposes that you run the cables deep underground instead. You run the logistics (e.g. it is more expensive, and it takes more time to repair) and decide that it is worth it, especially as it is the less hazardous option (less electromagnetic radiation so less health risk). In the end, you both get what you want, and you have succeeded in carrying out the initiative and fulfilling its purpose.

20 Stay calm

You should never lose your cool. It is important that you always have control of your emotions. As soon as you react, you open yourself up to unnecessary issues. You might say the wrong thing, do the wrong thing, make a rash decision, or make a disagreement personal. However, if you stay calm, you will let your opponents know that they cannot faze you, no matter how intense their resistance becomes.

This is a strategy to employ carefully. Sometimes your calmness can seem like provocation, especially if your opponents were hoping to get a rise out of you. In this case, you will want to complement your calmness with over-communicating the purpose of the initiative, and reiterating that you have no intention of fighting.

Staying calm also sets an example for your supporters, showing them how they ought to behave. If necessary, verbalize the importance of them being poised, and remind them that if they would like to vent, they should do it in private.

It is detrimental to the initiative if your support network provokes your opponents. If they lose their cool, they risk the initiative's success. Therefore, ensure that both you and your support network remain poised and do not rise to provocation.

21 Keep ego out of it

It is not about YOU. This is a fundamental thing to remember with any initiative. If you allow ego to be part of what you are trying to do, you risk the initiative being labeled as a personal initiative. That poses a serious issue. Many of your supporters will withdraw their support, and your opponents will use this to make sure that the initiative comes tumbling down.

Keeping your ego out of it is also important if your opponents start using personal insults or spreading rumors. If you let your ego become too involved, it will probably be "bruised" in the process, and you will be more likely to take things personally. As a result, you will not be able to control yourself. Eventually, you will lose your cool, express your negative emotions, and probably make it personal. From this point on, your initiative is almost guaranteed to fail.

To avoid all this, leave your ego at the door, forget about "me", and focus more on the initiative and the benefits it will bring to "all".

If you are a person whose ego is important, you need to take particular care as you prepare yourself to forgo it. You may want to consider having a person or group with you to act as a buffer so that you don't react negatively when your opponents start spouting personal insults and false claims, or when they attempt to ruin your reputation not just as a "leader", but as a person.

22   Create some distance

We all need a breather every once in a while. Sometimes there is not much you can do to quell your opponent's resistance, and you can wear yourself out trying. At this point, you must just give yourself (and others) some space. If you feel that you are getting nowhere, you just don't have the solution, your supporters are feeling pressured, you are personally exhausted, etc., then pull out and create some distance between you and your opponent (the source of the pressure).

There will be instances when the only thing that will get the opponent to back off is seeing concrete results, but these often take time. Creating some distance can buy the initiative some time to flourish and show these results.

At the more intense side of the spectrum, distance is not only an option but a necessity. You need to create distance to protect yourself, your supporters, and the initiative[8].

---

[8] When you choose to create some distance, that doesn't mean you ignore your opponents, but rather that you keep watch over them from afar. It is still important that you know what they are up to. Additionally, you should use the time which this strategy buys you to come up with creative solutions for dealing with your opponents and protecting your supporters and initiative.

23 Mentally and technically prepare yourself for the worst; it will get messy

You need to be in the right state of mind if you want the initiative to succeed. There is no doubt that things will get messy, especially with the more intense opponents. Sometimes the worst-case scenario may become a reality. When that happens, you need to make sure you are mentally and technically prepared, and this includes securing all the resources you need. If you are not prepared, the situation might catch you by surprise, and you may face some serious psychological stresses (e.g. you may panic) and technical issues (e.g. losing support). You need to ensure you are prepared, not just for your own sake, but for the sake of the initiative and your supporters.

Another way to think about this is to "expect the unexpected" and prepare yourself and your supporters. Work with your support network and look for solutions to every negative scenario you can think of. Outline how you would approach the situation, and what you would need to make sure the solution(s) addressed the issue. You should also try to think of ways to prevent these situations from becoming a reality in the first place. In both cases, you should map out what resources you would need. This way you won't waste time trying to get the initiative back on its feet, and you can use the time and efforts to push the initiative forward.

Another important strategy in preparing for the worst is to secure the necessary support from key players, ones who will help to quash your opponents' attempts to hurt you. For instance, seek the support of the majority of the constituency, or secure your authority's support. It will be harder for your opponents to succeed if they don't have your constituents' support, or for your colleagues to succeed if they don't have authority's support.

Whatever it takes, make sure you are technically prepared, as well as mentally prepared, to deal with messy situations. Don't let something you could have prevented be the downfall of a purposeful, beneficial initiative.

---

24   Fight with full force

Don't be afraid to take the fight to your opponents. There are times when you need to fight back to protect yourself, your supporters, and the initiative. When you do this, remember not to cross any legal, ethical, or moral boundaries. If you fight back but open yourself up to ferocious backlash then you will have fought back and lost.

Unfortunately, there are times when it will be challenging to fight back, especially in situations where close relationships are involved. In such situations, you may have to deal with many negative emotions, ranging from anger all the way to self-doubt.

It is important that you do not allow feelings of self-doubt, guilt, or shame to occupy your mind when you choose to fight back. Remember that you are protecting the initiative, not trying to hurt your opponent. Be careful not to let any anger you feel fuel the fight either. This will backfire, and you will likely do more harm than you intended to. You may also open yourself up to some backlash, even if you don't cross any boundaries.

Remember that "crush your enemy" should never be your first choice.

Fight back, but always keep what you are fighting for and why at the forefront of your mind. This will help you fight clean and achieve the best outcomes.

25 Be ready to compromise

There is no shame in compromising, and there will be situations where you will have to. It is not about personal pride. If a compromise is the best option on the table, take it. You need to always consider and ask yourself, "what is the best for the initiative?"

If the best option for the initiative is to give up on your approach, do so. If you need to choose one tactic over the other, do so. If you need to adjust the way you framed the initiative, do so. The point is that if you need to give a little to get a little, accept this. As long as the initiative is not suffering, compromise and negotiate. Of course, try not to give up too much, if possible. Think about maximizing the impact but minimizing the losses.

One extra step you need to take when negotiating is to consult with and prepare your supporters. You need to make sure that they are on board with your compromise, and that they accept the new terms after you and your opponents have reached a deal. Since you may not be able to address all your supporters, consider gathering a team of representatives that can report back to the different groups and get their feedback on the issue. If it is in the initiative's best interest to compromise, make sure you let your supporters know. You don't want them to feel like you have opted for a compromise because it was quick and easy.

26 Don't compromise on ethics or professionalism

"In matters of style, swim with the current; in matters of principle, stand like a rock"

– Thomas Jefferson

There are two components you should never compromise on: 1) ethical, moral, and legal principles, and 2) the purpose of the initiative. You must do what is in the best interest of the initiative, but compromising on your purpose or on matter of principles will actually be worse for the initiative than going into "battle" with your opposition.

Keep your supporters in the loop, but also prepare yourself to lose a few people along the way, especially if some of your supporters would have been willing to compromise on these matters.

In professional settings, you will need to consider another element: professionalism. No matter what the situation, you should never act in a way that is not professional. If you are asked to compromise and the person you are dealing with is not professional, you need to be wary of the potential deal. There is no guarantee that they will uphold their end of the bargain.

27 Mobilize with enthusiasm

Would you rather support an enthusiastic individual or a dispirited individual? Most of us would probably opt for the former. Remember that initiatives call for change, which many of us are not fond of. You need to counter that lack of enthusiasm with your own boundless excitement and energy for your project, demonstrating how thoroughly you believe in its success and the benefits it will bring.

Letting your enthusiasm inspire others will help to peak the interests of the more passive supporters, fueling them to become more active, as well as intriguing the neutrals enough that they may get involved and choose your side. As such, when you mobilize individuals, you need to do it with enthusiasm. Show those around you that you believe in your project, and you will help them believe in it too.

Of course, no matter how enthusiastic you are, there will be some people who will still be against you. Nonetheless, you will be in a better situation because you will have expanded your support network and shown everyone how passionate you are about achieving the end goal. This in and of itself will put pressure on your opposition.

28 Sell the benefits of the initiative

Although many of us may not admit it, we usually want to know what we stand to gain if we support a change initiative. In this case, the benefits of the initiative will probably be your strongest selling point, so highlight them. People might initially focus on the risks involved, and to counter that, you need to sell the initiative's benefits.

If you let people know what they will gain, they may be more likely to support you. In addition, if you over-communicate the benefits to all the people involved, you may find that some of your opponents will reconsider and decide to join your side, or at least decrease their intensity.

People will be more willing to bear some pressure, pain, and loss if they know that it will pay off in the end. Of course, you cannot sell false hope, but you can say that if the initiative succeeds then life will be better. Try to give them specific benefits that tie in with the initiative, so they can see concrete improvements that you can deliver on.

Change initiatives are risky because nothing is guaranteed, and you cannot know exactly what the future will be like, but you can do your best to make it as good as possible, and you should constantly highlight the potential rewards which the system will reap.

29 Remove the "Bad Apples"

What happens when your own team members, supporters, partners, allies, friends, etc., become a hindrance to the initiative's progress? It is unfortunate, but it does happen sometimes. Normally, most supporters would withdraw their support if they felt the initiative was not living up to their expectations, or if they felt that the risks outweighed the rewards. In other cases, however, some of your disgruntled "supporters" might not abandon you but might instead try to get you to change the initiative, so much so that they could become more of a nuisance than a supporter.

When you are faced with this situation, you need to confront them about their actions and how they are negatively affecting the success of the initiative (e.g. slowing it down, or ruining morale). If they don't change their tactics or withdraw their support, you need to create some distance between them and the rest of the group.

In a professional setting, you may have fellow team members who don't want to support the initiative, but also don't want to quit their jobs, so they decide to stay on the team and resist you from within. Of course, you cannot let people remain on your team if they are unwilling to lend a hand or at least voice their concerns and try to work with you to resolve them. If you cannot get these people back on your side, you need to find a way to create some distance. At times, unfortunately, this may mean terminating their membership (e.g. employees).

Whatever the situation, you need to remove bad apples before they infect the whole tree.

---

30   Bring in fresh, positive blood

Supporters will come and go, and you should always be on the lookout for more support. There are situations where you will need to assemble a team (e.g. corporate setting). In such situations, you may want to be a bit more selective about who you choose to be part of your team and your inner circle.

If possible, you want to bring in someone who is invested and enthusiastic about the initiative, someone who is interested in actively promoting it. This will not only keep the initiative's momentum going, but may actually boost it. Having a new, energetic, positive team member will also improve the team's morale, especially if the team has recently lost a key player.

In general, new team members are more excited at the prospect of helping out, so they will work harder to try to cement their position. Of course, this doesn't apply to every fresh face, and it shouldn't matter if it doesn't, provided they are doing their part in seeing the initiative's purpose fulfilled.

You cannot predict the future, so you cannot know if this fresh face will leave or stay, but for the time being, if their enthusiasm will boost the initiative and the team then, by all means, bring them on board.

31　Vigilantly monitor the system

Keep watch over what is happening in the system. You need to always consider the options you have at your disposal, but you cannot do that if you don't understand how the system works and where it is heading. The initiative cannot adapt to changing circumstances and keep up its momentum if you aren't aware of the system it is operating in.

It can be difficult, not to mention exhausting, to keep a constant watch on the system with your resistance trying to pull the initiative down. However, if you want the initiative to succeed, you need to know what adjustments can and must be made so that the initiative's purpose is fulfilled.

If you see any suspicious behavior, don't ignore it. Instead, try to investigate it further. It is better to have doubts about people's behaviors than to be naïve and assume people will not take their resistance to new levels. Of course, this doesn't mean that you should second-guess everyone's actions, or you could stray towards paranoia. Follow your instincts and investigate if something feels wrong.

Remember to utilize your support network. Ask your supporters to keep an eye out for any changes and report them back to you, and consult with them about any suspicious behavior.

You should always know about any development that affects the initiative, whether it is the next best idea, a small change, or suspicious behavior. Make sure you and your support network keep tabs on the system, so that you can constantly adapt to changing circumstances.

32   Ask for help

Your support network is there for a reason. Be ready to ask for help when you need it. When you keep your supporters in the loop and encourage a collaborative atmosphere, your supporters may offer assistance on their own. However, there will be times when you need to ask for help. Don't just wait around for your supporters to offer.

Call a weekly meeting where you can discuss new developments. Use these meetings to brainstorm more effective ways of keeping the initiative moving forward, and/or different techniques for dealing with your opponents. Listen carefully to everyone's suggestions. There is no doubt that the next great idea could come from your support network.

Consider setting up a communication system that allows your supporters to get in touch with you, and vice versa. It is possible that a weekly meeting might not work, so you need to make sure you have another way to communicate with your supporters, such as a collective email list, a group forum, or a group chat on a social media platform.

There will be times when you need access to resources, so remember to ask. After all, the initiative cannot move forward without them, and your supporters may be able to help you get them.

Don't hesitate to ask the relevant parties for help, whether it's for resources, keeping an eye on developments, offering up suggestions, informing you of suspicious behavior, or making sure your actions are what's best for the initiative.

---

33   Debug the initiative

Nothing is perfect, and that includes your initiative. You should constantly examine it to see if there are any flaws, weaknesses, blind spots, or errors. When you discover a "bug", try to repair it before it is too late, and your initiative fails.

Remember to take advantage of your support network as extra pairs of eyes when you look for "bugs" in the initiative. All individuals have blind spots, and sometimes we cannot see the weaknesses in our own ideas. You should always utilize the perspectives of others to check if there are "bugs" which you have overlooked.

Run every situation by your trusted supporters to double-check if your interpretations have any blind spots. It is likely that you have not considered every detail. It is rare for a person to be able to take in all the information a situation has to offer. When you consult your supporters, they will help to pinpoint different ways of looking at your initiative, highlighting important details you may have missed. This will help fill in any gaps your interpretations may have. Each one of your supporters will have their own, unique perspective, and this will increase your chances of capturing the situation in its entirety, avoiding unnecessary "bugs".

Do not forget your enemies and opponents in this situation. They will not hesitate to exploit the weaknesses, and this should increase the urgency of fixing the "bugs". Sometimes they will, quite publicly, let you know what is wrong with the initiative. Do not discount their views on the matter. Instead, listen to what they have to say, and if it holds any merit, you may want to investigate and address those weaknesses. In some situations, you may be able to ask them what they feel is wrong with your initiative, and they will let you know.

However you approach this strategy, make sure you are constantly checking your initiative for mistakes, so that you can move towards fulfilling its purpose with minimal hiccups. Although you may not cover every blind spot, weakness, or error, you can at least take care of some, and that will smooth the path your initiative takes.

34   Create, score, and celebrate a stream of small victories

Talking about the benefits might get people listening initially, but it will not be enough on its own. You need to show people evidence, no matter how small, of those benefits. One sure way to do this is to choose an approach to the initiative that allows you to split the initiative up into small, achievable tasks. This way, you can create goals, achieve them, and give your supporters, neutrals, and even your opponents a constant stream of evidence of the benefits you have been talking about.

When you do secure small victories, celebrate them and make them public. Do not do this as a way of flaunting your success, but as proof that the initiative is beneficial. This will boost the morale of your supporters and yourself. It may also demoralize your opponents, encouraging them to abandon their resistance.

Create opportunities for a stream of small victories, achieve them, and celebrate with the system as you continue to move forward towards progress.

---

35 Take responsibility for your mess

There will be hiccups along the way, and some of the mess will be your doing. You, as the source of the initiative, will make mistakes, slip-up and lose your cool, be ambushed, pick the wrong approach, let ego slip in, etc. It is natural and is bound to happen; you are undertaking a challenging endeavor. What is important is that you don't get too caught up with your mistakes and failures. Instead, you need to learn from them and move ahead. However, you must take responsibility for your mistakes. You cannot just brush them off.

Make sure that you offer up the necessary apologies to your supporters, opponents, and the rest of the system. After this, you can move forward with the initiative, learning not to repeat those mistakes.

Remember that your mistakes may point out some major flaws in your initiative, which you can then address. Take responsibility for your own mistakes and learn from them.

36 Double-check the sanity of the initiative

There will be times when you will ask yourself if the initiative is worth it. Although it usually is, it doesn't hurt to keep checking if your initiative will help more than it will harm. Don't leave this question only to moments of self-doubt. Make sure you also ask it when you are feeling confident. You might be able to make a sounder judgment.

Ask your supporters if they believe the initiative is worth it, but be careful you don't sow seeds of doubt in their minds. Instead, try to approach it objectively, and get their honest opinions. If the costs outweigh the benefits, you may want to reconsider. This doesn't mean that your initiative is bad, but it might be that you're trying to introduce it at the wrong time. If you and your supporters come to a consensus, reexamine it and then accept it.

A warning: whatever conclusion you draw, don't accept it without thinking two, three, even four times about it. It easy to imagine a situation where your exhaustion or frustration might affect your judgment.

37 Don't aim to be popular

An act of leadership is not a popularity contest, so don't let yourself get distracted from your initiative by trying to please everyone. It is not about YOU. It's about offering value to the system. It's also worth remembering that, by default, change is often not popular, so expect to disappoint a few people.

Still, you should not introduce an initiative that is completely unpopular. You don't want to alienate the entire system. Try to find an approach that suits your purpose, but also pleases some members of the system. In other words, try to listen to and satisfy others without losing sight of your goal.

38 Involve the members of the system in the initiative

To lessen your opposition, try to get the members of the system invested in the initiative. Involve them in the process, assign them roles or duties, and give them a sense of responsibility. You may be able to gain supporters before they can become your opponents.

Even once the initiative has its fair share of opponents, try to get the key players on the opposing team involved in the initiative. This way, a large section of the opposition may feel invested and support their key player.

For example, when I was working for a multinational news company, I decided to move the main office to a more isolated area of the city. Initially, many of the employees protested this decision. I looked for the most avid opponent and made him the project manager. This quelled the majority's resistance, and the project went through without any major issues.

39   Plan and deliberate

You should not jump into situations without planning ahead. When you consider confronting your opponents, it is unwise to do so without having a plan. This is not the type of situation where you should improvise from the start. Before moving ahead with confrontation, you need to:

- Study the situation.

- Understand what your opponents are up to.

- Examine your resources and how best to make use of them.

When you have examined all these elements, you can then begin to work with your supporters to come up with the optimal approach for confronting your opponents.

It is of paramount importance that you plan carefully because a mistake could mean serious damage, not only to the initiative, but also to yourself and your support network. Don't "wing it". Instead, study the situation and plan your moves.

40   Know when to confront

There is a time and a place for confrontation. Take a thorough look at yourself, your support network, your opponents, and the resources each side has. After you have studied the situation and the system, you will be able to decide when the right time for you to confront your opponents is. It is about gauging when confrontation will yield the desired results.

Take some time to consider where you stand in comparison to your opponents. If all signs point towards a successful confrontation, go for it, but make sure you are mentally and technically prepared. If you find that you need to wait for a little while, do so. The cost of losing is too great for you to rush into something you simply cannot win.

Whatever the situation, make sure you time your confrontation to suit what is best for your initiative. Do not hesitate when you think the time has come, but act decisively. Good timing and preparation can mean the difference between the initiative failing or succeeding.

41 Let them negotiate for you

Consider hiring a professional to represent you in all major negotiations, especially if you feel that someone else is better equipped to handle the negotiating. After all, a professional:

- Will know how to read the situation and other people.

- May be trained in strategy and tactics, especially in highly emotional situations. They will know when to act, when to negotiate, and when to stay silent.

- Will not have emotional stakes in the negotiation, so will be less likely to be provoked.

- Will be objective and able to negotiate rationally and effectively. Ultimately, they will get the best deal for the initiative.

In the meantime, you can focus on advancing the initiative, and finding other ways to deal with your opponents. Leave the negotiations to the experts with no emotional stakes. No matter how effective you are at negotiating in everyday situations, the amount of care and time you put into the initiative will affect your emotional behavior, making it easy for things to get out of hand. In turn, the initiative will suffer, and the system will be worse off for it.

42 Don't let conflicts and diversions distract you

Engaging your resisters and opponents will take effort. Your opponents have a repertoire of tactics under their belts, and one of these is diversion. They will attempt to distract you with petty conflicts so that they can prepare their main "blow" without having to worry about you stopping them. The moment that happens, your initiative's chances of success will start to decrease.

Be careful not to fall for their traps. If you feel that they are creating side issues or trying to "string you along", make sure you do not respond.

Try to avoid engaging your opponents before you understand what their motives are and whether the conflict serves the initiative in any way. If you don't, you risk being distracted, and the longer you stay distracted, the more likely it becomes that your initiative will suffer. Added to this, you will be caught up in conflicts that will exhaust you further, hurt you and your supporters, and possibly end your initiative.

43   Don't be provoked

Although this is one of the preemption strategies, it is equally important to continue it throughout your initiative. Dealing with opponents and enemies can be an emotional endeavor, and it increases in intensity the closer your relationship. There may be moments when you want to react irrationally, when you feel that they have taken their resistance too far. This is natural because of the care and effort you have put into the initiative. However, no matter how emotional and messy the situation becomes, do not be provoked. Sometimes, all it takes is a single mistake, and your opponents will seize the opening, bringing you and the initiative down.

Dig up those skills of strategic and tactical silence and inaction. Sometimes saying or doing nothing may be the preferable strategy. Study the situation and wait for the right time to engage your opponents (it may be that the right time is never).

When you pose a serious threat to your opponents, they will increase their resistance, and in doing so will also increase their attempts to provoke you. They are baiting you, waiting for you to act reactively and make a mistake. Instead, ignore their provocations and take some time to plan your next move. Even if you are ready to engage them, never behave reactively. It will always hurt the initiative, regardless of whether you win or lose.

44   Use your opponents' mistakes

Everyone makes mistakes, and that includes your opponents. Always know what your opponents are up to and keep a keen eye out for any slip-ups. The instant they get something wrong and make a mistake, you will be able to take advantage of it.

Depending on the magnitude of the mistake, you may be able to use it to encourage them to forgo their resistance. Sometimes, your strongest tool may come from your opponent. A mistake can mean the difference between success and failure, especially if both of you are on equal footing. Therefore, it is important that you think about how you can best use their mistakes to stop their resistance[9].

For instance, equally trained martial arts masters may spend some time making moves and countering them. It is not until one of them makes a mistake that the other one wins. If one of them fails to take advantage of the other master's mistakes, they may be unable to win the match.

---

[9] This does not mean that you should "crush them" when they make a mistake, although on rare occasions you might choose such drastic measures. Instead, you should use their mistake as a way of ending their resistance.

45 Be unpredictable

You may be watching your opponents, but your opponents are definitely watching you, and one of the worst things to be in this situation is predictable. If your opponents can guess your next few moves or find out what your strategy is, they can preempt, plan, and tailor counter-strategies to make sure you fail. Ensure you don't divulge any information (directly or indirectly) that they can use against you, especially if you are in the midst of a conflict. Remain adaptive, even before the situation calls for a change, ensuring that your opponents cannot accurately predict what you will do next.

You should always be clear about what approaches you have at your disposal. This will allow you to optimize your initiative by choosing the best strategy, and will also mean you can switch tactics without having to spend time working out a new approach. Your opponents will not have a chance to come up with a counter-strategy and halt the progress of the initiative. Make sure you are constantly shifting things around and keeping key information hidden. Being unpredictable can mean the difference between a successful initiative and a complete failure.

Remember to be discrete about your choice of strategy. Part of being unpredictable lies in carefully choosing who among your supporters needs to know your plans. Ideally, your supporters will not turn on you, but you cannot dismiss the possibility when you are in the middle of a confrontation.

46 Expand your repertoire of options

"Keep your options open." You may have heard this sentence before and you may have disregarded it. However, when dealing with resistance, you need to take it seriously. You need to make sure you keep expanding your repertoire of options. The more options you have, the more unpredictable you become, and the higher the chances are that your initiative will succeed.

If you have only a few options at your disposal, you may find yourself backed into a corner, and you may not be able to fight your way out without jeopardizing the initiative. If you have a lot of options to choose from, however, you may be able to wiggle yourself out of the corner, or avoid getting into it altogether.

For instance, imagine that you and your opponents have decided to negotiate. When they propose a specific deal, if you don't have alternative options, you may have no choice but to accept their deal. If you have alternatives, you are more likely to be able to negotiate from a position of strength.

Therefore, for the sake of your supporters and your initiative, keep expanding your options. In the end, if you have many options, you increase your chances of staying on top and you will avoid ever being predictable.

47 Don't be fainthearted or indecisive

Dealing with your opponents will occasionally require you to make quick and tough decisions. If you feel that you are not up to the task, you may need to reconsider what you are doing and whether you should be leading the initiative at all.

Leadership is not a task for those who are indecisive. You cannot hope to progress if you cannot make decisions. Saying, "I don't know," "It is fine either way," or "whatever suits the group" can all backfire. How can you inspire people if you cannot make a decision? How can you persuade people to stay on course in the face of resistance if you can't decide how to deal with your opponents? If you feel that you cannot make decisions under pressure, then dealing with resistance is not for you, and by extension, neither is leadership.

Furthermore, you must be willing to make the tough decisions. Some people are not cut out for this, but if you want the initiative to succeed, you must be prepared to make quick and difficult decisions when the situation calls for it.

Resistance will eat up the fainthearted and indecisive individual because when the going gets tough, you need to be up to the task and more.

48 Don't focus on winning — it is about fulfilling the purpose of the initiative

I cannot emphasize this point enough. You must always do what is best for the initiative, and not get distracted by trying to accumulate wins against your opponents. Remember that you did not introduce your initiative to get into battles, and you did not introduce it to win them. They are a side effect of positive change in the system, and should never become the focus.

Your main driver must be fulfilling the purpose of the initiative so that the system can continue to grow. Do not let personal goals or a desire to win every battle detract from that. Stay focused, engage your opponents only when it helps the initiative, and never let your wins or losses bear weight in terms of your direction.

49 Winning in confrontations demands self-discipline

Successfully dealing with resistance is contingent on self-discipline. If you cannot control your thoughts, emotions, and behavior then you will probably make mistakes that your opponents can take advantage of. You will also set a bad example for your supporters, and some of them may then abandon you.

Additionally, dealing with your opponents needs careful and strategic planning. If you are not able to control yourself, you will not be able to objectively consider the best course of action – which is a necessary condition for the initiative to succeed.

It will become more difficult, but also more vital, to exercise self-discipline as the resistance intensity increases, or when you are dealing with stronger opponents. There will be more provocation and more confrontation, and if you are not able to act responsively, you will not succeed.

---

50 Don't assume that you can always predict the moves of your opponent

---

No matter how much time you spend thinking about and studying your opponents, you still cannot accurately predict what they will do. There will be some moves that are unexpected, so prepare yourself for surprises. You will have to continue with your own progress and, when they show their hand, you will have to adapt and deal with their resistance.

Ideally, you should map out all possible scenarios and minimize what you need to worry about, but your opponents will have "aces in the hole", so just prepare yourself and your supporters for the possibility of a surprise.

51 Never underestimate your opponents

"There is no greater danger than underestimating your opponent."

– Lao Tzu

It would be unwise to assume that your opponents cannot defeat you. Even if you have won every battle, do not assume that you have won the war. You would be surprised what lengths people whose livelihood is threatened will go to.

There are many plot twists, surprises, and unexpected endings in blockbuster movies that revolve around how the underdog was underestimated. There are further examples in sports when a racer, boxer, team, etc., was pegged to lose the tournament, only to end up on equal footing, or even emerge victorious.

Make sure that you move forward, aiming to win confrontations and focusing on your initiative, but don't forget to keep your eyes on your opponents and their movements. Never let your guard down until you have fulfilled the purpose of the initiative.

52 Never humiliate your opponents

You are not in the business of making other people look bad. Your sole focus must be the initiative. It is neither about you nor them. Therefore, when you decide to deal with the resistance or engage your opponents, make sure you do so only with the intention of lessening or ending their resistance. There is no circumstance where you should resort to personal attacks. Instead, focus on their resistance, and don't drag them personally through the mud.

This continues to apply if you succeed in quelling their resistance. Don't start bragging or showing off, calling them names, or reminding them who won and who lost. These are childish, personal attacks that do not benefit the initiative. They go against the type of courteous and compassionate leadership we discuss in this book.

---

53   Do what is best for the system

Focus on doing the right thing for the system. This is the quintessential purpose of leadership. Whenever you say or do anything, make sure you think about how your actions will affect your supporters and the system as a whole. If your actions will cause more harm than good in the long run, consider other options. Even if you can see a course that will surely end the resistance, if the system will emerge worse off, you will need to find another path.

In the end, the purpose of proposing this change and going through all the associated trouble is to benefit the system. If you emerge victorious but harm the system in the process, you will have lost. Therefore, keep your supporters and the system at the forefront of your mind, and even consider consulting them if in doubt over a course of action. You might be surprised by how much they can help you in filtering the right actions from the wrong ones.

54 Success depends on doing the right thing, at the right time, and in the right way

Make sure you are always doing the right thing. To start off with, you should always follow universally accepted moral, ethical, and legal guidelines when you wish to introduce an initiative. Next, you need to make sure that your initiative is for the benefit of the system, not some personal goal.

Think carefully and choose the right time to carry out the initiative. If you are too early, the system may not be ready, and you will encounter difficulties (e.g. no support, stronger and more intense resistance). Alternatively, you may not be ready to deal with the resistance, even if the system is in desperate need and somewhat accepting of the initiative.

If you are too late, then the damage may already be done, the initiative will be futile, and you will need to come up with a new one to suit the major circumstantial changes. Alternatively, the resistance might have grown too strong to deal with, and you won't be able to fulfill the purpose of the initiative. Therefore, carefully choose the perfect window to carry out your initiative.

Make sure you also choose the right approach. This is more flexible. The approach must adapt to changing circumstances. As such, focus on choosing the best approach for the context. This will allow you to lessen resistance and increase the chances of the initiative succeeding.

It is only if you combine these three crucial elements that you will substantially increase your chances of success. The costs of failure will lead to losses for your supporters, yourself, and the system — your beneficial initiative will never bring about the necessary change.

55 Know when to accept temporary defeat

Surrender and defeat might be the last things on your mind. However, in some situations, you will need to retreat and accept defeat so that you can pick up the pieces and continue with your progress.

There may be times when your opponents win. It might be that they had an "ace in the hole", were stronger than you, or made use of your mistakes. You can make that defeat a temporary one if you surrender or retreat. If you keep fighting when it is obvious that you cannot win, you will exhaust your resources and lose supporters. You will be defeated permanently and, depending on how intense their resistance is, you might even pay a heavy price (e.g. your job, your life, your family).

Consider carefully what actions would be best for your supporters, the system, and the initiative. If this means letting go of a few victories, so be it. Don't let your pride, honor, ego, etc., stop you from choosing temporary defeat over a "fight till the end".

You cannot hope to win if you have exhausted all your resources, so for the sake of the system, consider choosing temporary surrenders. In the end, sometimes you have to retreat so that you can give the initiative a better chance to advance.

56 Don't burn the bridges between you and your opponents

Your opponents may not have always been, and may not always be, your opponents. After your initiative reaches its conclusion, the dynamics between you and your opponents may go back to the way they were before your initiative was introduced. In other cases, your initiative might create life-long opponents and enemies.

If possible, try to preserve the relationship, keeping the disagreement solely about the initiative, and not allowing your opponents to take it personally. This way, you can keep the "bridge" between you intact.

In the future, you may have to collaborate on a project, or you may need their support for another initiative. If you burn the bridge between you, it can prove difficult to approach them and ask for their support. That is why it is important not to discount your relationships with your opponents, provided they don't cross any boundaries from which the relationship cannot be salvaged (e.g. a messy divorce, illegal behavior).

57 Choose clarity or ambiguity, depending on the situation

Some scenarios will call for transparency, while other scenarios will call for ambiguity. This applies to your opponents and supporters. Before you divulge any information, consider the situation, and just how much information needs to be out in the open for the initiative to move forward.

Keep information on a need-to-know basis. If you are working with your opponents to try and find the best approach for both of you, you may need to divulge some information. However, you should consider how much detail they need to know so that you can come to an agreement. If you feel that you need to be completely honest about everything, then make sure you are, but be careful. If you feel that you will have the upper hand if you keep them guessing, choose to be ambiguous.

With regards to your supporters, don't be too quick to tell everyone everything. At the start, it would be naïve to trust all your supporters with game-changing or crucial information. Instead, you may want to be selective about who you tell and what information you give them. There will be some people that you can trust completely and you may be transparent with them, but there will be others who haven't earned your trust, and so you may choose to be ambiguous and selective.

Whatever you choose to do, and whoever you choose to tell, the first thing you need to do is think about the situation. If being transparent will lead to the best results for the initiative then that should be your choice, but if you find that ambiguity or even silence suit the situation better then go for these options.

58   Reflect on the purpose of the initiative

You may think that your initiative is for the benefit of the system and its constituents, but the system's constituents might see it differently.

If you believe that the real reason you introduced the initiative was for the benefit of the system then make it known, but not before you take some time to reflect on the matter. It is possible that although you have convinced yourself that your motives are pure, your initiative stems from a place of personal hunger or ambition. Before you move forward, reflect on the roots of your initiative and your actions. It may be that the initiative started out with the intention of helping the system, but with time became fueled by more personal ambitions.

Ask your supporters for their opinions, and even consult your opponents. Whoever you choose to talk to, make sure that you express the urgency of their honesty. Explain to them that you want to know if this initiative comes off as a personal endeavor, and whether it seems that your intentions are pure. Based on their information, you may want to consider either staying on your course, adjusting it to suit its initial purpose, or giving it up, at least for the time being.

Every now and then, take some time to reflect on the matter and ask your supporters and opponents to help you with your "sanity" check.

59 Be wary around people who have nothing to lose

Be careful when confronting your opponents; you may come across a few who have nothing to lose. These people can be dangerous, and you will need to watch your back with particular care. There are no limits to what they will do to see you fail and the initiative fall into ruin.

If you know anyone who fits into this category, you need to be extra vigilant and careful, because the more pressure you put on them, the more they will feel cornered. If they really have nothing to lose, they will cross boundaries without a moment's notice, and come after you with all they have got. At times, their attacks may come close to being lethal, either personally (e.g. they might attempt to take your life), socially (e.g. they might present false evidence to ruin your reputation), or professionally (e.g. they might ruin your career).

You need to distance yourself, keep a watchful eye on them, and be careful not to pressure them more than you have to. Be sure to warn your supporters too, and consider calling the relevant authorities. These people can easily flip from being opponents to being enemies, so watch out.

60 Show your strength, but without provocation

Your opponents are less likely to confront you if they know it is futile. Consider, then, exhibiting your strength. If you have a great number of supporters, let it be known. If you have key authority figures and decision-makers on your side, make it public. If you have more resources, and therefore you are able to take on conflict and emerge victorious, don't hide it. When you decide to show your hand, you let your opponents know how strong you are, and they will be less likely to confront and oppose you.

For instance, telling your existing and potential supporters and allies that authority is on your side and backing the initiative will increase their morale, breathing energy and life into their efforts, and ultimately increasing the quality of their support. Your supporters will want to get into authority's good books, and the first step is joining the side authority is rooting for. Their increased involvement will boost the strength of your side, and the chances of success for your initiative will increase significantly.

Added to this, when your opponents see that authority and a large support network are behind the initiative, they will be demoralized and discouraged, slowing down and decreasing the ferocity of their resistance.

If it is publicly known that authority is behind an initiative, resisting said initiative may become synonymous with resisting authority itself. That is something some of your opponents will be unwilling to do, so they will back off, either joining your team or becoming neutral.

Showing your strength will also deter potential opponents as they may be reluctant to start resisting your initiative if it could be interpreted as an attack on their authority's wishes, as well as possibly upsetting their colleagues.

You want to be tactful and authentic in showing your strength. The last thing you want is for your support network or authority to feel used or manipulated for personal gain. Do not brag about your support, but inform your authority and support network that you will be letting the system know who is backing your initiative. Express your appreciation for their support and thank them for their help in making the initiative a possibility.

Take care not to provoke your opponents or make it personal. You are showing your hand only because you wish to avoid further resistance and confrontation, not to challenge them. If you provoke them, it will defeat the purpose of this strategy, and you will incur unnecessary, and possibly expensive, losses.

61 Investigate to see if there is more to their resistance than meets the eye

There will be times when your opponents seem relatively quiet, calm, and collected. This can be deceiving because you might assume that they are no longer opposing you. Although this might be the case, don't just ignore the situation. Instead, investigate thoroughly to see if there is more to their quietness than meets the eye. It is quite possible that they are plotting behind closed doors and attempting to lull you into a false sense of security.

There is another possibility when you deal with the quieter resisters. Although they will not be too vocal or obvious in their resistance, they may still be indirectly actively opposing you. Many backstabbers, schemers, and saboteurs tend to be quiet about their intentions and schemes.

This might be more common than you think. Most people don't like conflict, and instead will resort to underhand tactics to put an end to your initiative. They may parade as neutrals, passive opponents or, in some cases, as your supporters.

It is important that you don't open yourself up to such surprises. Instead, if you have your doubts, investigate and see if there is more to their resistance than meets the eye.

62 Involve relevant authorities

When things get really nasty, your opponents may cross legal and ethical boundaries. If that happens, don't try to deal with them on your own. Instead, gather evidence of the illegal activities and present it to the relevant authorities.

Don't let your opponents hurt you or your supporters without acting. You should never let your rights be taken away from you or your supporters. If you feel that some serious boundaries have been crossed, don't waste your time trying to deal with your opponents; just let the authorities step in. Meanwhile, you can focus on advancing your initiative and keeping up its momentum.

63 Take care of yourself physically, mentally, emotionally, and spiritually

Dealing with resistance is exhausting. You cannot hope to take on your opponents and succeed if you don't give yourself some breathing room along the way.

Resistance challenges all aspects of your being from the physical to the emotional to the mental, and even to the spiritual. This is one of the reasons it can be dangerous. The good news is that you can overcome this, but you need to take care of yourself. Some people enjoy meditating, others enjoy vacationing, others enjoy spending time with family and friends, while others might just like to take some time alone. Whatever gives you peace of mind and helps to refresh you, go for it.

This strategy is not about escaping or temporarily forgetting your worries, which would just be postponing the inevitable. In fact, when you came back to face your issues, you would experience the same concerns and stresses, and you would not have done any-thing to take care of yourself — you would have just pressed pause and then picked up where you left off. Instead, find a way to rest your body, mind, and spirit.

Consider healthy habits such as a proper sleep schedule, a proper diet, and sufficient exercise. In addition, you should consult others and ask for their help if it allows you a little breathing space to de-stress. Remember that you shouldn't be afraid of asking oth-ers for help.

You need to take care of yourself so that you can deal with resistance and move forward with your initiative. It will allow you to tackle challenges with a fresh mind and consider new ways to handle your opponents.

64 Take care of your supporters

You are not in this alone. You can't be. There are other people involved, and not all of them will be standing on the opposing side. You will have supporters, allies, and partners, and you cannot leave them to fend for themselves. You will want to take measures to protect them as well as yourself. After all, they are watching your back and if you don't watch theirs, they may give up, or even join the opposing side. You will find yourself with fewer supporters, and your initiative will crumble.

Make sure you inform them of all the dangers they may be facing. Give them information which pertains to their well-being, or which may help them protect themselves. Remember that they can make better decisions if they are well-informed and aware of any potential dangers. Prioritize their welfare to ensure your initiative stays strong and that those who side with you are rewarded for their efforts.

65 Tailor your approach to your target audience

Every person requires a different approach or amount of information before they make a decision. When you introduce your initiative, you shouldn't assume that everyone will be on your side. It may not be because they don't support what you are doing however. They may have simply not understood the reasons behind the initiative, or what benefits they will reap if they support it.

You need to try and guard against losing their potential support. Repeating information about the purpose of the initiative is a good start, but the delivery method is crucial and must vary depending on who you are speaking to. Try to tailor your approach to the person or persons sitting across from you.

Pick the right frame. If you go for a more inclusive, wider frame, more people will feel that their role is important and that the benefits also apply to them. However, that is just one aspect of tailoring your approach. You will need to also consider how best to explain what it is that you are doing, why you are doing it, and what the possible outcomes are. Some people like to hear as much detail as you can provide, while others just want a straightforward explanation, not a "sales pitch". Some people may want to map out the pros and cons before making their decisions, so make sure you provide them with the information they need. Whatever their preferences, you will want to make sure that you tailor the frame to fit with your audience.

66 Work to minimize the damage

Resistance puts up a fight, and even when you win, you will still experience some losses. At times, these losses may be greater than you had anticipated, so you need to look for ways to minimize them. After all, your purposeful leadership initiative is intending to make the system better, adding value to other people's lives and helping them in their journey of survival and growth. As such, you cannot in good conscience accept unnecessary damage for the sake of seeing your initiative succeed.

That is why it is important to think of creative ways to minimize the negative impact. This could be in the way you introduce your initiative. Consider whether you can at least soften the blow for those involved, including your opponents. Remember you are not out to hurt others, but to help them. It is, unfortunately, part of the process that some people may lose out, and that is reason enough to try to soften the blow.

For instance, if your initiative incurs some financial cuts, and some people may lose their jobs, you might consider trying to help ease them back into another job, or keeping their benefits (e.g. insurance) for up to a year.

67 Actively and authentically listen to all parties involved

Always keep the door open for anyone who wishes to discuss, debate, offer a suggestion or opinion, etc. When you sit down and talk to them, you must keep an open mind, show them empathy and compassion, and actively and authentically listen to what they have to say. Usually, this sort of active listening is a preemptive measure, but between introducing the initiative and fulfilling its aim, there will be times when people want to voice their concerns. Whether you are just talking or you are trying to negotiate, make sure you listen carefully to what they have to say.

You cannot hope to deal with an opponent if you don't give them the chance to express their concerns, issues, opinions, etc. At times, their concerns will point to legitimate flaws in your initiative, things you may not have thought out fully. Make sure you hear them out.

You might be surprised by how many opponents will back off when you genuinely care about their concerns, listen to them, and work with them to creatively come up with mutually beneficial solutions.

68 As with a game of chess, think about your moves ahead of time and plan your strategy

Even once you have introduced your initiative, you should always consider all possible moves which you could make to ensure the initiative's success is as smooth as possible. There is no doubt that you should have considered the different options at your disposal when you planned your initiative, but there will have been changes and new circumstances which you haven't accounted for since then.

For instance, your most keen supporters may actually decide it is not worth the trouble and quit, an authority figure might suddenly withdraw their support, or your most ferocious enemy could come to terms with your initiative and support you. Whatever the case, you need to constantly think ahead and plan. With every changing circumstance, new paths diverge in different directions, and you should make sure you know what paths are open to you.

Remember, purposeful leadership is adaptive and can move down various different paths to fulfill its aim. Therefore, as the circumstances shift, make sure your initiative shifts with them.

In addition to this, you will need to revise your strategy as your opponents make movements and revise theirs. Just as a change in circumstances affects your plans, it will affect your opponents'. As they change and come up with countermeasures, you need to do the same. In a game of chess, you don't only consider what your next move is, but what vulnerabilities that move will open up. If you understand what options are available for both you and your opponents, you can better see how they might respond to your plans.

Don't sacrifice your key pieces because you failed to take the time to consider all the measures and countermeasures.

69 Use patience, silence, and inaction wisely and strategically

Remember those preemptive strategies, patience and silence? You need to utilize them when dealing with your opponents, although this can be difficult. These two techniques are valuable because they offer you time to think well and act responsively. They will help you control your emotions, which might otherwise sky-rocket as the conflicts intensify and your opponents increase their resistance.

This doesn't mean that you should stay silent all the time, or that you should wait for something to happen. The strategy lies in knowing when to use these techniques wisely so that they work in your favor. It is about understanding when you should stay silent and let your opponents talk, complain, or rant, and knowing when it is time to say your piece, voice your plans, and explain the purpose of your initiative.

Remember that silence can also be used to figure out the true intentions of your opponent. When you stay quiet and listen, you can understand what your opponent is saying on the surface, and what they really mean deep down. With their true intentions clear, you can act accordingly.

Let us add a third technique: inaction. As with patience and silence, inaction has a particular place. Sometimes, situations call for inaction so that your initiative can continue to move forward. You will be required to do nothing except watch and bide your time for the right moment to make your move. In some instances, your move will be to make no move. That in and of itself is a play.

For instance, in the 1940s, African-Americans were not allowed to play in the major baseball leagues. However, Jackie Robinson made history as the first African-American ballplayer to play in

those leagues. Throughout his career, he experienced a lot of resistance, including physical, emotional, and mental resistance. He
knew that to make history and change the landscape of the game,
he needed to just play the game, and he could not react to any resistance. He kept his mouth shut, did what he needed to do, and
gave it his all. Only through inaction was he able to pave the way for
future African-American athletes and make the sport solely about
the game and not the skin color of its players.

These three can be powerful tools and techniques if used properly. It is all about thinking before you act or speak, and being wise
and strategic when you apply them.

70 Be wary of competition

In a professional setting, there will be people who are opposing
you, not only because your initiative is inconveniencing them, but
also because they are competing with you. It is possible your co-
worker is going after a specific promotion, has their own initiative,
wants authority's approval, etc. When you are standing in the way
of people's progress, they will oppose what you are doing, even if
they agree that it is potentially beneficial. They will see your initiative as an obstacle stopping them from achieving their goals.

One way to overcome this is to talk to them about what their
issues are. If there is a way that you can help them, and in return
gain their support, then do it. If you feel that you can involve them
in the initiative to get their support, go for it. Whatever tactic you
choose, make sure that you are not in the dark about the real reasons behind their opposition. If you are not the cause and you are
able to resolve it, do so.

Make sure that their competition does not stand in the way of your progress, and keep an eye out for any competitive reasons they may be resisting you.

71 Never provoke authority

Authority in this context is the entity that has the power to influence your initiative. They are able to control your access to resources, make the journey of your initiative easier or harder, and give you specific permissions and powers (e.g. give you power over decision-making process). Their support also tends to increase the credibility of your initiative, which in turn will decrease the number of opponents, while also increasing the number of supporters. Usually, they have the power to veto whatever you are doing. They can confiscate your resources or alter your supporters' loyalties if they don't like your initiative.

For these reasons, you need to make sure that not only do you keep authority satisfied, but that you never provoke or challenge them. If you do, your initiative will suffer consequences that might make it difficult to continue your journey. You cannot hope to challenge authority and get away with it.

If you do provoke them, it will not only affect you and the initiative, but it will also decrease the size of your support network and increase your resistance. People who see that you are provoking authority will either remove their support (supporters), or they will intensify their resistance (opponents). Whoever they are, their interests lie with a pleased authority, not a provoked one. Therefore, be careful not to do anything that could be misconstrued as a provocation or challenge towards authority.

72 Use authority to gauge the system overall

Authority is given its power and authorization by the system in which it resides. It is always keeping an eye on the system, since its continued existence is dependent on the system being satisfied with its services. It almost always knows what is going on in the system. As such, authority serves as a good barometer to gauge how the overall system is feeling towards your initiative. Most of the complaints, issues, and opposing views will be relayed to authority, so they will know what concerns people have with the initiative.

Keeping an eye on authority will let you monitor the pressure on the system. If the system is not working in harmony, your authority will seem upset or fazed, while if the majority of the system is cooperating, they will seem satisfied.

Pay attention to how authority is interacting with the system, listen to them, focus on their tones of voice, gestures, body language, facial expressions, etc. If something feels off, there is probably more resistance than you know about. Focusing on authority will give you a better understanding of how the system is reacting to your initiative, and you can see whether you need to slow things down or speed them up.

73 Make sure authority is on board

Remember, authority is a force which is stronger than you are, which holds your fate and the fate of your initiative in its hands. They have the power to put an end to what you are doing, but they also have the power to make your journey easier. It depends which side they are on. For the sake of the initiative, you will want to consult with your authority. This will help to get the ball rolling, but will also ensure that fewer obstacles stop you on the way to fulfilling the initiative's purpose.

It is recommended that you do not move forward with your initiative if you don't have authority's approval. If you have not asked for it before introducing the initiative, you should consider pausing the initiative until you get the go ahead.

If your authority is not on your side, moving ahead without their support may be perceived as a challenge to their position, and they will use their power to bring you down. The more intense their resistance is, the more likely it becomes that your initiative will incur heavy losses, and may even fail.

To avoid such situations, you may want to consider putting things on hold until you have cleared the air between you and your authority figures. Let them know what you are doing, why it will work, how it will benefit them and the system, and remove possible misunderstandings. Address all their concerns and explain yourself thoroughly.

In short, do what you must and tell them all they need to know to get them on board. It can make the difference between success and failure.

74 Stay close to authority and always keep them informed

Authority is taking a risk with you when they decide to back your initiative. They will need constant reassurance about your competence and loyalty. They will want to know that you are worthy of their support. It is important that you keep them in the loop about every development.

You need to make sure they stay on your side, and keeping them in the loop will give them a role to play and keep you on their good graces. They will then help you with whatever obstacles you may face, and give you access to anything at their disposal that will help in fulfilling the initiative's purpose.

You should constantly inform them of new developments, ideas, plans, wins, losses, or advancements in the initiative. This way, they will know exactly how the initiative is unfolding. In general, authority hates surprises; to them, a surprise means that there are things under their control that they are not aware of. This makes them wary, and they may feel that you are exposing them to risks. When authority does not have all the information, they cannot make calculated, well-considered decisions. When things flare up between you and your opponents, your uninformed authority will have to deal with a mess they were not prepared for, one they might have prevented had they been informed of the situation.

Additionally, when they are informed about every change, no matter how small, they will trust you more, and believe that you are competent. They will appreciate and value your transparency. They will feel safer and have peace of mind knowing all they need to know.

This strategy also helps as a preemptive move to guard against your opponents' attempts to shake authority's trust in you.

Your opponents may try to exaggerate the risks involved in the initiative. They will twist information and create rumors about you and the initiative in an attempt to get authority to withdraw its support. However, if authority knows what is going on, they will be able to dismiss this information as false. This will discredit your opponents and shake authority's trust in them.

It is not enough to have authority on your side but predominantly uninvolved, because if the circumstances shift in a way that is not in their best interest, you will find them withdrawing their support, along with their resources, power, and access.

To guard against this situation and keep them satisfied, stay close to them and regularly notify them about anything related to the initiative before, during, and after every step. This will strengthen your relationship with them, making it easier to fulfill the initiative's purpose, and will shield you against your opponents lobbying authority to their side.

75 Attend to authority's warnings

Authority will issue warnings if they are unhappy. These warnings may come in the form of hesitation or silence, while at other times authority will be more vocal. Be sure to attend to them; the warnings will point to something about the initiative that is upsetting authority, and may signal that your relationship with authority is shaky. Consider slowing your initiative down or halting it so that you can clear the air. They have so much power over your fate and the fate of your initiative that you should not move forward if they are issuing warnings.

Respond to these warnings by approaching authority and voicing your suspicions that something is amiss. This may open up a conversation, and help you get to the root of their resistance.

Under no circumstances should you ignore these warnings. The longer you do so, the more likely it becomes that they will turn into actions. Additionally, ignoring them may give authority the impression that you are challenging them. They will act to bring your initiative down, and the power and resources at their disposal will serve as major obstacles, which can be taxing to deal with.

When authority issues a warning, pause and address it, unless you wish to take on a "giant".

76 Be careful not to give authority a reason to "punish" you

Authority cannot be effective if its formal position and power are not acknowledged and respected. A manager, CEO, president, or parent cannot be effective if they are ignored. For this reason, authority is highly sensitive when it comes to asserting its place in the system; otherwise, it would risk losing its role.

That is why an act of defiance or insubordination is usually met with firmness (even if you do nothing to provoke them), not only to set the record straight and punish insubordination, but also to send a clear message to everyone in the system that such insubordinate behavior will not be tolerated.

Be careful not to give authority an excuse to flex its muscles and display its power. It will publicly reprimand and punish you for ignoring, undermining, or challenging it. This will put a strain not only on your initiative, but on your continued survival in the system. Tread lightly around authority, while being clear and transparent. If you are doing everything above board, authority will rarely have a reason to come after you.

---

77 Build a relationship with higher authority

With a stronger support network, the initiative will be better off, especially in the face of resistance. If you have a chance to build a relationship with the higher levels of authority (e.g. executives, heads of family, heads of state), go for it. However, make sure that when you try to convince higher authority to join your side, you are not treading on anyone's toes. You don't want to create conflict with your own direct authority (e.g. boss) because you chose to befriend their authority. This could be dangerous if they misinterpret your attempts as a challenge.

Instead, try to find a way of befriending higher authority that will not seem intimidating to your authority. This is important because if they feel challenged before you have solidified your relationship with the "higher-ups", they will probably convince their authority that you are a "bad investment". Therefore, try to build a relationship with the "higher-ups", but don't create more conflict.

A good relationship with higher levels of authority will give you credibility, decrease the number of resisters, help you build a stronger support base, and allow you to take on stronger opponents. This is especially important if your initiative is targeting an authority figure. If you have their "bosses" on your side, you will not suffer as many negative consequences as you would if you were alone.

78

If your purpose is worthwhile, prepare to push forward against authority

What happens when your initiative is working towards removing authority figures from their positions? Or if your authority does not give you their blessings? You will probably face a lot of resistance, and you may lose supporters, either of their own volition or as "collateral damage". At this point, it is important that you examine your reasons for carrying out the initiative. If you feel it is worth it, prepare yourself for a tough battle, but stay on course.

If you have the support of other authority figures, the road might be a bit easier, although it will still be tough. Focus on your purpose and push forward, keeping up the momentum of the initiative. In addition to this, warn your supporters about the battle ahead, especially when authority cranks up its resistance. Expect some of your supporters, allies, and partners to leave; they may feel that challenging authority is too risky, and they might not be ready to commit to it. Some of them may even join ranks with authority.

So, I reiterate, make sure you believe that your initiative is worth the trouble. If it is both valuable and beneficial, you will always have supporters, even in the face of authority, but if it is not, expect many of your supporters to abandon you.

79   Assert your authority

In some areas of your life, you will hold a position of authority, whether you are an elected official, a manager, a team leader, a parent, or an older sibling. You will hold specific powers over the fate of others, and you will have access to resources within the system. If the situation calls for it, you may need to assert your authority over others. However, in the context of leadership, you should only use your authority for the sake of the initiative, and not for personal reasons.

If necessary, you can use your authority to deal with resistance, but be careful not to provoke or threaten your opponents; that will only intensify their resistance. Also, make sure that your relationship does not become too casual (e.g. in a professional setting), and that you are still their authority.

You can (and should) encourage discussions and accept opposing opinions, but at the end of the day, individuals need to follow your instructions. You can be flexible, but sometimes you will have to put your foot down.

It depends on the situation, but when you can use your authority to quell the resistance, or at least decrease it, you should do so. However, remember that you need to be fair, respectful, ethical, etc.

80 Always be willing to learn

You will not always have the best approach to carrying out your initiative, dealing with resistance, or rallying supporters. It does not hurt to keep an open mind and be willing to learn, even from your opponents. The beauty of our technological advancements is that we are afforded a wealth of information right at our fingertips. You no longer have to start from scratch. Instead, you can read up on what others have done and adjust it, or build on it, to suit your own purpose.

Consult with your supporters, research whether there have been any similar cases for precedence, look at what other people are doing, or even ask your opponents. Sometimes, the greatest insights and lessons will come from your opponents. Don't leave any source of relevant and beneficial knowledge untapped if you can access it. When you make mistakes, be willing to learn from them. There may be a better way of doing something which you failed to consider, but you will not improve your future strategy if you are not willing to learn.

It is important that you don't discount any opportunity to learn, especially when dealing with resistance. You need to adapt, and that cannot happen without learning. You should research historical cases and study people who have effectively dealt with a variety of opponents. There is no doubt that there are many approaches used throughout history, but not all of them were new. They were adapted from previous examples and techniques.

Therefore, save yourself some trouble and learn from others, from their mistakes, from your own mistakes, or from the advice of opponents and supporters. This will allow you to implement strategies that have worked in the past, and adapt them if necessary.

81 Constantly innovate and create exceptional value

Aim to always add exceptional value; this will set your initiative apart from other more ambitious personal or organizational interventions and innovations. The point of a leadership initiative is to add value to the system. If you are not constantly working towards that goal, your initiative may not be worth all the resistance and hardships you may face.

Always work towards learning, adapting, and creating different initiatives that you know will add exceptional value. Sometimes this means revolutionizing an entire industry, and at other times it might mean helping a few people live slightly improved lives. It is not about the quantity of value added, it is about the quality.

Constantly create and innovate, searching for an initiative that will elevate people's lives. This alone will set you above your opponents and put you ahead in the game. Of course, you will still face resisters, but they will fall behind you, and the system's constituents will notice improvements brought about by your initiative, and start to support you.

82 Never fight fire with fire

When someone fights dirty, you don't want to follow suit. This doesn't mean that you should sit on the sidelines. You should fight, but keep in mind that there are boundaries you should not cross. You should not resort to any illegal, unethical, or immoral actions, no matter how much you feel you want to "give them a taste of their own medicine". This retaliatory mindset will only get you into more trouble, so don't take the bait and fight dirty.

Instead, whenever your opponents "bring on the heat", you should study their resistance and think about how best to deal with them. The initiative is more important than petty fights, and there are usually better ways to deal with your opponents and enemies than retaliation. Therefore, avoid fighting fire with fire. Deal with opponents in a way that neutralizes their resistance, but benefits the initiative.

---

83 Protect your reputation

In some situations, your opponents may come after your character and reputation. They may attempt to create rumors, dig up past mistakes and "skeletons in closets", use your mistakes against you, divulge personal information, twist your words, or resort to other ways to ruin your reputation. You should expect that some of your opponents will cross moral boundaries. It is important that you don't allow such actions to surprise you, let alone discourage you. You will need to get ahead of them so that your opponents' attempts will be invalid and useless.

You may choose to:

- Keep all relevant individuals apprised of developments with the initiative.

- Publicly express any conflicts of interest. This way your opponents cannot make it seem like the initiative is serving a personal purpose.

- Divulge personal information that might be used against you, giving your reasons as to why these are not a testament to your current character.

- Point out the success of the initiative, highlighting in the process that you are doing all you can to make sure the system benefits.

- Ask influential members to provide testimonials of your current character.

- Consider turning the supposed "weaknesses" or "negative character traits" into strengths. Explain how your past negative experiences have actually helped you to learn and become a better person.

It is preferable to address these issues before your opponents have managed to spread any unwanted information. Even if people trust you, these attempts may sow the seeds of doubt in them. Some people may decide that they cannot come to terms with this information and so withdraw their support. If you lose your reputation, it will be harder for people to trust you, so they will be less likely to support you and the initiative. This is the last thing you want, so protect your reputation.

84 Consider tactically putting your initiative on hold

There will be times when the best thing to do for your initiative is to put it on hold. As with everything related to an act of leadership, this needs to serve the purpose of the initiative. If you reach a situation where the best tactic to adopt is temporarily putting the initiative on hold, go for it.

You may consider this tactic when you need to make midcourse corrections. If you come across developments such as new information, a different interpretation of the situation, victories or losses, or changes to the environment, you will need to consider putting the initiative on hold. This will let you use the information to make the necessary corrections.

If you feel that your initiative is creating unwanted conflict with authority, you should consider this option and temporarily pause what you are doing. If you don't, you risk provoking your authority, since they may see your lack of response and the continuation of your initiative as an act of provocation.

Sometimes you may feel that you need time to gather some more support and change tactics to strengthen your initiative. If that is the case, you will want to freeze it and work on building up your support network. This way, your initiative may better withstand its opponents when it begins moving again.

Pausing the initiative may also be used to handle your opponents. If you wish to calm them down, you might have to put things on hold so that you can address their concerns, find an approach that quells their resistance, or come up with a strategy to deal with them and break their momentum. Whatever the situation, consider taking a break from advancing your initiative so that you can focus on slowing, and possibly stopping, your opponents' resistance.

In another instance, you could consider using this strategy as a negotiation tactic. If you are negotiating with your opponents, pausing your initiative can be used as a gesture of good faith. You can say that you have paused what you are doing to show them that you are willing to come to a mutually beneficial agreement. This will give you a bargaining chip and convey to your opponents that you truly want to resolve matters and move forward in the best way possible.

Finally, you can use this strategy to reflect on your initiative and its purpose. Although putting the initiative on hold is usually used to ensure that you clear a path for it, sometimes you may want to reconsider what you are doing. It might be that your initiative is not working, it is not the right time to introduce it or, for whatever reason, you feel the initiative must be postponed. Therefore, reflect on matters, and if you feel you need to rethink your initiative altogether, a good first step is putting things on hold.

85   Give authentic credit to authority

Usually, you cannot move forward with your initiative unless authority lends you their support, grants you permission, and at times gives you access to necessary resources (e.g. funds). Therefore, it seems natural and fair that you need to give them credit for their assistance. This also has other advantages. When you give them credit, you let them know that you appreciate what they are doing. This, in turn, will encourage them to keep on supporting you, and may even encourage them to increase their support.

Furthermore, this could be considered an expression of your loyalty towards them. Loyalty is one of the main attributes authority looks for, so they will highly appreciate it and might show their gratitude by further increasing their commitment to you and the initiative.

If you can, consider giving them credit publicly, not only to make your appreciation known, but also to send a message to everyone else that authority is backing the initiative up, and that in essence, it is "their initiative". This will again increase the support for the initiative and decrease the resistance against it. Added to this, most authority figures would like people to know that their efforts are bringing results and that their decision to back you up has proven to be the right one.

86   Give credit to your supporters

You need to acknowledge the help of those pushing the initiative forward, not only because it is the right thing to do, but also to express the significance of their support and the pivotal role they are playing in fulfilling the purpose of the initiative. This will revitalize them and make them feel appreciated, which in turn will ensure that they keep their supportive momentum going, and possibly even increase it.

When you give other people credit for doing their part, you will demonstrate that the initiative is not an individual effort, but a collective one. Your supporters will respect you for that and increase their support. In addition, you will gain the respect of your opponents, and possibly their support (this is more likely from the passive opponents than the active ones). When they see that you are all working as a group to benefit the system, they will be encouraged to join in.

Authority is always watching, and when you give credit where credit is due, they will also respect you for it. The loyalty and appreciation you show your support network will increase your authority's support for the initiative.

Furthermore, giving your supporters and others credit for their help and the roles they are playing will strengthen your relationship with them. As such, you will build relational capital, which you can utilize later on in the initiative if you need it. The stronger your relationship with your supporters, the more likely they will be to remain loyal to you and the initiative, and the less likely it becomes that your opponents will succeed in seducing them over to the other side.

Finally, be generous when you give your supporters credit. This will invigorate them and, as such, they will support you more enthusiastically — which increases the chances of success. This should not be seen as a ploy to manipulate them. Genuinely express your gratitude and give them well-deserved credit. In the terms of your initiative, success is not a personal accomplishment, but a group venture.

87 Never criticize or blame your passive or passive-aggressive resisters

Even if your opponents are working against you, there is no excuse for criticizing or blaming them. Remember that you don't want to make the resistance personal, nor do you want your opponents to think that you are taking it personally. Therefore, avoid criticizing and pointing fingers, especially when you are dealing with the less active resisters.

If you feel that this is idealistic, consider it from a strategic perspective. Your passive and passive-aggressive resisters are still not actively working against you. If you start pointing fingers at them, it may rile them up and could potentially push them further up the intensity spectrum. The more you criticize them, the higher the chances of them intensifying their resistance.

In addition, constant berating from your side will make it easier for your active opponents to rally these individuals into more active stances, as well as to cement their resistance. In turn, this will make it harder for you to deal with them. As they become more intense opponents, you are less likely to succeed in turning them into supporters.

All in all, criticizing your less active opponents will do more harm than good. Instead of berating them, attempt to rally them to your side, and avoid giving your opponents the tools to strengthen their opposition.

---

88 Expose and discredit your opponents; don't blame them

Ensure you know the difference between discrediting someone using factual evidence and blaming them based on personal opinions. Don't start a blame game by pointing fingers at your opponents. Instead, focus on the purpose of the initiative and its benefits. This way, you will not get caught up in distracting conflicts and unnecessary arguments over who is to blame for something.

There may be times when your opponents will spread malicious rumors, attack your reputation, or twist or fabricate information in an attempt to discredit you and your initiative. In any of the above situations, you may need to consider exposing them and discrediting their attempts with a response based solely on the factual evidence.

You need to expose the truth, not for your own gain, but to counter their attempts to discredit you. If you do not get ahead of them, you risk losing current and potential supporters, as well as increasing your opponents. You need to protect your supporters and others from falling prey to your opponents' manipulative efforts.

Therefore, don't hesitate to expose the truth behind your opponents' malicious attempts, as long as you do so by presenting facts and objective evidence. Don't resort to personal attacks, pointing fingers, and criticizing your opponents. It does not help you to start an unnecessary conflict. Instead, be truthful and factual, so others can understand what is really going on, without getting the impression that you are making the attacks personal.

For instance, in 1993, *Virgin Atlantic Airlines* won a case against *British Airways*. As part of the settlement, British Airways apologized to Richard Branson and to Virgin Atlantic for using questionable and possibly illegal strategies to gain a competitive edge. Focusing solely on evidence, Virgin Atlantic was able to expose their competition's inappropriate attacks. This helped Virgin Atlantic get back on good footing and protect their customers from being manipulated with misinformation.

89 Avoid conflict and head-on collisions when possible, but do what it takes to protect yourself and the initiative

You should avoid getting into conflicts and butting heads with your opponents whenever you can. It will not only be distracting, but it might harm your initiative. Conflicts are costly; you will lose time, resources, supporters. Responding to attacks is risky, and often unwise. However, this does not mean that you should always avoid conflict.

If you find that you need to resort to head-on collisions with your opponents, don't hesitate to engage fiercely. Sometimes, avoiding conflict could mean risking the success of the initiative. If this is the case, you need to kick your countermeasures into high gear and prepare yourself and your support network for the upcoming conflict.

Having said that head-on collisions need to be the last resort. Consider instead:

- Negotiations,

- Mediations,

- Creative solutions that will deal with the reasons for the resistance,

- Giving things time to calm down.

In short, consider every possible "peaceful" mechanism for dealing with the situation before opting for head-on collisions. This will often be cheaper and less risky.

---

90 Do Favors

There is a psychological concept called the *law of reciprocity*. The gist of it is that when you do someone a favor, they will feel obliged to return that favor. Therefore, in the context of the initiative, you will want to do as many favors for others as you can, so people will respond in kind. However, it is important that you do people favors not for the sake of collecting favors, but as a service to them. If they feel like you are manipulating them, they will be less likely to help you out.

In other words, unlike a "quid pro quo" situation, you are doing them a favor not on the condition that they return it, but because it helps them in some way.

Helping others will let you build relational capital and stronger bonds with the individuals involved. Consider this strategy even before you start your initiative. When the time comes for you to introduce the initiative, people may avoid opposing you because you have helped them in the past, or they may jump at the opportunity to support you and return a favor you did for them. In either case, doing favors for others will help to decrease resistance, increase support, and give your initiative a solid chance at success.

91 When mobilizing, target the mind and the heart

For others to accept your proposed purposeful initiative, you need to consider two fronts on which you must mobilize them: 1) mind and 2) heart.

Firstly, start by appealing to their intellect and rationality. You need to lay out all the details of your initiative, starting with what the issues are, why change is necessary, how you propose to fix things, and what their roles in making this initiative a success could be. While appealing to the mind, you will explain all your reasoning behind the initiative and build a picture of a potentially better reality. When they can see that your initiative makes sense and is beneficial, they may be intrigued and wish to join your side.

However, this might not be enough. You should also appeal to their hearts. Many people are unmotivated by dry statistics and facts, and may be disinterested in a better reality unless they have a sense of what it will feel like.

You need to engage their emotions to inspire them. When you mobilize individuals towards a purposeful initiative, you need to highlight the benefits by appealing to their 9-Ds.

Ultimately, feelings of fear and hope drive most people. People shy away from things that they fear and run towards things that give them hope. You need to make sure that when you introduce your initiative, or even the idea of it, you bear this in mind. Link the benefits of your initiative to their hopes. Let them know the risks and the potential for loss, but also let them know how you plan to minimize these factors. Talk to them about the elevated reality you are aiming for, engaging their hopes and dreams. Of course, you should not manipulate or lie to them, but be honest and tailor your explanation to highlight the hopes and ease the fears.

Together, these frames will help you mobilize supporters, decrease opponents, and introduce an initiative that has a good chance of success. Therefore, present your arguments, give them all the information they need, but also appeal to their emotions. Both fronts are needed; one alone will not give you the desired effect.

As an example, I will refer again to my decision to move the head office of the company I worked for to another area. At the time, this was a hassle for many of my employees. However, when it came to distributing information about the move, I targeted their minds and their hearts.

I started with an approach explaining why it made sense: the new location was where all media and news corporation would be. To add to this rational explanation, I appealed to their emotions by printing 3-D renderings of the new head offices, showcasing the elegant furniture, beautiful views, and exquisite design. When people saw what their new offices would look like, they felt a sense of pride and joy. Suddenly, the proposed workplace became a reality they could imagine, and the design appealed to their emotions. After targeting these two fronts, I found my employees became enthusiastic about moving.

92   Battles should be won before they are fought

"The supreme art of war is to subdue the enemy without fighting"

– Sun Tzu

Conflicts with opponents are always dangerous and unpredictable because, as much as you try to guess what your opponent will do, you will not always get it right. There will always be some miscalculations on your part, as well as some surprises on theirs. It is hard to accurately predict every potential strategy and countermeasure your opponents might employ. However, you should still try to figure out as much as possible about how your opponents will move.

Remember that conflicts will incur costs, ranging from the time spent all the way to losing part of your support network (e.g. some people will decide to leave because it is too stressful). Therefore, you should avoid taking part in a conflict if you are not prepared to deal with the costs. Unfortunately, you will not be able to avoid conflicts all the time, and you will need to take part in a few because it is necessary for the success of the initiative. Spend time preparing yourself prior to engaging in the conflict. This preparation will lead to better results and bring fewer costs to you and your supporters.

To the best of your ability, factor in all the information you have on your opponents so that you can avoid unnecessary miscalculations. In addition, factor in and expect that there will be some surprises you were not able to account for. If you prepare yourself thoroughly, many conflicts will essentially be won before you even engage in them.

93 Don't always revert to your default thinking

Every person has their own individual, default way of thinking. Some people are pessimists, others are optimists. Some people are skeptics, others are believers. Some people are distrusting, others are trusting. Some people have a tendency to over-interpret a situation, searching for deeper meanings when there are none, while others are less inquisitive. As Sigmund Freud once said,

"Sometimes a cigar is just a cigar"

Not everyone will think the same way, and they tend to interpret things based on their preferred way of thinking. They will analyze information within the scope of their default mindset. Although this may prove beneficial at times, it can also limit one's ability to consider different angles and perspectives.

You need to make sure that you don't always fall back on your default way of thinking when you are interpreting the environment at a given moment. Each situation you find yourself experiencing will be different. As such, each of these different situations will require different ways of thinking. Only by opening your mind can you study the situation, the issues it presents, the options it opens up, and which solution you should use to deal with the situation and reach the best possible conclusion.

If you hope to understand your opponents and supporters, predict what your opponents may do, and consider what options you have at your disposal, you cannot filter every situation through the same mindset. This will limit your interpretation and increase the risk of miscalculations. In turn, a miscalculation will affect your choice of strategy, and if you choose the wrong one or a suboptimal one, you may not be able to deal with the resistance effectively.

"To a man with the hammer, everything looks like a nail"

– Mark Twain

Not everything is a nail, so be flexible with your thought process. Adopt many ways of thinking so that you can understand all the facets of the situation, and pick the most appropriate interpretation.

---

94   Adapt the tactics when necessary

Just as each individual has a default way of thinking, people also have their own preferred repertoire of tactics, ones which have worked well for them in the past. Some people prefer to opt for a defensive strategy, while others prepare for the offensive. Some people are meticulous and slow, while others are efficient and fast.

Unfortunately, relying on the same set of tactics will not always be good for your initiative. It is essential to recognize that not every situation will call for the same set of tactics. It is important to adapt the tactics to the context. When you find that your tactics and options are not working for the initiative, you will need to find and adopt new ones. If you don't, you will not be able to do what is best for your initiative and/or resolve situations in the best possible way. Constantly expand your repertoire and try different combinations of strategies.

95 Make smart use of your relationship network

Every person has something to offer, whether it is connections, skills, expertise, or other forms of support. Relationships are valuable when they offer something beneficial. Your relationship network is made up of the people you have a connection with, and they are the people you should go to when you need support. You should have a good understanding of what each individual has to offer in terms of the initiative. They may be useful in a:

- **Practical Sense.** They may have technical expertise, access to resources, or other practical skills that may make the journey of the initiative smoother. They may also offer you a creative solution based on their area of expertise.

- **Moral Sense.** They may be the voice of reason, constantly checking your interpretations and actions to make sure you don't cross any ethical or moral boundaries.

- **Emotional Sense.** They may offer comfort and support, especially in the highly emotional atmosphere of resistance. For instance, you may need someone to help keep you calm, and they might offer you chances to decompress and express your emotions in a healthy way so that you don't have an outburst in front of your opponents.

- **Social Sense.** They might have good social skills and strong relationships. They may be easy to talk to and they may be on good footing with most people in the system. Their strong people skills could be used to help you lobby more supporters and try to convince your opponents to give up their resistance.

- **Political Sense.** They may know the ins and outs of the system, and be able to help connect you to the key influencers. They might have important connections and know how to navigate the system. They can help you get a step ahead of your opponents by talking to the right people and moving smoothly through the system.

- **Spiritual Sense.** They may bring out the best in you, calm you down, highlight the virtues within you. You will need all this when dealing with resistance, because it will challenge your very spirit.

So, when dealing with your opponents, you will need to leverage all the benefits that these different relationships provide. Whether it is providing the proper backing to protect you, the right tools to tackle opponents, heading a meditation class, or offering up resources, creative ideas or solutions, know which skills your individual supporters are strong in, and utilize them accordingly.

Note: be smart and accept the help your relationship network has to offer. If there is one particular right time to make use of your network, it is the moment you decide to introduce the initiative, especially since you have invested so much time in building and strengthening your relationship with these individuals. Therefore, approach them and ask them for their support and their unique help in their specialized areas.

96 Learn to live with the heat without internalizing it

Resistance manifests itself in different ways, often emotionally. Your opponents will express their resistance with a myriad of negative emotions, including anger, frustration, disappointment, fear, panic, sadness, anxiety, etc. All these expressions will be directed at you, which is a normal, human reaction considering the element of uncertainty that is attached to purposeful change.

You cannot stop this from happening, but what you can do is expect these emotions, process them, and learn how to absorb them without being hurt by them. This is an important step in dealing with resistance. You need to be able to take the heat without internalizing it and making it personal. After all, it is not about you as a person, but about the initiative and people's reactions to it. If you can't avoid internalizing, you risk their emotions getting to your core and creating negativity which could dissuade you from continuing your initiative.

Your role in the game includes introducing the initiative and dealing with the heat of resistance. This may be quite difficult, especially when the intensity of resistance is higher up the spectrum. However, your initiative cannot move forward if you are not able to take the heat and stay focused.

Leadership is a difficult endeavor because it can get highly emotional, chaotic, and messy. It is disruptive, moving people's lives around and changing the status quo. Therefore, do your part and learn how best to navigate the heat, for your sake and the sake of the initiative and its beneficial purpose.

97 Don't allow your initiative to become an extension of yourself

I have been saying that you should not take your opponents' resistance personally. However, this includes not making the initiative itself personal. The initiative is just an initiative, not a personal conquest or proposition. You are introducing it for the purpose of benefiting the system, and not for yourself. Don't make the initiative an extension of yourself. After all, you might have to change it, put it on hold, and sometimes you may even have to postpone or abandon it.

Therefore, don't own it. Don't make it a large emotional investment and, most importantly, don't make it about you. It is an initiative or intervention, meaning it is something external to you; the journey it will take is not fully in your control. If you ignore these facts, it will be harder for you to adjust the initiative, make changes, accept criticisms, alter your interpretations, etc.

98 Don't be over-compassionate

Empathy and compassion are at the root of leadership, so they are crucial attributes to have. However, this does not mean that you should allow compassion to get in the way of the initiative. You should not be so compassionate that you sacrifice the collective good. There is such a thing as being overly compassionate.

Of course, you need to be empathetic so that you can understand your opponents' issues and concerns. Furthermore, you need to resort to these fundamental attributes while trying to find creative ways of dealing with the resistance. However, you will need to look for methods which allow you to exercise your compassion without negatively influencing the initiative.

Sometimes, you will want to give people the benefit of the doubt, to put yourself in their shoes, and to try, to the best of your abilities, to understand what is bothering them and how you can help. However, at other times, you will need to confront your opponents and even engage in conflict. Don't let compassion stop you from engaging in necessary conflicts, confrontations, and sometimes head-on collisions with your opponents.

Put bluntly, don't use compassion as an excuse to avoid necessary conflict. Engaging in conflict does not mean that you are not compassionate. Indeed, it is compassion that allows you to see that conflict is necessary, and that it will benefit the collective good. You can still be compassionate and do the right thing for the initiative, your supporters, and the system overall.

Finally, don't let your opponents abuse your compassion. If they know that most of the time you "ask questions first" and try to understand their side before engaging in conflict, they may take advantage of this and use your compassion to buy themselves time to bring your initiative down. Therefore, be compassionate with them, but if you are getting nowhere, you should consider more direct options and other solutions.

99 Stay close to your opponents

Keep an eye on your opponents and stay close to them. Try to encourage communication between you. This will give you an "in" with them. You will have a better chance of understanding what they are thinking and planning to do, and you will be more prepared for their resistance and countermeasures.

In addition to this, if you communicate, you increase your chances of building connections and a rapport with them. This will make them more likely to listen to your side of things, so you can better express your plans and intentions. You may also be able to clear up any misunderstandings that they may have, and, in some cases, neutralize their resistance.

Finally, you will see a more personal side to your opponents, and they will hopefully see the same in you. This will help you build bridges, maintain relationships, and ease the tension that comes with the opponent-opposed relationship.

100 Accept casualties publicly

Inevitably, an act of leadership will result in losses on both sides. You should do your best to minimize these, but unfortunately, you will not be able to prevent them or come out unscathed. You need to accept that you will have casualties, and you will need to let your supporters, your opponents, and the system overall know that too. Make it clear to them that there will be collateral damage.

Some people will fall through the cracks, no matter how hard you try to minimize harm.

The point of being open about this is you want to send a signal to the system, especially your opponents, that you are not afraid of confrontation, not intimidated by resistance, and you are ready to suffer the inevitable consequences of pain and loss that come with introducing an initiative. If your opponents sense a low pain tolerance on your end, they will jump at the opportunity to use it against you.

101 Make an accurate interpretation of the situation and the resistance

For you to move forward with the initiative, you need to understand the dynamics of the situation and the resistance you are facing. You cannot hope to make the right moves if you have not accurately interpreted the situation, and you will not be able to deal with your opponents if you don't correctly diagnose the intensities of their resistance and the roles they are playing.

Don't fool yourself with wishful thinking and the constructed illusion of a reality you would prefer to believe in. If you twist reality, you will misinterpret the situation and you will not be able to deal with resistance effectively. In turn, this will open your initiative up to vulnerabilities and blind spots, which your opponents will take advantage of. Instead, focus on seeing the resistance for what it is, and accept the reality of your situation.

Reality wins, every single time

102 Communicate in advance about your initiative

Let people know what your initiative is all about before you go ahead and introduce it. Elaborate on its purpose, its benefits, what it involves, and how it aims to create a better reality. This will not only reduce misunderstandings or misinterpretations of your intentions, but people are more likely to respect you for being clear and transparent about what you plan to do. Added to this, if you prepare the system for your initiative ahead of time, people will be less likely to act surprised when you introduce it.

Take the time to give everyone involved a detailed explanation of what you are going to do, why you are going to do it, how you are going to do it, what the costs might be, what the risks might be, and what the benefits might be. This will give people time to prepare for its introduction. Additionally, it will give you clues about who your potential supporters and opponents are.

Remember that communicating in advance decreases the chances of blame. There is no doubt that some people will still point fingers after you have explained and elaborated on your initiative and all its aspects, but you will avoid making opponents out of people because you did not give them enough time to process the initiative. You will also avoid giving your opponents a chance to say that they were caught by surprise.

There is no downside to letting people know that you are planning an initiative, but there is one if you keep it to yourself and "surprise" the system. Be clear, transparent, and upfront; you will have fewer opponents to deal with.

103 Frequently review your map of existing and potential supporters, opponents, and authority

Progress is dynamic, and the environment is constantly changing. Sometimes people will switch "camps" between supporters, resisters, and neutrals. In other words, depending on how the initiative is unfolding, people may decide to switch allegiances or become neutral. As such, the map you prepared in the preemptive stage will not remain the same. Changes will happen, and these will affect where people appear on your breakdown. You will need to consult and possibly update the map with every emerging development.

As you score wins or losses, the dynamics between you and the system will change. People will begin to have second thoughts. When you score wins, some of your resisters may join your side or become neutral, while neutrals may decide to join you. When you lose, your supporters may become afraid of backing a failing initiative, and might become neutrals, or even resisters.

Intensities change as well. For instance, after a win, passive supporters may become active in their support, while active-aggressive resisters may become passive-aggressive. After a loss, passive resisters may become active in their resistance, or active resisters may become active-aggressive.

As new developments emerge, make sure you study the situation and frequently update your map. You should consider consulting it on a regular basis, even if there haven't been major changes; there might be some subtle differences you have missed. An accurate map of the system will allow you to effectively deal with your resistance, give you an idea of who you can and can't trust, and perhaps even offer some indication of who you can and cannot convince to join you.

104 Experiment and test before going public, so that you can gauge reactions

Before you introduce your initiative to the system, you may want to consider testing the waters. If you want to increase the chances of success for the initiative, consider experimenting with it on a smaller scale. For instance, if you plan to introduce an initiative across your whole organization, consider starting with just one department. This way, you will get a general overview of how the system might react to the initiative. In addition, you will see what impacts it has and what consequences come out of it. You will know what does and does not work. You will also get a clear idea of the possible trajectory of your initiative — how it will unfold. This will help you immensely.

When you gather up all this information you will (among other things):

- Understand how people may react to your initiative.

- See what its strengths and its weaknesses are.

- Know if it has any blind spots.

- See what types of resistance you might face.

- Understand what people liked and dislike about the initiative and the approach you used.

You can gather up all this information and use it to refine your approach before you adopt it on a larger scale. In short, this gives you the chance to predict how things will unfold, and this will allow you to prepare yourself and your strategies for potential opponents. It will also give the system an opportunity to prepare for what is to come. You will be able to fix any kinks to make sure you increase the chances of success, while also minimizing the resistance you will face.

PART THREE

THE 36 SCENARIOS

HOW TO USE THE STRATEGIES/PRINCIPLES SECTION

In this third part, I am going to dedicate an independent sectionfor each role, with its varying intensities. I will start each section with a small introduction of the role, how the people playing this role may resist you, and the nuances that make each type of opponent special. After the introduction, the section will move ahead in more detail, combining the roles and intensities to present you with 36 different scenarios. In addition, I will list the recommended strategies (by their corresponding numbers in part two) that apply to each combination of role and intensity for you to use as you wish. In some cases, I will add a note to a strategy for you to consider in addition to what has been already explained in part two. Think of these additions as something to bear in mind if you choose to apply the strategy. To avoid repetition, I will only mention these additions once, but in some cases they apply to the intensities that follow as well.

The number and applicability of the strategies will vary depending on the role and intensity. I would recommend that you use your own discretion when deciding how to use the strategies, in what order, and with what level of emphasis.

The structure of this part is intended to make it easier for you to make the best use of this book. My hope is that when you face opponents in the future, you will identify the role in which you are experiencing resistance, and then specify which intensity — based on the explanations in chapter 4 (part one) — your opponents fit into. Then you can go to the section dedicated to that specific combination of role and intensity and see what strategies you can apply to deal with their resistance.

The list of strategies is comprehensive and it covers the subject to a great extent, but I would like to emphasize that this list is by no means absolute. Therefore, I recommend that you apply your wisdom and life experiences to come up with your own strategies, ones that you feel will deal with your opponents. Ensure that they serve the purpose of fulfilling your leadership initiative, effectively, efficiently, morally, ethically, and with minimum cost.

Enjoy and good luck!

A selection of 36 strategies/principles have been grouped in the table on the next page. They are considered fundamentals that apply in the first 30 scenarios starting with "personal passive" and ending with "constituents malevolent". Archenemy, the 31st scenario, has its own table with specific selections, and will be presented in its own sub-chapter.

To avoid unnecessary repetition, I have included the Fundamental Strategies/Principles table here. Please remember to take these strategies into consideration when you deal with resistance from any of the first 30 scenarios. Take some time to examine these strategies before moving forward into the scenarios.

Fundamental Strategies/Principles

4	Always be kind and courteous	14	Stay focused on your purpose
9	Objectively diagnose the root of their resistance	5	Always be compassionate and empathetic
18	Don't make it personal or take it personally	67	Actively and authentically listen to all parties involved
52	Never humiliate your opponents	43	Don't be provoked
6	Over-communicate	19	Think creatively
63	Take care of yourself physically, mentally, emotionally, and spiritually	102	Communicate in advance about your initiative
10	Be conscious of the cultural codes of conduct and protocols	21	Keep ego out of it
17	Stay close to your support network	51	Never underestimate your opponents
20	Stay calm	86	Give credit to your supporters

Fundamental Strategies/Principles

65	Tailor your approach to your target audience	97	Don't allow your initiative to become an extension of yourself
95	Make smart use of your relationship network	98	Don't be over-compassionate
96	Learn to live with the heat without internalizing it	90	Do favors
94	Adapt the tactics when necessary	93	Don't always revert to your default thinking
91	When mobilizing, target the mind and the heart	46	Expand your repertoire of options
92	Battles should be won before they are fought	103	Frequently review your map of existing and potential supporters, opponents, and authority
101	Make an accurate interpretation of the situation and the resistance	99	Stay close to your opponents
72	Use authority to gauge the system overall	104	Experiment and test before going public, so that you can gauge reactions
100	Accept causalities publicly	50	Don't assume that you can always predict the moves of your opponents

PERSONAL SCENARIOS

Remember that this role denotes your family, friends, and social contacts (neighbors, club members, religious or spiritual group, etc.), who probably constitute an important part of your life. They may live under the same roof as you, you may see or talk to one another daily, and you may share a rich, long relationship with them. In some ways, they may be the most deeply rooted presence in your life. A big part of understanding this subcategory lies in understanding the relationship, with its history and shared experiences. It is loaded with emotions, and is generally not a rational, exchange-based relationship.

In addition, you usually expect people in this subcategory to be supportive of the changes you wish to make. However, there are times when they will not agree with what you are doing, and they will express their opposition in varying ways depending on how they perceive your change initiative, and how it relates to your relationship and its history. This may frustrate you and lead to disappointment and feelings of betrayal.

Furthermore, in these relationships, conflicts will bring up residual feelings and thoughts left from previous conflicts. Frustrations and bottled-up emotions are more likely to surface. This makes these relationships sensitive, so changes tend to agitate them more easily than other relationships.

This can be quite a tricky subcategory. Both parties have certain expectations, and leadership initiatives tend to create issues related to these expectations. The emotional nature of the relationship coupled with these expectations, might make it difficult for the both of you to keep the conflict from becoming personal. All your interactions, including resistance, will carry a deeply emotional element, which makes them more delicate, and makes negative reactions potentially more extreme.

When you introduce an initiative that upsets someone in this subcategory, they will more than likely feel betrayed, and may feel that your willingness to forego your loyalties, even if for a good cause, is a personal attack on them. Emotions will run high, and it may reach a point where they harbor animosity towards you. It could be quite difficult to subdue these emotions without giving up on your initiative.

You should also remember that if you make an opponent or enemy out of a person in this subcategory, they may take everything they know about you, your secrets, vulnerabilities and weaknesses, and use them against you. After all, depending on how close the relationship is, they will know which buttons to press to get a rise out of you. This can easily escalate the conflict out of control: it may become nasty and put a strain on your lives and relationship.

For instance, in a family business, if the relationship between family members or stakeholders becomes sour, it can threaten the survival of the business, because personal relationships can be irrational and highly emotional.

The good news is that your history can also work in your favor, with shared experiences and intimacy serving to mitigate their opposition and maintain your relationship. For instance, couples can get on each other's nerves sometimes, but they stay together because there have been more good times than bad times through-out their relationship. Remember to focus on the good times when-ever you encounter this sort of conflict, and don't let bad feelings override good memories.

PERSONAL: PASSIVE

Usually, people in the personal subcategory feel comfortable enough to confront you with their issues. However, that doesn't mean that they will be active in their resistance. Sometimes, you will introduce a change that they are uncomfortable with, and they will express their resistance indirectly.

In this case, members of this subcategory value the relationship enough to give you the benefit of the doubt. They are still not supportive of what you are doing, but they trust you enough to not make a big deal out of it. Instead, they will stay quiet for the most part, and will claim that they have no opinions on the matter, or that they are waiting for some results before they make a definite decision.

The tricky part here is picking up on their hesitation and understanding that their indecisiveness points to an issue that you may wish to address. Even if they don't pose a direct threat, if you leave their hesitation unattended to, it can easily intensify. They can be patient only for so long; if you don't change your approach, try to convince them that you are doing the right thing, or address their concerns in some way, they may decide to kick their resistance up a notch or two.

Given the emotional element in this subcategory, their resistance may point to something more than just passive resistance. You need to be careful, because sometimes you may wish to let them cool off before talking about it, while at other times you will need to approach them and address the issue directly. Dealing with them starts with you figuring out what their passive resistance is down to.

It's also important to remember that they may indirectly influence other people. Their hesitation can make others doubt your intentions and the initiative.

RECOMMENDED STRATEGIES/PRINCIPLES

- **2** ✓ **Respect the history of the relationship**
- **7** ✓ **Over-communicate your interest in listening to their point of view**
- **1** ✓ **Ensure any negativity doesn't become contagious**
- **3** ✓ **Limit the conflict to the relevant issues**
- **61** ✓ **Investigate to see if there is more to their resistance than meets the eye**
- **27** ✓ **Mobilize with enthusiasm**
- **28** ✓ **Sell the benefits of the initiative**
- **38** ✓ **Involve the members of the system in the initiative**
- **15** ✓ **Maintain the momentum of your progress**
- **34** ✓ **Create, score, and celebrate a stream of small victories**
- **87** ✓ **Never criticize or blame your passive or passive-aggressive resisters**

PERSONAL: PASSIVE-AGGRESSIVE

Many of us may have been on the receiving end of a friend's or family member's silent treatment or sarcastic comments. Usually, the issues are related to a mistake on our end, or an earlier misunderstanding. However, in the context of an initiative, this presents a more serious problem.

In this case, they still value the relationship, and as such, they will be less likely to openly express their concerns. However, their resistance will show in their body language, their tone of voice, their retorts, or their silence. If you are observant, you will pick up on these signs and know that something is wrong, that the initial absence of their resistance didn't mean they were happy with the initiative.

Passive-aggressive resistance from someone you expect support from demonstrates that something is wrong, and that they expect you to resolve it. Think about your relationship in the long-term, how the conflict might affect it, and what you can do to minimize the damage.

If you value the relationship, you will usually want to get to the bottom of what is troubling them. Engage them in a conversation so you can understand the root of their resistance, and then work on resolving it. However, do so carefully and delicately, because things can easily spiral into a highly emotional atmosphere, intensifying their resistance in the process.

This is a crucial point because passive-aggressive resisters are one step away from being an active form of resistance. Heed their warnings and avoid crossing this boundary — more active resistance tends to increase considerably. At this point, you still have a chance to salvage the situation without too much trouble. If you let their resistance go unchecked, they may misinterpret the situation, feeling that you don't care about them, or about your loyalties and commitments to them.

RECOMMENDED STRATEGIES/PRINCIPLES

2 ✓ **Respect the history of the relationship**

7 ✓ **Over-communicate your interest in listening to their point of view**

3 ✓ **Limit the conflict to the relevant issues:**
It is easier for your opponent in this role to focus on and remember past mistakes, issues, and other unrelated problems. Make sure their resistance is not focused on these issues.

1 ✓ **Ensure any negativity doesn't become contagious:**
At this intensity, passive-aggressive resistance may be noticed by others in your personal or social circles. As such, you need to make sure that the tension between you and your resisters doesn't spread.

11 ✓ **Keep the fire contained**

61 ✓ **Investigate to see if there is more to their resistance than meets the eye:**
It is possible that their passive-aggressiveness is a warning of more intense resistance brewing behind closed doors. Therefore, use this strategy carefully.

27 ✓ **Mobilize with enthusiasm**

(12) ✓ **Don't provoke them**

(28) ✓ **Sell the benefits of the initiative**

(15) ✓ **Maintain the momentum of your progress**

(38) ✓ **Involve the members of the system in the initiative**

(34) ✓ **Create, score, and celebrate a stream of small victories**

(42) ✓ **Don't let conflicts and diversions distract you:**
At a personal level conflicts can be distracting, especially when opponents are not being completely open about what is troubling them.

(82) ✓ **Never fight fire with fire**

(87) ✓ **Never criticize or blame your passive or passive-aggressive resisters**

(74) ✓ **Stay close to authority and always keep them informed:**
Usually, in personal relationships, the authority is part of the personal circle. They might be a family member, or head of the neighborhood watch. Although, you may not need it, it can sometimes help to consult with whoever the authority is and keep them in the loop.

PERSONAL: ACTIVE

In this scenario, your opponents will be more vocal in their resistance. They will convey their thoughts and feelings openly to you. They may feel hurt, question your loyalty, bring up similar past events, etc. At this point, they are genuinely interested in understanding why you are introducing such a risky change. They still value your relationship, but they are starting to question your loyalty. It is possible that there have been a few arguments and fights in the past that might lead them to react this way.

Their resistance may be irrational and based on feelings, which will put immense emotional pressure on you. Their actions will hurt and disappoint you, and it might be quite difficult for you not to take it personally. You need to be careful, because if you say or do something wrong, things may flare up even more, and the argument will lead them to intensify their resistance. It is a delicate situation, and so must be dealt with as such.

In addition to this, conflicts within your personal circle may create a ripple effect that involves others within the circle, or even spreads to other areas of your life. It is unfortunate, but it would be naïve to assume that other aspects of your life will not be affected. For instance, a conflict with your neighbor in a gated community may affect other neighbors, your family, or your overall quality of life. It is also possible that in this emotionally charged atmosphere, your opponent will bring other unrelated issues to the surface.

RECOMMENDED STRATEGIES/PRINCIPLES

2 ✓ **Respect the history of the relationship**

7 ✓ **Over-communicate your interest in listening to their point of view:**
At this intensity, they may have some doubts about your willingness to resolve issues. By using this strategy you can reassure them that you care about their opinions and concerns.

31 ✓ **Vigilantly monitor the system**

61 ✓ **Investigate to see if there is more to their resistance than meets the eye**

1 ✓ **Ensure any negativity doesn't become contagious:**
When they are actively resisting you, there is a higher chance that others in your social/personal circle will be affected, directly or indirectly. Consider focusing on this strategy to make sure you avoid unnecessary tension with other parties.

3 ✓ **Limit the conflict to the relevant issues:**
If you are experiencing this type of resistance, it will be easier for your resisters to bring up other irrelevant issues perhaps relating to past arguments. In fact, it may fuel their resistance further, so do your best to focus on the relevant issues, while expressing your willingness to address the other issues in time.

11 ✓ **Keep the fire contained**

66 ✓ **Work to minimize the damage**

(12) ✓ **Don't provoke them**

(23) ✓ **Mentally and technically prepare yourself for the worst; it will get messy:**
It is a highly emotional situation, and their active opposition might make you feel conflicted. You will need to be careful. At this intensity, they may still hesitate to start revealing your secrets and vulnerabilities. However, prepare yourself so that you are better able to tackle their resistance; just in case they plan to bring out the worst and use it against you.

(74) ✓ **Stay close to authority and always keep them informed:**
Things have escalated so now might be the time to involve authority, so that things don't get out of control. Consider staying close to authority and letting them know what is going on every step of the way.

(16) ✓ **Create and nourish your support network:**
It can be hard to ask people in your personal circles to choose sides. However, from this level onward, you need to make sure you have people by your side. Make sure that the difficult situation does not stop you from asking people to support your initiative.

(64) ✓ **Take care of your supporters:**
In this scenario, this strategy also involves making sure your supporters are not dragged into conflicts and tensions with the resisters, especially if they themselves have a strong relationship with the resisters.

(36) ✓ **Double-check the sanity of the initiative**

33 ✓ **Debug the initiative:**
Dealing with personal relationships can cloud your judgment and may make you susceptible to over-looking the "bugs" in your initiative. It is crucial that you are constantly examining your initiative for potential weaknesses that can be used against it.

58 ✓ **Reflect on the purpose of the initiative:**
Dealing with people who you care about can be tricky in many ways (e.g. emotional, mental), but your purpose can help you stay focused and push forward.

35 ✓ **Take responsibility for your mess**

69 ✓ **Use patience, silence, and inaction wisely and strategically:**
It may quite difficult to utilize this strategy without straining your personal relationships, but at times you might need it so that you don't do something you'll regret.

54 ✓ **Success depends on doing the right thing, at the right time, and in the right way**

40 ✓ **Know when to confront:**
Knowing whether you have prepared enough is harder when you are faced with individual in your personal circle. However, at times you will need to confront them, and you must see if you have the necessary resources to do so.

89 ✓ **Avoid conflict and head-on collisions when possible, but do what it takes to protect yourself and the initiative**

84 ✓ **Consider tactically putting your initiative on hold**

55 ✓ **Know when to accept temporary defeat**

25 ✓ **Be ready to compromise:**
You should always have this option on the table when dealing with this subcategory. At this intensity, you need to be ready to use it whenever it could help resolve issues.

26 ✓ **Don't compromise on ethics or professionalism**

13 ✓ **Consider involving mediators:**
Active resistance at the personal level maybe harder to deal with than you think. The situation can be quite emotional, so you may need to consider getting a neutral party to do the rational thing.

41 ✓ **Let them negotiate for you:**
The emotional atmosphere can make it difficult for you to negotiate with your opponents. Avoid putting yourself in a position where you might do something you will regret and let professionals negotiate for you.

15 ✓ **Maintain the momentum of your progress**

27 ✓ **Mobilize with enthusiasm**

28 ✓ **Sell the benefits of the initiative**

83 ✓ **Protect your reputation:**
Opponents in this scenario have information that they could use to harm your reputation. At the active level, they may hold some leverage over you. Consider what you need to do to make sure that your reputation is not tarnished. If it means you need to be more open about some past experience or secret, make sure you are.

42 ✓ **Don't let conflicts and diversions distract you:**
A personal and close relationship makes it easier for your opponents to distract you. You need to stay focused on your initiative.

48 ✓ **Don't focus on winning – it is about fulfilling the purpose of the initiative:**
You are not in this to win or prove that you are right, and this is especially true when dealing with people in your personal life. Instead, focus on your initiative and its purpose.

80 ✓ **Always be willing to learn**

68 ✓ **As with a game of chess, think about your moves ahead of time and plan your strategy**

45 ✓ **Be unpredictable:**
They know a lot about you. That is why it is important that you try to switch things up and remain unpredictable.

82 ✓ **Never fight fire with fire**

56 ✓ **Don't burn the bridges between you and your opponents**

PERSONAL: ACTIVE-AGGRESSIVE

It is possible that you may do something that others in your circle will see as a personal attack on them. They may feel betrayed that you have taken such a step to uproot their lives. As a result, they will take it personally and will make it personal, focusing on you and not the initiative. It will get nasty, painful, and might even become vicious. This sort of opposition usually stems from the emotional side of your relationship, and from unmet, high expectations held by both parties — you expect them to support you, while they expect you to uphold your loyalties and commitments.

In this situation, unrelated issues may eventually dominate the conversation. For instance, what was an argument with your flatmate about changing the furniture becomes an argument about how you are a selfish individual. It will get messy quickly and it will hurt — remember that people in the "personal" subcategory are more likely to know what upsets you. This, along with the emotionally charged vibe, can make it challenging for you not to take their "attacks" personally.

Even if you do manage to stay calm, the commotion surrounding your relationship will probably still spill over to other people in your circle. In fact, your opponents may try to convince people not to support you. This will force others to choose a side, and if you don't try to resolve the issue, you will not only open yourself up to more intense resistance, but an increased number of resisters. Relationships in the "personal" subcategory are entangled, with one negative relationship affecting others.

Make sure you don't try to avoid your opponents, even if at times you want to. Avoiding them may be seen as a statement that you don't care for the relationship anymore, and you risk losing this person or creating further conflict with them by hurting their feelings.

RECOMMENDED STRATEGIES/PRINCIPLES

2 ✓ **Respect the history of the relationship**

7 ✓ **Over-communicate your interest in listening to their point of view**

31 ✓ **Vigilantly monitor the system**

61 ✓ **Investigate to see if there is more to their resistance than meets the eye**

1 ✓ **Ensure any negativity doesn't become contagious:**
At this intensity, it may be difficult to keep the tensions from affecting other parties, but you should still do your best to minimize this.

3 ✓ **Limit the conflict to the relevant issues**

22 ✓ **Create some distance**

11 ✓ **Keep the fire contained**

12 ✓ **Don't provoke them**

23 ✓ **Mentally and technically prepare yourself for the worst; it will get messy**

83 ✓ **Protect your reputation**

47 ✓ **Don't be faint-hearted or indecisive:**
Take some time to examine whether you are up to the task. There is no shame in admitting you cannot go through with it while the people in your personal life are exhibiting resistance at this intensity. Therefore, before you move forward reflect and consider whether you can or should do this.

74 ✓ **Stay close to authority and always keep them informed**

16 ✓ **Create and nourish your support network**

64 ✓ **Take care of your supporters**

32 ✓ **Ask for help:**
Although you may hesitate to involve others, at times you will need it. Therefore, don't dismiss this strategy because you don't wish to "burden" others with your resistance. After all, they may be facing it too.

54 ✓ **Success depends on doing the right thing, at the right time, and in the right way**

66 ✓ **Work to minimize the damage**

69 ✓ **Use patience, silence, and inaction wisely and strategically**

40 ✓ **Know when to confront**

89 ✓ **Avoid conflict and head-on collisions when possible, but do what it takes to protect yourself and the initiative**

49 ✓ **Winning in confrontations demands self-discipline:**
Winning in general means you need to have some control over yourself and your actions. In this scenario, you need to be even more in control. Emotions will run very high and your opponents may start exposing your secrets and vulnerabilities, so get a hold of yourself if you want to keep the initiative going.

42 ✓ **Don't let conflicts and diversions distract you**

48 ✓ **Don't focus on winning – it is about fulfilling the purpose of the initiative**

25 ✓ **Be ready to compromise**

26 ✓ **Don't compromise on ethics or professionalism**

13 ✓ **Consider involving mediators**

41 ✓ **Let them negotiate for you**

15 ✓ **Maintain the momentum of your progress**

36 ✓ **Double-check the sanity of the initiative**

84 ✓ **Consider tactically putting your initiative on hold**

33 ✓ **Debug the initiative**

58 ✓ **Reflect on the purpose of the initiative**

35 ✓ **Take responsibility for your mess**

80 ✓ **Always be willing to learn**

68 ✓ **As with a game of chess, think about your moves ahead of time and plan your strategy**

45 ✓ **Be unpredictable**

57 ✓ **Choose clarity or ambiguity, depending on the situation**

82 ✓ **Never fight fire with fire**

56 ✓ **Don't burn the bridges between you and your opponents**

(88) ✓ **Expose and discredit your opponents; don't blame them:**

If your personal opponents are doing something wrong or are attempting to sway others using your previous faults, or anything that warrants disproving, consider this strategy. However, remember that you should frame it in a way that does not blame them.

PERSONAL: MALEVOLENT

It is unpleasant to find yourself facing such intense resistance from your own personal circle. Nonetheless, it may happen, especially if your initiative creates a lot of change or robs those around you of something they consider essential. It may be that you are asking too much, that you are risking too much, without any obvious reward. As such, they will see your intervention as a personal attack, and naturally they will return this in kind.

This is not only about resisting your initiative – it is about you. In a personal relationship, an initiative alone will not usually cause this type of intense resistance. At worst, it would usually warrant active resistance. When someone shows this kind of resistance, it means that: you are at fault, seriously hurting them somehow, you have ignored their earlier resistance attempts, refused to listen to them, or there is something fundamentally wrong with your relationship.

In the first cases, you will need to acknowledge your mistake, apologize, and do what you can to salvage the situation, but it will be difficult. However, in the last case, your opponent no longer values your relationship. At this point, there is so much pent-up emotion that when you introduce an initiative that negatively affects them, they burst.

This person will use all they know about you, personal information, secrets, etc., to expose your "skeletons", spread rumors, and push all your buttons. It is an emotional, challenging situation, and you will need all your willpower to control yourself and stay calm. People who weren't originally involved may suddenly be forced to choose sides. All the bottled-up issues will come gushing out, and any minor or major arguments you have had with this person will be out in the open. There really is no limit to what they might say or do to make it personal for you, and it will be an immense challenge for you not to take it that way. It is a nerve-wracking situation, but one which you need to deal with, even if it seems easier to just avoid it.

RECOMMENDED STRATEGIES/PRINCIPLES

(23) ✓ **Mentally and technically prepare yourself for the worst; it will get messy:**
This strategy is needed now more than before. The lines your opponents will cross may shock you. The situation will get nasty and you will need to make sure you are prepared for the worst your opponents can throw at you.

(47) ✓ **Don't be faint-hearted or indecisive**

(22) ✓ **Create some distance**

(73) ✓ **Make sure authority is on board:**
There will be times when you need to make sure that you involve the authority in the situation, and that you make sure they support what you are doing.

(74) ✓ **Stay close to authority and always keep them informed:**
This scenario has the potential to cause a distressing situation. Having authority on your side can prove to be a beneficial and necessary strategy.

(16) ✓ **Create and nourish your support network**

(64) ✓ **Take care of your supporters**

(32) ✓ **Ask for help**

(83) ✓ **Protect your reputation:**
With all the inside information they have on you, it is crucial that you consider how they may tarnish your reputation, and how you can combat their attempts.

(31) ✓ **Vigilantly monitor the system**

(42) ✓ **Don't let conflicts and diversions distract you:**
Since they know your weaknesses, and vulnerabilities, they may know exactly how to distract you and divert your attention. Be careful.

(59) ✓ **Be wary around people who have nothing to lose:**
When your personal circle feels like they have nothing to lose — they are going all out — expect all your secrets to be unveiled. Be careful of these individuals. This intensity and this role make them one of the worst resistance scenarios you will face, especially if they feel like they have been backed into a corner.

(61) ✓ **Investigate to see if there is more to their resistance than meets the eye**

(60) ✓ **Show your strength, but without provocation**

(11) ✓ **Keep the fire contained:**
It may seem like you cannot contain the "fire", but you must do what you can to make sure they don't do something you can never forgive or forget. Try your best to calm things down, avoiding more intense and messier resistance.

12 ✓ **Don't provoke them**

54 ✓ **Success depends on doing the right thing, at the right time, and in the right way**

66 ✓ **Work to minimize the damage**

68 ✓ **As with a game of chess, think about your moves ahead of time and plan your strategy**

69 ✓ **Use patience, silence, and inaction wisely and strategically**

48 ✓ **Don't focus on winning — it is about fulfilling the purpose of the initiative**

89 ✓ **Avoid conflict and head-on collisions when possible, but do what it takes to protect yourself and the initiative**

55 ✓ **Know when to accept temporary defeat:**
It might be best for all involved if you accept that your opponent poses too much of a threat to you. With all the information they may have on you, going against them might do more harm than good to the overall system. Consider this strategy carefully.

25 ✓ **Be ready to compromise:**
Even if they do things that make you question your relationship, be willing to use this strategy — even if your relationship will never be the same. Limiting their resistance may help you achieve your purpose, while avoiding unnecessary humiliation and possible defeat.

26 ✓ **Don't compromise on ethics or professionalism**

(13) ✓ **Consider involving mediators:**
At this intensity this strategy could make the difference between successful negotiation or more intense resistance.

(41) ✓ **Let them negotiate for you**

(15) ✓ **Maintain the momentum of your progress**

(84) ✓ **Consider tactically putting your initiative on hold**

(36) ✓ **Double-check the sanity of the initiative**

(33) ✓ **Debug the initiative**

(58) ✓ **Reflect on the purpose of the initiative**

(35) ✓ **Take responsibility for your mess**

(80) ✓ **Always be willing to learn**

(39) ✓ **Plan and deliberate**

(40) ✓ **Know when to confront**

(49) ✓ **Winning in confrontations demands self-discipline**

(24) ✓ **Fight with full force:**
You may need to work extra hard to put your emotions aside for this strategy, given the close relationship you have or have had with your resisters. Also bear in mind that no one wins, so don't rush to use it. You will risk your relationship with your resisters, and with other individuals you both have a strong relationship with (e.g. a divorce affects the children too.).

(44) ✓   **Use your opponents' mistakes:**
The heat and emotion will lead to mistakes on your resisters' part, so consider applying this strategy, as long as it won't make matters worse for you in the future.

(88) ✓   **Expose and discredit your opponents; don't blame them**

(57) ✓   **Choose clarity or ambiguity, depending on the situation**

(45) ✓   **Be unpredictable**

(81) ✓   **Constantly innovate and create exceptional value**

(82) ✓   **Never fight fire with fire:**
At this intensity, with the highly emotional atmosphere, it may be hard, but you need to always keep this strategy in mind.

(62) ✓   **Involve relevant authorities:**
Malevolent personal opponents will make your life "hell", and if you find out that they are doing something illegal, you need to get authorities (in this case the law) involved, even though this may be hard because of your relationship with the opponent .

SUBORDINATES SCENARIOS

In most professional settings, you have individuals working for you, who may be members of your team. Ideally, your team members and subordinates will be on your side, helping you fulfill the purpose of your intervention. It is your subordinates' basic duty to do their job, and they are obliged to follow their superior's (i.e. you) instructions. This is the nature of the hierarchy. Provided that the instructions are in line with the agreed upon nature of their job, and that what is asked of them is legal and ethical, they cannot refuse to do their job if they have accepted its terms and conditions in a signed contract. That is why anything less than being fully supportive of their boss is a violation of the working relationship.

This doesn't mean that they don't have the right to voice their concerns and opinions, but they are still contractually obliged to carry out their duties and do their job. If they don't, it is a breach of their contract and can be considered an act of insubordination. From your perspective, as a boss, tolerating acts of insubordination will seriously undermine your authority and diminish the chances of your initiative surviving and growing. You simply cannot afford people who are insubordinate, you should never compromise on this. This is a professional relationship and so you don't carry emotional pressure on your shoulders, as you would with personal relationships.

Despite all this, there will still be people who will resist you. They may decide not to do the work, to go on protests, or to become spies for the competition. What degree of resistance they opt for will depend on how they perceive your initiative and what you are asking them to do.

One trick which might allow you to avoid their resistance altogether is to preempt it by making sure you communicate all the information clearly. This includes:

- Distributing and explaining their roles and responsibilities.

- Laying the rules, regulations, policies, protocols, and procedures out for them in detail.

- Making sure that your subordinates are capable of fulfilling their expectations and that there are no practical obstacles standing in their way (e.g. they haven't been trained for the job, or they don't have the resources to get the job done [money, connections])

SUBORDINATES: PASSIVE

Given the power difference, many of your subordinates may be less inclined to oppose what you are proposing, especially since it is for the benefit of the system and is clearly not a personal quest. However, some of them will opt for passive resistance.

The fact that you are their "boss" will affect how willing they are to voice their concerns. There is an element of fear when dealing with authority figures, so it may be that, because of this power differential, they will be afraid to voice their opposition. Even if you haven't given them the impression that you discourage opposing views, they may assume that this is the case, and keep their opinions to themselves.

Unfortunately, it can be quite difficult for you to discern whether your subordinates have an issue with what you are doing. However, they may display some signs of discontent, hesitation, and indecisiveness, and possibly even avoid talking to you unless it is necessary. Look for patterns of behavior that suggest there could be an underlying issue.

Noticing behavioral changes presents you with an opportunity to check if they know what is expected of them: it could be that what seems like opposition is actually them not knowing what to do, or it could be that they do not have all the tools to get the job done. You can resolve this issue by communicating effectively and regularly.

Luckily, passive opposition from subordinates is not a serious situation, since the job is still being done. As long as progress is not obstructed, and things are moving forward, this intensity will not present much of an issue. It may also be resolved with time as they start to see your initiative bearing fruit. However, you should keep monitoring the situation, and let them know you are doing so. They may be less likely to resist you if they know that you are keeping an eye on everything that is going on in the workplace.

RECOMMENDED STRATEGIES/PRINCIPLES

7 ✓ **Over-communicate your interest in listening to their point of view**

1 ✓ **Ensure any negativity doesn't become contagious**

15 ✓ **Maintain the momentum of your progress**

27 ✓ **Mobilize with enthusiasm**

28 ✓ **Sell the benefits of the initiative**

34 ✓ **Create, score, and celebrate a stream of small victories**

79 ✓ **Assert your authority:**
Dealing with your subordinates requires you to be firm and "let them know who is boss", but at this intensity you don't need to be too firm or you risk being provocative. You want to come off as fair and understanding, but you don't want to risk giving them enough leeway to intensify their resistance.

60 ✓ **Show your strength, but without provocation**

87 ✓ **Never criticize or blame your passive or passive-aggressive resisters**

(73) ✓ **Make sure authority is on board:**
In this case, this refers to your authority. You will want to make sure that your superior approves of what you want to do. This will help you deal with your subordinates.

(74) ✓ **Stay close to authority and always keep them informed**

(38) ✓ **Involve the members of the system in the initiative:**
Involving your subordinates in your initiative means giving them more responsibility than they already have. This vote of confidence from your end may turn your passive resisters into supporters.

(31) ✓ **Vigilantly monitor the system:**
The fear of your retribution and power over their fate may mean that they decide to resist you actively but bide their time until they have the upper hand. They may know that if you catch wind of what they are planning, you have the authority to put an end to it. Keep an eye on the system so you know if there is any behind-the-scenes planning.

(61) ✓ **Investigate to see if there is more to their resistance than meets the eye**

(29) ✓ **Remove the "Bad Apples":**
Be careful not to act too hastily, but if you feel that the source of resistance is one of your subordinates, you may want to nip their opposition in the bud rather than allowing it to spread.

(42) ✓ **Don't let conflicts and diversions distract you**

(35) ✓ **Take responsibility for your mess**

83 ✓ **Protect your reputation:**
It may just be that the external façade of their resistance is passive, but they are working to discredit you or harm your reputation. Remember that they have insider knowledge, and bear this strategy in mind.

SUBORDINATES: PASSIVE-AGGRESSIVE

Sometimes you will find that your subordinates promise to do something, and then fail to follow through. At other times, they might ignore you when you talk to them but apologize moments later and claim that they didn't hear you. They may take their time handing in a report, or getting a task done. Certainly, this sometimes happens without pointing to resistance; your subordinates are human, and nobody is perfect. However, if this becomes a pattern, then it indicates passive-aggressive resistance: they are not happy with what you are doing so they are not cooperating.

It may be that your position as their superior makes them afraid to confront you or voice their concerns, and it's possible that they would actually be more resistant than passive-aggressive if not for this fear. Bear in mind that they may be biding their time or trying to rally other resisters.

Of course, they are your subordinates and you cannot tolerate even passive-aggressive resistance. This resistance raises alarms about how effective your authority is. You cannot ignore it and, ideally, you should not let it intensify; it is a direct challenge to your authority. If left unchecked, their resistance may intensify, and they will slow things down or, worse, influence others to oppose you.

You can still salvage this critical situation. They are not actively resisting you, even if they intend to in the future, so you have an opportunity to fix things.

RECOMMENDED STRATEGIES/PRINCIPLES

(7) ✓ **Over-communicate your interest in listening to their point of view**

(1) ✓ **Ensure any negativity doesn't become contagious**

(79) ✓ **Assert your authority**

(60) ✓ **Show your strength, but without provocation:**
In this case, you might simply do something to remind them of your authority and emphasize who else supports your initiative.

(73) ✓ **Make sure authority is on board**

(74) ✓ **Stay close to authority and always keep them informed**

(85) ✓ **Give authentic credit to authority**

(15) ✓ **Maintain the momentum of your progress**

(27) ✓ **Mobilize with enthusiasm**

(28) ✓ **Sell the benefits of the initiative**

(34) ✓ **Create, score, and celebrate a stream of small victories**

(64) ✓ **Take care of your supporters:**
Some of your subordinates will be your supporters. If you take care of them it may cause a ripple effect. Your passive-aggressive subordinates may reconsider.

(38) ✓ **Involve the members of the system in the initiative**

31 ✓ **Vigilantly monitor the system**

61 ✓ **Investigate to see if there is more to their resistance than meets the eye**

29 ✓ **Remove the "Bad Apples"**

33 ✓ **Debug the initiative:**
It is important that your initiative doesn't have weaknesses. Since your subordinates will be working on it with you, they will know all the intricacies of it. If you leave a gap for them to take advantage of, you may lose.

35 ✓ **Take responsibility for your mess**

89 ✓ **Avoid conflict and head-on collisions when possible, but do what it takes to protect yourself and the initiative:**
Although you would most likely win, head-on collisions are expensive. It is also true that going for head-on collisions may be exactly what fuels the resistance of your more passive and passive-aggressive subordinates.

45 ✓ **Be unpredictable:**
It can be difficult to know who to trust and who not to trust among your subordinates. To protect your initiative you need to remain unpredictable.

83 ✓ **Protect your reputation**

87 ✓ **Never criticize or blame your passive or passive-aggressive resisters**

SUBORDINATES: ACTIVE

There will be times when your team members feel that what you are doing is directly going against them. They may feel cheated, robbed of specific necessities/luxuries, asked to do more than they would like to, etc. When this happens, they may opt for a more active approach.

How they will go about expressing their resistance will vary. They may decide to voice their concerns, asking to discuss them with you. In other scenarios they may opt for an alternative route and decide to arrange protests or sit-ins. In whatever way they express their resistance, the bottom line is that they are not willing to cooperate, and they are openly telling you that. Of course, they are within their rights to express their opinions, but given your position, you can utilize your authority to quell their resistance.

You need to examine the situation, the initiative, and yourself to get to the bottom of what the issue might be. If you find that you are asking them to do something that is not within the parameters of the contractual agreement, you will need to adjust to get back on track. However, if you find that you are not in violation of the agreement and that you are conducting yourself legally, ethically, and morally, you will need to move forward. You might warn them that they need to do their jobs or you will have to let them go. Either way you cannot have anyone on your team or payroll who is actively resisting you.

RECOMMENDED STRATEGIES/PRINCIPLES

7 ✓ **Over-communicate your interest in listening to their point of view**

1 ✓ **Ensure any negativity doesn't become contagious**

11 ✓ **Keep the fire contained**

79 ✓ **Assert your authority**

60 ✓ **Show your strength, but without provocation**

23 ✓ **Mentally and technically prepare yourself for the worst; it will get messy:**
Your team members actively turning against you can be shocking and, at times, unexpected. Things could spin out of control, especially if many of your subordinates exhibit this form of resistance. You need to be mentally and technically prepared to deal with their resistance, otherwise they will catch you off-guard and you may find yourself dealing with more than you anticipated.

47 ✓ **Don't be faint-hearted or indecisive:**
Dealing with your subordinates' resistance can shake you. As such you need to keep this strategy in mind so that you can prepare yourself to make the "tough" decisions when you need to.

68 ✓ **As with a game of chess, think about your moves ahead of time and plan your strategy**

73 ✓ **Make sure authority is on board**

(74) ✓ **Stay close to authority and always keep them informed:**
As soon as you experience active resistance, you should make sure that authority is aware of the situation, otherwise your subordinates may have the upper hand if they choose to complain to your authority.

(75) ✓ **Attend to authority's warnings:**
In this case, we are talking about your authority, if s/he tells you to calm things down then consider this strategy. If you are the authority, then it doesn't apply.

(85) ✓ **Give authentic credit to authority**

(16) ✓ **Create and nourish your support network**

(64) ✓ **Take care of your supporters**

(53) ✓ **Do what is best for the system**

(31) ✓ **Vigilantly monitor the system:**
It is a mark of a good authority to know what is going on in the system. Being vigilant will help you spot your existing opponents, and also weed out potential ones. You will be able to see if there are any underhanded schemes. Remember that your subordinates' fear of retribution might cause them to opt for more hidden resistance.

(61) ✓ **Investigate to see if there is more to their resistance than meets the eye**

(22) ✓ **Create some distance:**
Give your subordinates some space to cool down. Since you are their authority, this will also serve to send them a warning that their resistance is unacceptable.

(29) ✓ **Remove the "Bad Apples"**

(30) ✓ **Bring in fresh, positive blood**

(54) ✓ **Success depends on doing the right thing, at the right time, and in the right way**

(66) ✓ **Work to minimize the damage**

(69) ✓ **Use patience, silence, and inaction wisely and strategically**

(89) ✓ **Avoid conflict and head-on collisions when possible, but do what it takes to protect yourself and the initiative**

(39) ✓ **Plan and deliberate**

(40) ✓ **Know when to confront:**
Although you will likely win if you confront them, this should not be something you take lightly. You will waste time and you will create further tension among your other subordinates. Confrontation may end up hurting you more than helping you, if used unwisely.

(59) ✓ **Be wary around people who have nothing to lose**

(24) ✓ **Fight with full force:**
It may sometimes be necessary for you to bring all your power to the table. It is important that you are decisive and take the necessary action to protect your initiative.

(44) ✓ **Use your opponents' mistakes**

(42) ✓ **Don't let conflicts and diversions distract you**

49 ✓ **Winning in confrontations demands self-discipline**

26 ✓ **Don't compromise on ethics or professionalism:**
As part of this strategy, you need to let your subordinates know that you will not tolerate undue resistance and lack of professionalism.

15 ✓ **Maintain the momentum of your progress**

34 ✓ **Create, score, and celebrate a stream of small victories**

36 ✓ **Double-check the sanity of the initiative**

33 ✓ **Debug the initiative**

35 ✓ **Take responsibility for your mess**

37 ✓ **Don't aim to be popular:**
Although you may want to stay the "cool boss" at times, don't let that thought or "hunger" stop you from doing what is necessary.

80 ✓ **Always be willing to learn**

62 ✓ **Involve relevant authorities:**
You may not have the power to remove your subordinates from your organization, so you will need to ask whoever does have this power.

83 ✓ **Protect your reputation**

45 ✓ **Be unpredictable:**
It is important that you remember to switch things up, as your subordinates may be familiar with your tactics. This will diminish their chances of coming up with the right counter-strategy.

SUBORDINATES: ACTIVE-AGGRESSIVE

At this stage, your subordinates will have an issue with you to the degree that they will lobby against you. The work you are asking them to do is likely to be affecting some of their dimensions in a way that they view as unacceptable. They may try to go over your head and speak to your authority to get you to stop what you are doing, and will attempt to gather their own supporters to oppose you.

In this case, they are no longer part of your team. Your subordinates have crossed the line. They are not only refusing to support you, but they are actually trying to ruin your intervention. This situation is more urgent than active subordinates, and you will need to take swift and immediate action. It is no longer simply about the fate of your initiative, but about your own fate and reputation.

Their resistance will speak volumes about your reputation as an authority figure. If you permit such insubordination to continue, many people will start to doubt your effectiveness as an authority.

The conflict will consume your energy, and it will challenge you mentally, emotionally, and possibly physically. Your subordinates have worked with you and they will know your professional vulnerabilities, trade secrets, the inner working of the initiative, etc. They may use this information in an attempt to discredit you and ruin your reputation, bringing your initiative down in the process.

You should not allow it to reach this stage if you can do anything to prevent it. However, if you do end up here, you need to swiftly and decisively deal with their resistance, before they have a lasting impact, not only on the initiative, but on your reputation.

RECOMMENDED STRATEGIES/PRINCIPLES

(7) ✓ **Over-communicate your interest in listening to their point of view:**
In some cases, your subordinates are crucial for the initiative's success. In such a scenario, you may want to over-communicate your interest in hearing their perspectives; despite their intense resistance.

(23) ✓ **Mentally and technically prepare yourself for the worst; it will get messy**

(47) ✓ **Don't be faint-hearted or indecisive**

(53) ✓ **Do what is best for the system:**
This must always be on your mind. Don't let their resistance cloud your judgment. Don't let their insubordination be the trigger for unnecessary conflicts, hesitations, or anything else that harms the system.

(1) ✓ **Ensure any negativity doesn't become contagious:**
The aggressive tactics can help your subordinates to recruit more of their peers to their side. Do your best to take the necessary steps and avoid more negativity on your team.

(11) ✓ **Keep the fire contained**

(84) ✓ **Consider tactically putting your initiative on hold**

(31) ✓ **Vigilantly monitor the system**

(79) ✓ **Assert your authority**

(60) ✓ **Show your strength, but without provocation**

(73) ✓ **Make sure authority is on board**

(74) ✓ **Stay close to authority and always keep them informed**

(85) ✓ **Give authentic credit to authority**

(75) ✓ **Attend to authority's warnings**

(83) ✓ **Protect your reputation**

(61) ✓ **Investigate to see if there is more to their resistance than meets the eye**

(59) ✓ **Be wary around people who have nothing to lose**

(42) ✓ **Don't let conflicts and diversions distract you**

(22) ✓ **Create some distance:**
When you distance yourself from a subordinate, this sends a message to the rest of the team (possibly the system) that this person or group is to be avoided. This may disarm your resisters, as well as, give them time to cool down.

(29) ✓ **Remove the "Bad Apples":**
In this situation, you cannot leave any opponents on your team, or you risk poisoning the rest of the team. Remove all the "bad apples" if you can.

(30) ✓ **Bring in fresh, positive blood**

(16) ✓ **Create and nourish your support network**

(64) ✓ **Take care of your supporters**

(68) ✓ **As with a game of chess, think about your moves ahead of time and plan your strategy**

54 ✓ **Success depends on doing the right thing, at the right time, and in the right way**

89 ✓ **Avoid conflict and head-on collisions when possible, but do what it takes to protect yourself and the initiative**

66 ✓ **Work to minimize the damage**

15 ✓ **Maintain the momentum of your progress**

34 ✓ **Create, score, and celebrate a stream of small victories**

69 ✓ **Use patience, silence, and inaction wisely and strategically**

33 ✓ **Debug the initiative**

35 ✓ **Take responsibility for your mess**

39 ✓ **Plan and deliberate**

40 ✓ **Know when to confront**

44 ✓ **Use your opponents' mistakes**

49 ✓ **Winning in confrontations demands self-discipline**

24 ✓ **Fight with full force**

26 ✓ **Don't compromise on ethics or professionalism**

80 ✓ **Always be willing to learn**

62 ✓ **Involve relevant authorities:**
Once again, if you don't have the power to dismiss people from your team, you may need to turn to the relevant authority. If your subordinates start acting illegally, this might be the police.

88 ✓ **Expose and discredit your opponents; don't blame them:**
Even if you have the authority, you should not use it to blame your subordinates. This would be counterproductive, instead focus on discrediting their attempts.

57 ✓ **Choose clarity or ambiguity, depending on the situation**

45 ✓ **Be unpredictable**

SUBORDINATES: MALEVOLENT

There is a possibility that your subordinates are scheming behind your back. They might appear to follow instructions, but instead secretly plan ways to ruin your initiative and your career. They may create rumors about you and relay their false claims to your boss. They may fabricate emails and use them as evidence. If you do not figure out what they are up to, you may end up paying a heavy price.

Your position of authority may push these opponents to be secretive. In this case, it can be quite difficult to discern what they are up to. It will take all of your skills, vigilance, and diligent monitoring to determine whether someone is harboring malevolent intentions, but you must prioritize finding out, or the price could be high. They know the ins and outs of your initiative, so they will know exactly where to strike. Unfortunately, you cannot always predict what this kind of opponent will have in store, and you may get hit a few times.

You need to try not to let it reach this stage. You will rarely encounter anyone who resists with such intensity from the beginning – usually they start with lesser resistance – so keep an eye on any escalation among your opponents and address it as quickly as possible.

If you do find any of your subordinates operating at this intensity, you must count them out as your subordinates. They harbor enough animosity towards you at this point that they no longer see themselves in this way. They obviously cannot work for you anymore, meaning that you should not have them on your team. If given the chance, they may stay on the team to spy on your progress so that they can backstab you at a later time. They may be feeding other opponents information so that they can gain the upper hand, or they may be sabotaging your interventions from the inside. They may even be willing to break the law if it gets the job done and will hurt you.

For instance, Leen Schaap — a fire chief in Amsterdam — received multiple death threats from his subordinates for trying to change the status quo. In response to his attempts to diversify a dominant Caucasian male culture in the fire department, his subordinates issued many threats against his life. This is one example of how malevolent subordinates might resist a leadership initiative.

RECOMMENDED STRATEGIES/PRINCIPLES

23 ✓ **Mentally and technically prepare yourself for the worst; it will get messy:**
Since they probably don't count themselves as your subordinates, they may opt for some really harmful tactics. Prepare as thoroughly as you can, especially if they have in-depth knowledge of your initiative.

47 ✓ **Don't be faint-hearted or indecisive**

58 ✓ **Reflect on the purpose of the initiative**

11 ✓ **Keep the fire contained**

12 ✓ **Don't provoke them**

73 ✓ **Make sure authority is on board**

74 ✓ **Stay close to authority and always keep them informed**

(85) ✓ **Give authentic credit to authority**

(31) ✓ **Vigilantly monitor the system**

(59) ✓ **Be wary around people who have nothing to lose**

(29) ✓ **Remove the "Bad Apples"**

(30) ✓ **Bring in fresh, positive blood**

(61) ✓ **Investigate to see if there is more to their resistance than meets the eye**

(42) ✓ **Don't let conflicts and diversions distract you**

(79) ✓ **Assert your authority**

(60) ✓ **Show your strength, but without provocation**

(83) ✓ **Protect your reputation:**
Your reputation maybe the first target on their list. Do what you must to guard yourself, the initiative, and the system.

(16) ✓ **Create and nourish your support network:**
It can be difficult for some of your supporters to be involved in conflicts that target their coworkers, and possibly their friends, so make sure you address concerns of this sort.

(64) ✓ **Take care of your supporters**

(32) ✓ **Ask for help:**
At this intensity, it would be wise to accept all the help you can get. Holding authority over your subordinates means you are expected to "keep them in line", but there are times when you cannot. Don't shy away from asking others for help.

(53) ✓ **Do what is best for the system**

(68) ✓ **As with a game of chess, think about your moves ahead of time and plan your strategy**

(54) ✓ **Success depends on doing the right thing, at the right time, and in the right way**

(66) ✓ **Work to minimize the damage**

(84) ✓ **Consider tactically putting your initiative on hold**

(75) ✓ **Attend to authority's warnings:**
If your authority is asking you to take your initiative down a notch, that means that the pressure on the system is too great. Heed that warning or you will risk losing one of your most significant supporters.

(15) ✓ **Maintain the momentum of your progress**

(34) ✓ **Create, score, and celebrate a stream of small victories:**
This is geared more towards maintaining your support network. Showing progress will help to improve your credibility, which your opponents may attempt to tarnish.

(26) ✓ **Don't compromise on ethics or professionalism**

(35) ✓ **Take responsibility for your mess**

(89) ✓ **Avoid conflict and head-on collisions when possible, but do what it takes to protect yourself and the initiative**

(69) ✓ **Use patience, silence, and inaction wisely and strategically**

(39) ✓ **Plan and deliberate**

(40) ✓ **Know when to confront**

(44) ✓ **Use your opponents' mistakes**

(49) ✓ **Winning in confrontations demands self-discipline**

(24) ✓ **Fight with full force**

(62) ✓ **Involve relevant authorities**

(88) ✓ **Expose and discredit your opponents; don't blame them**

(45) ✓ **Be unpredictable:**
Malevolent subordinates may try to dismantle your initiative from within, and they have a higher chance of success if they know what you plan to do. Therefore, be careful about how much information you share.

(57) ✓ **Choose clarity or ambiguity, depending on the situation**

COLLEAGUES SCENARIOS

Your colleagues are people who have the same status as you in the organizational hierarchy. You may find yourself dealing with them on a regular basis, and your cooperation and collaboration with one another are necessary to allow the organization to work at the optimal level. You may collaborate with them on multiple projects, and they might be instrumental to the success of your initiative, especially if it is dependent on their cooperation.

However, sometimes you just don't see eye to eye with your colleagues, and anything you do that threatens them, or doesn't benefit them, may be met with resistance. This can create some unwanted conflict and dysfunction within the organization, conflict that will not be appreciated by your shared authority — since s/he will count it as conflict within her/his team.

In addition, you don't have authority over your colleagues, so you cannot use your status as a way to deal with them and quell their resistance.

Apart from the above difficulties, sometimes your colleagues may resist you not because of your initiative, but because you are competing over resources. They need funding, authority's approval, supporters, etc. They may have their own initiatives, plans, or agendas, and they will see you as a competitor or threat to said plans.

They may try to delay your work by withholding necessary information (e.g. contracts, legal documents), lobbying against you, rallying other colleagues to protest, spreading rumors, or going after your personal life.

In addition to that, these individuals may be team leaders, and therefore they will have subordinates who highly value their opinions. This means that the resistance they show could be shared with their subordinates, introducing another group of opponents.

COLLEAGUES: PASSIVE

Passive resistance may be a sign that they haven't bought into your initiative yet. In other words, your colleagues may not be convinced by what you are proposing, because they don't see the benefits for themselves. However, they may be willing to wait it out.

They may resort to passive resistance only to give you some time to prove that your initiative is the right one. If you take too long to show them results, they may decide to actively resist what you are doing.

Remember that you work with these individuals, you see them daily, and they are also the major pool from which you recruit your support. Added to this, you have a professional relationship that is contingent on collaboration. Furthermore, your colleagues may have their own teams, so they hold leverage over others in the organization, and if they are hesitant to give you their support, you are unlikely to have their team members' support — another key faction that would aid the success of your initiative.

Therefore, even if your colleagues are only being passive opponents, you will need to address or resolve the issues, or their resistance may intensify, and could put a strain on your initiative.

There is another dynamic you need to consider. You colleagues may be jealous of or competing with you. In the case of jealousy, they might see the benefits your initiative has, but they will also see that you are gaining attention and increasing your reputation in the eyes of authority and the system. In the case of competition, remember that they might see you as an obstacle to the resources they need for their own initiatives. They may not be able to actively resist you — especially if authority is on your side — so they opt for more passive resistance.

Finally, their passive resistance may disguise more intense resistance. You will need to keep an eye on them, just in case there is something more brewing beneath the surface.

RECOMMENDED STRATEGIES/PRINCIPLES

2 ✓ **Respect the history of the relationship**

7 ✓ **Over-communicate your interest in listening to their point of view**

1 ✓ **Ensure any negativity doesn't become contagious**

3 ✓ **Limit the conflict to the relevant issues:**
There is a possibility that you are collaborating on other projects. Make sure that their issues with your initiative don't affect those projects.

11 ✓ **Keep the fire contained**

12 ✓ **Don't provoke them**

73 ✓ **Make sure authority is on board:**
Given the lack of a power differential, having authority on your side may help to keep your resisters at bay; or quell their resistance.

74 ✓ **Stay close to authority and always keep them informed**

(15) ✓ **Maintain the momentum of your progress**

(27) ✓ **Mobilize with enthusiasm:**
At this intensity, your colleagues may not be convinced yet. However, by keeping up the enthusiasm you may be able to bring them to your side.

(28) ✓ **Sell the benefits of the initiative**

(34) ✓ **Create, score, and celebrate a stream of small victories**

(85) ✓ **Give authentic credit to authority**

(60) ✓ **Show your strength, but without provocation:**
When it comes to your colleagues, this strategy is a strong tool to make them question their resistance.

(16) ✓ **Create and nourish your support network**

(64) ✓ **Take care of your supporters**

(38) ✓ **Involve the members of the system in the initiative**

(31) ✓ **Vigilantly monitor the system**

(61) ✓ **Investigate to see if there is more to their resistance than meets the eye**

(53) ✓ **Do what is best for the system**

(54) ✓ **Success depends on doing the right thing, at the right time, and in the right way**

(56) ✓ **Don't burn the bridges between you and your opponents**

(35) ✓ **Take responsibility for your mess**

(80) ✓ **Always be willing to learn**

87 ✓ **Never criticize or blame your passive or passive-aggressive resisters**

62 ✓ **Involve relevant authorities:**
You may not have the power to deal with your re-sisters, so consider authorities who can. Even if you feel it is unwarranted to take this strategy, it will help strengthen you and send a message to your colleagues at this intensity, and higher intensity, that you are protected.

COLLEAGUES: PASSIVE-AGGRESSIVE

If your colleagues are affected to a higher degree than their passive counterparts, then you will find them trying to hinder your progress. Although, in this case they will not (at least apparently) resort to active measures, even passive-aggressive resistance can affect your initiative significantly.

If you are working with your colleagues, passive-aggressive opposition can have serious consequences, since their inaction will slow things down for you. You need to pick up on any signs of this type of resistance, whether it's the famous silent treatment, or a consistent failure to hand in whatever documents, reports, etc., you expected them to hand in. It can become quite difficult for you to work in the same environment as people who are actually taking steps to slow things down for you.

It can also get tricky when your colleagues are not doing anything, but their team members are resisting you. You cannot be sure whether they are doing it for their boss or of their own volition. Unfortunately, your colleagues will sometimes resort to such sly tactics to affect the initiative while keeping their hands clean.

Finally, remember that your colleagues may use passive-aggressive resistance as a guise to hide more active opposition, and they may be competing with you. Instead of showing their hand they will try to slow you down, so they can get ahead with their own agendas, removing any edge your initiative may offer you. The appearance of passive-aggressive resistance also means they can avoid the confrontation which comes with active resistance, and the possible negative consequences associated with it (e.g. authority potentially reprimanding them for creating unnecessary conflict).

RECOMMENDED STRATEGIES/PRINCIPLES

2 ✓ **Respect the history of the relationship:**
In this case it is about how much you value a cooperative and working relationship.

7 ✓ **Over-communicate your interest in listening to their point of view**

1 ✓ **Ensure any negativity doesn't become contagious**

3 ✓ **Limit the conflict to the relevant issues**

11 ✓ **Keep the fire contained**

73 ✓ **Make sure authority is on board**

74 ✓ **Stay close to authority and always keep them informed:**
At this intensity, your colleagues may postpone your work and hinder your progress indirectly — they won't be doing their job. If authority knows what every member is expected to do, you will avoid unnecessary conflict with authority.

85 ✓ **Give authentic credit to authority**

16 ✓ **Create and nourish your support network**

64 ✓ **Take care of your supporters**

12 ✓ **Don't provoke them**

15 ✓ **Maintain the momentum of your progress**

27 ✓ **Mobilize with enthusiasm**

28 ✓ **Sell the benefits of the initiative**

(60) ✓ **Show your strength, but without provocation**

(34) ✓ **Create, score, and celebrate a stream of small victories**

(38) ✓ **Involve the members of the system in the initiative**

(8) ✓ **Consider some "quid pro quo"**

(23) ✓ **Mentally and technically prepare yourself for the worst; it will get messy**

(31) ✓ **Vigilantly monitor the system**

(61) ✓ **Investigate to see if there is more to their resistance than meets the eye**

(70) ✓ **Be wary of competition**

(42) ✓ **Don't let conflicts and diversions distract you**

(53) ✓ **Do what is best for the system**

(54) ✓ **Success depends on doing the right thing, at the right time, and in the right way**

(68) ✓ **As with a game of chess, think about your moves ahead of time and plan your strategy**

(39) ✓ **Plan and deliberate**

(32) ✓ **Ask for help**

(75) ✓ **Attend to authority's warnings:**
From this intensity onward, word of your colleagues' issues and concerns will eventually get back to authority. Make sure to utilize this strategy if you sense some hesitation from authority.

(69) ✓ **Use patience, silence, and inaction wisely and strategically**

(33) ✓ **Debug the initiative**

(58) ✓ **Reflect on the purpose of the initiative:**
It is possible that competition between you and your colleagues might push you to create a leadership initiative. It is important that you truly examine the purpose of your initiative and make sure that it is not for the sake of getting ahead of your colleagues. Use this strategy wisely.

(35) ✓ **Take responsibility for your mess**

(83) ✓ **Protect your reputation**

(80) ✓ **Always be willing to learn**

(66) ✓ **Work to minimize the damage**

(56) ✓ **Don't burn the bridges between you and your opponents**

(82) ✓ **Never fight fire with fire**

(45) ✓ **Be unpredictable**

(87) ✓ **Never criticize or blame your passive or passive-aggressive resisters**

COLLEAGUES: ACTIVE

If your colleagues feel that your initiative is slowing down their own or is asking them to risk something they are unwilling to give up, that will be incentive enough for them to adopt a more active stance. After all, you have minimal leverage over them and they are not obliged to do what you ask of them.

They will lobby their supporters, subordinates, and other colleagues to work against you and try to put an end to what you are doing. In most cases, your colleagues also have some sway with your boss, at least more than your subordinates. Therefore, when they try to lobby against you, they may go to your shared authority and try to convince them to stop what you are doing. They may also hold some sway with your constituents, so if they can persuade them to withdraw their support, you may face some major hiccups along the way.

If the success of your initiative is dependent on your colleagues, they will slow things down, possibly using their own authority to deny you access to their resources or assets. Since you don't have power over them, you might want to try asking your boss to give you access to the needed resources. However, you need to be careful about this, since your colleagues will not like you going over their heads, and it will negatively affect your relationship and harm you in the future — it might come back to bite you.

However you choose to go about it, attempt to address their concerns and resolve the opposition between you. It is crucial that their opposition does not intensify, because the success of the initiative might be in their hands.

RECOMMENDED STRATEGIES/PRINCIPLES

7 ✓ **Over-communicate your interest in listening to their point of view**

3 ✓ **Limit the conflict to the relevant issues**

11 ✓ **Keep the fire contained**

12 ✓ **Don't provoke them**

23 ✓ **Mentally and technically prepare yourself for the worst; it will get messy**

68 ✓ **As with a game of chess, think about your moves ahead of time and plan your strategy**

31 ✓ **Vigilantly monitor the system**

61 ✓ **Investigate to see if there is more to their resistance than meets the eye**

42 ✓ **Don't let conflicts and diversions distract you**

70 ✓ **Be wary of competition**

73 ✓ **Make sure authority is on board**

74 ✓ **Stay close to authority and always keep them informed:**
From this intensity onward, you will need to stay very close to your authority; especially if your colleagues have a good relationship with them.

71 ✓ **Never provoke authority**

75 ✓ **Attend to authority's warnings**

(16) ✓ **Create and nourish your support network:**
The relationship some of your supporters may have with your opponents could affect this strategy, so be open with your supporters and make sure they are with you 100%.

(64) ✓ **Take care of your supporters**

(32) ✓ **Ask for help:**
In addition to other forms of help, from this scenario onward, consider asking your authority or your supporters to speak to your opponents and try to convince them about your initiative. It is possible that hearing the benefits of the initiative from someone else might do the trick.

(83) ✓ **Protect your reputation:**
The lack of power differential means that your colleague's word is as strong as yours. Therefore, work diligently to avoid doubts about your reputation spreading to your supporters and the rest of the system.

(53) ✓ **Do what is best for the system**

(47) ✓ **Don't be faint-hearted or indecisive:**
Going against people who may have once been part of your support network, or who are collaborating with you on other projects, may be quite difficult. Therefore, take the necessary time to consider this aspect before you keep moving ahead with your initiative.

(54) ✓ **Success depends on doing the right thing, at the right time, and in the right way**

(48) ✓ **Don't focus on winning — it is about fulfilling the purpose of the initiative:**
You may be tempted to score points with your supporters and authority by showing them a few wins. Although there is nothing wrong with that, make sure that it does not become your main focus.

(69) ✓ **Use patience, silence, and inaction wisely and strategically**

(66) ✓ **Work to minimize the damage**

(25) ✓ **Be ready to compromise:**
Sometimes your authority may ask you to compromise, be willing to apply this strategy if that happens.

(8) ✓ **Consider some "quid pro quo":**
In this category, your opponents may be more willing to help if you offer to help them in return. Consider using this strategy to get your active opponents (and others) on your side, or at least to lessen their resistance.

(13) ✓ **Consider involving mediators**

(15) ✓ **Maintain the momentum of your progress**

(27) ✓ **Mobilize with enthusiasm**

(28) ✓ **Sell the benefits of the initiative**

(34) ✓ **Create, score, and celebrate a stream of small victories**

(38) ✓ **Involve the members of the system in the initiative**

(26) ✓ **Don't compromise on ethics or professionalism**

(84) ✓ **Consider tactically putting your initiative on hold**

(58) ✓ **Reflect on the purpose of the initiative**

(33) ✓ **Debug the initiative**

(35) ✓ **Take responsibility for your mess:**
Getting ahead of your opponents by admitting your mistakes can catch them off-guard, so consider using this strategy if you find that you are in the wrong anywhere.

(22) ✓ **Create some distance:**
This may involve you temporarily tabling other projects you are collaborating with your colleagues on for a time. This way you give them, and possibly yourself, time to "cool down" and avoid creating tension in other unrelated projects.

(39) ✓ **Plan and deliberate**

(40) ✓ **Know when to confront**

(55) ✓ **Know when to accept temporary defeat**

(89) ✓ **Avoid conflict and head-on collisions when possible, but do what it takes to protect yourself and the initiative**

(60) ✓ **Show your strength, but without provocation:**
Make sure that you don't flaunt your strength in their face. They may use such actions against you, and you may actually lose your support and source of strength — they will not be afraid to take this to authority, since they are already active.

(44) ✓ **Use your opponents' mistakes**

(49) ✓ **Winning in confrontations demands self-discipline**

(85) ✓ **Give authentic credit to authority**

(24) ✓ **Fight with full force**

(62) ✓ **Involve relevant authorities:**
From this intensity onward, consider involving individuals who have the power to sway your colleagues. Although you may not need to raise legal concerns, it helps to have authority informed. It will ensure that nothing unethical or illegal is happening, and will also send a message to your opponents that they should not cross any such boundaries.

(45) ✓ **Be unpredictable**

(77) ✓ **Build a relationship with higher authority**

(80) ✓ **Always be willing to learn**

(88) ✓ **Expose and discredit your opponents; don't blame them**

(56) ✓ **Don't burn the bridges between you and your opponents**

(82) ✓ **Never fight fire with fire**

COLLEAGUES: ACTIVE-AGGRESSIVE

There will be times when your most aggressive resistance will come from within the workplace. Your active-aggressive colleagues will not hesitate to try and stop what you are doing. They may go straight to the boss and try to twist things to suit their perspective. They may try to propose an alternative initiative that will counter yours. They may set out campaigns aimed at showing the faults in your initiative. They may also encourage your constituents (if applicable) to forgo their support. They will go after your supporters to try and sway them to their side, or at least attempt to get them out of your support network.

Remember that, once again, they may only be open about some of their resistance, and they may be planning a sabotage while pretending they are only protesting. You need to be careful, because their word may be as credible as yours, especially if you don't have evidence to support the fact that they are scheming against you.

RECOMMENDED STRATEGIES/PRINCIPLES

(7) ✓ **Over-communicate your interest in listening to their point of view**

(1) ✓ **Ensure any negativity doesn't become contagious**

(3) ✓ **Limit the conflict to the relevant issues**

(23) ✓ **Mentally and technically prepare yourself for the worst; it will get messy:**
At this intensity, things will get nasty, so prepare yourself to deal with it.

(47) ✓ **Don't be faint-hearted or indecisive**

(16) ✓ **Create and nourish your support network**

(64) ✓ **Take care of your supporters**

(32) ✓ **Ask for help**

(73) ✓ **Make sure authority is on board**

(74) ✓ **Stay close to authority and always keep them informed**

(71) ✓ **Never provoke authority**

(85) ✓ **Give authentic credit to authority**

(75) ✓ **Attend to authority's warnings**

(77) ✓ **Build a relationship with higher authority**

11 ✓ **Keep the fire contained**

12 ✓ **Don't provoke them**

83 ✓ **Protect your reputation:**
Now, more than ever, you need to make sure that your reputation is not tarnished. Your colleagues have the power to spread rumors and blow issues out of proportion.

31 ✓ **Vigilantly monitor the system**

61 ✓ **Investigate to see if there is more to their resistance than meets the eye:**
Although they may be out in the open, make sure that they don't have more aggressive strategies in store for you — they may be malevolent.

42 ✓ **Don't let conflicts and diversions distract you:**
You will need to think about other projects you may have in collaboration with them. It is possible that they may use these projects and create issues to distract you.

53 ✓ **Do what is best for the system**

54 ✓ **Success depends on doing the right thing, at the right time, and in the right way**

69 ✓ **Use patience, silence, and inaction wisely and strategically**

68 ✓ **As with a game of chess, think about your moves ahead of time and plan your strategy**

66 ✓ **Work to minimize the damage**

60 ✓ **Show your strength, but without provocation**

25 ✓ **Be ready to compromise:**
It is possible that at this intensity, your opponents may be creating too much disruption to the system. If your authority approaches you and asks you to make compromises then prepare yourself to do as they ask.

45 ✓ **Be unpredictable**

8 ✓ **Consider some "quid pro quo"**

13 ✓ **Consider involving mediators**

41 ✓ **Let them negotiate for you**

15 ✓ **Maintain the momentum of your progress**

27 ✓ **Mobilize with enthusiasm**

28 ✓ **Sell the benefits of the initiative**

34 ✓ **Create, score, and celebrate a stream of small victories**

26 ✓ **Don't compromise on ethics or professionalism**

36 ✓ **Double-check the sanity of the initiative**

80 ✓ **Always be willing to learn**

48 ✓ **Don't focus on winning — it is about fulfilling the purpose of the initiative**

84 ✓ **Consider tactically putting your initiative on hold**

33 ✓ **Debug the initiative**

58 ✓ **Reflect on the purpose of the initiative**

(35) ✓ **Take responsibility for your mess**

(38) ✓ **Involve the members of the system in the initiative:**
When you apply this strategy, remember to highlight the benefits your initiative will have for your opponents.

(89) ✓ **Avoid conflict and head-on collisions when possible, but do what it takes to protect yourself and the initiative**

(22) ✓ **Create some distance**

(39) ✓ **Plan and deliberate**

(40) ✓ **Know when to confront**

(44) ✓ **Use your opponents' mistakes**

(62) ✓ **Involve relevant authorities:**
You may have to turn to authority for help, because you might not be able to pressure your colleagues on your own.

(24) ✓ **Fight with full force**

(49) ✓ **Winning in confrontations demands self-discipline**

(55) ✓ **Know when to accept temporary defeat**

(57) ✓ **Choose clarity or ambiguity, depending on the situation**

(88) ✓ **Expose and discredit your opponents; don't blame them**

(56) ✓ **Don't burn the bridges between you and your opponents**

82 ✓   **Never fight fire with fire:**
The intensity of their resistance, coupled with the relationship you may have with your opponents, may anger you. Make sure you don't return their actions in kind.

COLLEAGUES: MALEVOLENT

Your colleagues can be a force to be reckoned with. They have an insider view of your intervention, and they may be harboring animosity towards you. That is a troubling combination. In this case, the survival and growth of your career and your reputation are at stake.

As a malevolent resister, they may not express their intentions, but may resort to more devious tactics. They may spend their time scheming your downfall while giving you a friendly smile every morning.

In some cases, you will know that they are opposing you. For instance, they might be known to associate with your rivals, other opponents, or a competing party (e.g. parliamentary members work together but belong to different parties). However, at other times, it may be quite difficult to ascertain their position before they actually do some damage. This damage will vary in its type and effect.

They may try to tarnish your reputation, use what they know about your initiative to bring it down, create rumors, twist information and feed it to your shared authority, etc. They might exploit areas where your work intersects with theirs. They may use those intersections to sabotage and destroy your initiative. They will go about their work normally but, whenever they can, they will create difficulties and obstacles for you.

RECOMMENDED STRATEGIES/PRINCIPLES

(23) ✓ **Mentally and technically prepare yourself for the worst; it will get messy:**
Because the level of resistance is now so high, and you are on equal footing with your opponent, the situation could easily escalate and turn nasty, and you must be ready for this.

(47) ✓ **Don't be faint-hearted or indecisive**

(16) ✓ **Create and nourish your support network**

(64) ✓ **Take care of your supporters:**
Your colleagues may target your supporters. They might use the relationships they share with them to hurt them, damage their reputations, or manipulate them. You need to look after your supporters and ensure they are protected.

(73) ✓ **Make sure authority is on board**

(71) ✓ **Never (ever) provoke authority**

(74) ✓ **Stay (very) close to authority and always keep them informed**

(32) ✓ **Ask for help**

(75) ✓ **Attend to authority's warnings**

(85) ✓ **Give authentic credit to authority**

(77) ✓ **Build a relationship with higher authority**

(60) ✓ **Show your strength, but without provocation**

(11) ✓ **Keep the fire contained**

(68) ✓ **As with a game of chess, think about your moves ahead of time and plan your strategy**

(31) ✓ **Vigilantly monitor the system**

(61) ✓ **Investigate to see if there is more to their resistance than meets the eye**

(42) ✓ **Don't let conflicts and diversions distract you**

(59) ✓ **Be wary around people who have nothing to lose**

(83) ✓ **Protect your reputation**

(53) ✓ **Do what is best for the system:**
In this scenario this includes taking care of and protecting yourself and your supporters.

(54) ✓ **Success depends on doing the right thing, at the right time, and in the right way**

(66) ✓ **Work to minimize the damage**

(22) ✓ **Create some distance**

(15) ✓ **Maintain the momentum of your progress**

(27) ✓ **Mobilize with enthusiasm:**
Faced with intense resistance, your supporters may begin to reconsider their support, so you need to make sure you focus on maintaining their enthusiasm.

(28) ✓ **Sell the benefits of the initiative (to your supporters)**

(34) ✓ **Create, score, and celebrate a stream of small victories (for your supporters)**

(36) ✓ **Double-check the sanity of the initiative**

(80) ✓ **Always be willing to learn**

(81) ✓ **Constantly innovate and create exceptional value:**
If you are providing value to the system, authority will see you as an asset, and your supporters and the system will appreciate and value your contributions. This will set you apart from your colleagues, who may be on equal footing otherwise, and will help you gain the support needed to deal with your colleagues' resistance.

(84) ✓ **Consider tactically putting your initiative on hold**

(58) ✓ **Reflect on the purpose of the initiative**

(35) ✓ **Take responsibility for your mess**

(89) ✓ **Avoid conflict and head-on collisions when possible, but do what it takes to protect yourself and the initiative**

(69) ✓ **Use patience, silence, and inaction wisely and strategically**

(41) ✓ **Let them negotiate for you**

(39) ✓ **Plan and deliberate**

(40) ✓ **Know when to confront**

(44) ✓ **Use your opponents' mistakes**

(62) ✓ **Involve relevant authorities:**
Take the time to consult and inform all the relevant authorities. These range from your "boss" to the police (in case there is any illegal activity).

(29) ✓ Remove the "Bad Apples":
If possible, try to remove or dismiss them. Usually, you won't have the power to do this yourself, but you can give evidence of malevolent resistance to the authority who does.

(49) ✓ Winning in confrontations demands self-discipline

(24) ✓ Fight with full force

(55) ✓ Know when to accept temporary defeat

(45) ✓ Be unpredictable

(57) ✓ Choose clarity or ambiguity, depending on the situation

(88) ✓ Expose and discredit your opponents; don't blame them

(82) ✓ Never fight fire with fire

AUTHORITY SCENARIOS

There are situations where you are considered a subordinate, and the power differential is not in your favor. Authority likely holds your fate in their hands. In general, there is nothing to worry about, because you should almost always have an amicable relationship with your superiors. You should get their approval before you make changes and seek their support to help boost the success of your interventions. However, things may not always go smoothly.

Putting the Personal subcategory aside, this role is the next most challenging one to deal with. You may struggle to exercise leadership or introduce an initiative without the relevant authority's consent.

They have the right to say yes or no, and they have the power to enforce their decisions. Added to this, they control the resources that you might need in order to carry out your initiative, whether these are tangible (e.g. money, people) or intangible (e.g. approval).

Having authority as your opponent in a work environment, regardless of their intensity, can carry a huge amount of emotional stress. The authority can impact the survival and growth of your career, which cannot continue to flourish, or even exist, without authority's consent.

Even having authority figures as neutrals should not be an option. It is highly recommended that you do not start your initiative before getting their consent. If they are neutral, that means one of three things: 1) they hold no stake in the initiative and the subject of the initiative is irrelevant (in that it does not impact their survival and growth); 2) the initiative is significant to them, but they trust you enough to delegate the decision and responsibility to you; or 3) the initiative is significant to them, and their neutrality is an indirect message that they object.

Whatever the case, neutrality on significant, beneficial initiatives should not be something you accept, because if the initiative is significant and relevant to authority, and you fail, they will come down hard on you. That is why the general rule is:

Never rock the boat without the explicit consent of the captain

Their support helps to guarantee that they will not resist you and will offer access to the resources that you need, but it also means that they will have your back against other opponents. You will need their support, especially when it comes to dealing with colleagues, constituents, competition, and subordinates.

To stay on authority's good side, you need to be loyal and professional. They need to know that you can be trusted, and that you are skilled enough to pull the initiative off. They will see you as a resource for their own success. The minute you stop being a resource and become a liability, you enter a dangerous zone. If they feel you cannot do the job, or that they cannot trust you, they will have to let you go.

To get their support on an initiative you will need to convince them on two fronts:

- **The risk involved**. Authority needs to know that the risk involved is minimal, that there is no real risk, or at least that the initiative will not put them in any danger. If the initiative will create a mess that authority will have to clean up, they will probably not give you their support.

- **The benefits they will reap.** You will need to convince them that the initiative will benefit them, not just that system. They need to know that if they back the initiative, its success will move them personally forward, that they will be praised for backing it, and that it will help them achieve their own objectives. If the initiative doesn't contribute to their success, then they will be less likely to back you up, and your initiative will lose a key player.

If your initiative negatively affects authority, they will resist you, and this is never a good thing. You will need to watch out for them and keep an eye on them to make sure that they are always in support of the initiative. The moment you lose them, you risk not only your initiative, but your career, your reputation, and your existence in the system.

Although you may not want to challenge them, there will be times when the problem you are seeking to rectify lies with the authority (e.g. corruption, Ponzi schemes, discrimination) and you have to take them head on. Just think about the civil rights movements, revolutions, coup d'états, and whistle-blowers. In these cases, you need to make sure you have an extremely strong support network, because the moment you challenge the elephant, you need to be ready for the stampede that will follow.

AUTHORITY: PASSIVE

Ideally, you want to begin an initiative that your authority approves of, given the power they hold over you and your fate in the organization or system, which means that your initiative will have a hard time without their support and resources.

Occasionally, however, you will find a situation in which they do not give you their blessings, but don't do anything to stop you. Alarms should be going off. They may be passive, but with authority it tends to be more that they are indifferent to what you are doing, and even this should concern you. This signifies that their confidence in you has been shaken, and they are having second thoughts about your loyalty and professionalism.

Of course, being passive doesn't mean they are not monitoring the situation. They will keep an eye on you but will not do anything to stop you. The only way you will realize that they are being passive opponents — assuming that you have asked for and received their blessing before you started — is if you pay close attention to their behavior. If you realize that their enthusiasm has dropped, and their support has become somewhat passive (e.g. they don't make decisions when you need them to, not answering your questions), then you know that something is awry.

Usually when authority are passive, they are acting this way to send you an indirect warning. Their silence and indecisiveness are intentional and are aimed at telling you that you need to adjust the initiative (e.g. switch your approach). If you don't, they will intensify their resistance and withdraw their resources. That is why, in this case, it is crucial that you make sure that they are not harboring unexpressed animosity towards the initiative.

Addressing their passiveness must be first on your list of priorities. You need to figure out what has changed. Find out what part of the initiative is potentially upsetting them. Without this information, you cannot move forward. If you don't deal with their concerns, the authority may increase their intensity and decide to stop what you are doing. Remember they have power over resources and your fate. If they say no, even after they have previously said yes, then it is not a suggestion.

RECOMMENDED STRATEGIES/PRINCIPLES

71 ✓ **Never provoke authority:**
Don't do anything that you know would provoke them, directly or indirectly. It is true that your initiative may provoke them, but in this scenario take their passiveness as a warning and make sure you address it so that they don't feel challenged — which would provoke them.

7 ✓ **Over-communicate your interest in listening to their point of view**

87 ✓ **Never criticize or blame your passive or passive-aggressive resisters**

1 ✓ **Ensure any negativity doesn't become contagious:**
Make sure that the tensions between you and your authority are not made public. The last thing you want is a "me vs authority" situation, because you risk losing your current and potential supporters.

(73) ✓ **Make sure authority is on board:**
Your opponents' resistance may stem from the fact that you did not get their approval before moving forward. Make sure you do what is necessary to rectify this.

(74) ✓ **Stay close to authority and always keep them informed:**
At this intensity, you can still remedy the situation. Their resistance may stem from a lack of proper information as the initiative progresses. Make sure you let them know what is going on at all times.

(85) ✓ **Give authentic credit to authority:**
You may find that the reason authority is opposing you is because you didn't give them credit. Make sure you check if that is the case.

(60) ✓ **Show your strength, but without provocation:**
This strategy is to be used delicately in this subcategory. Your opponents will feel challenged if you show them your strength. However, it may help to let them know that you have people on your side. If a majority of the system, or your boss's own authority, is siding with you, they may reconsider their resistance. Be careful not to provoke them. If this strategy is used unwisely, it can easily do more harm than good.

(27) ✓ **Mobilize with enthusiasm**

(28) ✓ **Sell the benefits of the initiative**

(80) ✓ **Always be willing to learn**

(39) ✓ **Plan and deliberate**

(75) ✓ **Attend to authority's warnings:**
In this subcategory, this refers to your authority's authority.

(76) ✓ **Be careful not to give authority a reason to "punish" you:**
Passive resistance is a warning. If you move further without addressing it, you may find that they will "punish" you.

(77) ✓ **Build a relationship with higher authority**

(34) ✓ **Create, score, and celebrate a stream of small victories**

(31) ✓ **Vigilantly monitor the system**

(61) ✓ **Investigate to see if there is more to their resistance than meets the eye:**
Make sure that their passivity is not an indication of more intense resistance. Consider that authority doesn't need to share its strategies, thoughts, opinions, etc., with you.

(36) ✓ **Double-check the sanity of the initiative**

(33) ✓ **Debug the initiative**

(35) ✓ **Take responsibility for your mess**

(58) ✓ **Reflect on the purpose of the initiative**

(48) ✓ **Don't focus on winning — it is about fulfilling the purpose of the initiative:**
This is crucial when it comes to authority, since winning may be quite a difficult feat.

(84) ✓ **Consider tactically putting your initiative on hold**

AUTHORITY: PASSIVE-AGGRESSIVE

It is alarming in itself to have authority against you, even if they are expressing only mild resistance towards your intervention. Passive-aggressive authority may ignore you, withhold resources, take a long time to respond to you, send an organization-wide email subtly targeted at you, or anything else that might slow the initiative down. You should carefully consider any such resistance; it is the beginning of authority telling you that they are not happy with what you are doing, and they may be one step away from telling you to stop your initiative.

Their confidence in your loyalty and competency has significantly dropped.

In this case, there is no leeway. They are not giving you time to see if the initiative will succeed and create the beneficial change you are proposing. They are sending you a warning: they have an issue with the initiative. These warnings should be obvious to you. Something will change between you and your authority, and your initiative will start moving slowly or grind to a halt. This is a state of emergency; you will need put everything on hold while you address their concerns and the root of their resistance.

If authority do not want something to happen, they generally have the power to make sure it does not. They are not obliged to wait for your results, but they can be swayed to. Depending on your professional relationship and history — especially if you are trustworthy and competent — you may convince them to wait, but you will need to go to them and convince them that there is minimal risk and the potential for high rewards.

RECOMMENDED STRATEGIES/PRINCIPLES

7 ✓ **Over-communicate your interest in listening to their point of view**

71 ✓ **Never provoke authority**

23 ✓ **Mentally and technically prepare yourself for the worst; it may get messy:**
Even if they are passive-aggressive authority is not to be trifled with. When you think about what could happen, remember to take into account the power authority has over the system. As such you can imagine how messy this can potentially become, even at this intensity. Be careful.

1 ✓ **Ensure any negativity doesn't become contagious**

47 ✓ **Don't be faint-hearted or indecisive:**
With authority opposing you, you need to examine your resolve intensely.

64 ✓ **Take care of your supporters:**
Even at this intensity, if your supporters catch wind of the tension between you and authority they may quit.

25 ✓ **Be ready to compromise**

73 ✓ **Make sure authority is on board**

74 ✓ **Stay close to authority and always keep them informed**

85 ✓ **Give authentic credit to authority**

(60) ✓ **Show your strength, but without provocation**

(75) ✓ **Attend to authority's warnings**

(76) ✓ **Be careful not to give authority a reason to "punish" you:**
In this scenario, it is about heeding their warnings and trying to de-escalate the situation. Don't do anything to further aggravate them.

(77) ✓ **Build a relationship with higher authority:**
Mainly this is about informing the higher authority — if possible — and developing a relationship with them.

(31) ✓ **Vigilantly monitor the system**

(61) ✓ **Investigate to see if there is more to their resistance than meets the eye**

(68) ✓ **As with a game of chess, think about your moves ahead of time and plan your strategy**

(69) ✓ **Use patience, silence, and inaction wisely and strategically**

(54) ✓ **Success depends on doing the right thing, at the right time, and in the right way**

(56) ✓ **Don't burn the bridges between you and your opponents**

(82) ✓ **Never fight fire with fire**

(66) ✓ **Work to minimize the damage**

(83) ✓ **Protect your reputation:**
You need to do what you can to keep your reputation intact, the power differential means that your word will often be overpowered by theirs.

(27) ✓ **Mobilize with enthusiasm**

(28) ✓ **Sell the benefits of the initiative:**
When you do this, make sure you show them that the rewards far outweigh the risks. This may encourage them to reconsider their position.

(34) ✓ **Create, score, and celebrate a stream of small victories**

(84) ✓ **Consider tactically putting your initiative on hold**

(36) ✓ **Double-check the sanity of the initiative**

(33) ✓ **Debug the initiative**

(58) ✓ **Reflect on the purpose of the initiative**

(35) ✓ **Take responsibility for your mess**

(80) ✓ **Always be willing to learn**

(55) ✓ **Know when to accept temporary defeat**

(39) ✓ **Plan and deliberate**

(87) ✓ **Never criticize or blame your passive or passive-aggressive resisters**

(78) ✓ **If your purpose is worthwhile, prepare to push forward against authority:**
If you are opting for this strategy, you are targeting authority. Do what you can to protect yourself, your supporters, and the initiative. It is going to get difficult and messy fast. Be careful and focus on your purpose.

AUTHORITY: ACTIVE

You should try your best not to come across this situation, if possible. Authority will issue direct orders, or instructions, to stop what you are doing. They will be upfront and let you know that they don't like what you are doing. You are shaking the system, and they do not approve.

It could be that they initially expressed their support and faith in you and the initiative, but somewhere down the line they lost confidence in it or its benefits no longer serve them. At that point, they will express this form of resistance and ask you to stop what you are doing. If you don't do as they ask, they will see it as a provocation or challenge, and they will retaliate bluntly and come down with full force, asserting their authority and intensifying their resistance.

If they are actively working against you then you know that the journey is going to be quite difficult. After all, they can deny you access to resources that you need to implement purposeful change. They have the ability to stop you in your tracks and even push you into organizational limbo.

Furthermore, when authority makes it known that s/he has an issue with what you are doing, this may turn some individuals in the system against you, as well as encourage your more passive opponents to intensify their resistance.

RECOMMENDED STRATEGIES/PRINCIPLES

1 ✓ **Ensure any negativity doesn't become contagious**

7 ✓ **Over-communicate your interest in listening to their point of view**

23 ✓ **Mentally and technically prepare yourself for the worst; it will get messy**

47 ✓ **Don't be faint-hearted or indecisive**

71 ✓ **Never provoke authority**

73 ✓ **Make sure authority is on board:**
Clearly, if they are resisting you, authority is not on board, but you should not progress until they are. If you are targeting your authority (meaning they will never support you), try to make sure that their authority is on board instead.

74 ✓ **Stay close to authority and always keep them informed:**
This can sometimes help to get you back in their good graces. This strategy is also important to remember for the higher authority who is on your side. At this intensity, you need to be on good terms with the higher-ups.

75 ✓ **Attend to authority's warnings:**
This may be the last chance you have to remedy things. Stop what you are doing and focus on addressing authority's concerns.

83 ✓ **Protect your reputation**

(16) ✓ **Create and nourish your support network**

(12) ✓ **Don't provoke them:**
This includes not provoking the supporters of authority.

(11) ✓ **Keep the fire contained:**
The backlash at this intensity would be immense, so you need to make sure that you don't let the situation escalate.

(25) ✓ **Be ready to compromise:**
At this intensity, compromise should be at the forefront of your mind. Even if you are targeting your authority, it is important to remember that they still have power over your fate in the system, so if you can lessen their resistance by compromising, do it.

(54) ✓ **Success depends on doing the right thing, at the right time, and in the right way**

(66) ✓ **Work to minimize the damage**

(68) ✓ **As with a game of chess, think about your moves ahead of time and plan your strategy**

(69) ✓ **Use patience, silence, and inaction wisely and strategically**

(13) ✓ **Consider involving mediators**

(41) ✓ **Let them negotiate for you:**
Make sure that this does not backfire on you. Always attend the meeting, but don't do the negotiating. Your absence may be seen as a challenge to your opponents' authority.

(76) ✓ **Be careful not to give authority a reason to "punish" you**

85 ✓ **Give authentic credit to authority**

77 ✓ **Build a relationship with higher authority**

60 ✓ **Show your strength, but without provocation**

27 ✓ **Mobilize with enthusiasm**

28 ✓ **Sell the benefits of the initiative**

31 ✓ **Vigilantly monitor the system**

61 ✓ **Investigate to see if there is more to their resistance than meets the eye**

59 ✓ **Be wary around people who have nothing to lose:**
If authority does not have anything to lose, you need to make sure you have your back well-guarded.

36 ✓ **Double-check the sanity of the initiative**

33 ✓ **Debug the initiative**

58 ✓ **Reflect on the purpose of the initiative**

35 ✓ **Take responsibility for your mess**

84 ✓ **Consider tactically putting your initiative on hold**

55 ✓ **Know when to accept temporary defeat**

80 ✓ **Always be willing to learn**

82 ✓ **Never fight fire with fire**

56 ✓ **Don't burn the bridges between you and your opponents**

62 ✓ **Involve relevant authorities:**
In other words, involve the higher-ups if you need protection from your authority.

22 ✓ **Create some distance:**
Authority's grip on the system makes this difficult. You will need to try and limit your interactions, since distancing yourself from the residing power may not be possible.

39 ✓ **Plan and deliberate**

88 ✓ **Expose and discredit your opponents; don't blame them:**
This applies to situations when you are trying to remove the authority because they are the source of the issue.

78 ✓ **If your purpose is worthwhile, prepare to push forward against authority**

AUTHORITY: ACTIVE-AGGRESSIVE

In this case, the people in power have a real issue with what you are doing, and the journey will be immensely difficult. The odds are so greatly staked against you that it might seem nearly impossible for your initiative to succeed. After all, your authority's subordinates will fall into line at a snap of their fingers, and you are going to be faced with a massive resisting force.

Added to this, your boss probably holds your own fate in his/her hands and could ruin your career easily. Your survival in the system is in danger. Authority might transfer you into another department, demote you, give you a promotion that requires you to travel to another location, or assign you so many tasks that you have no choice but to abandon your initiative.

When you go head to head with an elephant — authority — you chances of survival are slim. You are now authority's issue, not just your initiative, and their countermeasure will be to target you. This is an urgent situation and you will need to do whatever you can to get your authority to settle down, or better yet, get behind what you are doing. Unfortunately, if s/he is active-aggressively resisting you there is little chance that you can do much to curb her/his resistance.

There are situations where you are targeting authority and will need to go head-to-head with them — your initiative demands it. When this happens, they will go into survival mode, and will come at you full-force. The power they hold over the system will depend on their level of authority, but the more power they have, the more fiercely they will retaliate. Remember that they will have more influence, more supporters, better access to resources, etc., than you do. If you believe that your initiative is necessary, and it aims to challenge authority, be ready to face extreme backlash.

RECOMMENDED STRATEGIES/PRINCIPLES

(7) ✓ **Over-communicate your interest in listening to their point of view**

(23) ✓ **Mentally and technically prepare yourself for the worst; it will get messy:**
They have access to resources, people, and power. The potential conflicts will challenge your spirit and your resources, so be prepared for the intense resistance.

(47) ✓ **Don't be faint-hearted or indecisive**

(59) ✓ **Be wary around people who have nothing to lose**

(77) ✓ **Build a relationship with higher authority**

(54) ✓ **Success depends on doing the right thing, at the right time, and in the right way**

(68) ✓ **As with a game of chess, think about your moves ahead of time and plan your strategy**

(66) ✓ **Work to minimize the damage**

(11) ✓ **Keep the fire contained**

(12) ✓ **Don't provoke them:**
If you provoke authority's supporters, you risk intensifying authority's resistance further, which could endanger your own support network.

(83) ✓ **Protect your reputation:**
It will be put to the test, so make sure that there is nothing substantial that can be used against you.

16 ✓ **Create and nourish your support network:**
This will be difficult because not many individuals
will be willing to join you against authority. However, you will need them more than ever at this
intensity, so gather whoever you can to your cause.

64 ✓ **Take care of your supporters**

32 ✓ **Ask for help**

31 ✓ **Vigilantly monitor the system**

61 ✓ **Investigate to see if there is more to their
resistance than meets the eye**

73 ✓ **Make sure (higher) authority is on board**

71 ✓ **Never provoke authority:**
Even if your initiative has provoked them, make
sure that you personally do not provoke them.

85 ✓ **Give authentic credit to (higher) authority**

74 ✓ **Stay close to (higher) authority and always
keep them informed**

75 ✓ **Attend to authority's warnings:**
This is also predominantly about the higher authority. If it has reached this stage with your authority,
they are no longer warning you.

76 ✓ **Be careful not to give authority a reason to
"punish" you:**
Make sure they don't have a justification for pun-
ishing you, because at this intensity they will try.

60 ✓ **Show you strength, but without provocation**

25 ✓ **Be ready to compromise**

13 ✓ **Consider involving mediators**

41 ✓ **Let them negotiate for you**

55 ✓ **Know when to accept temporary defeat**

84 ✓ **Consider tactically putting your initiative on hold**

36 ✓ **Double-check the sanity of the initiative**

33 ✓ **Debug the initiative:**
At this stage, it is of paramount importance that your initiative does not have any "bugs". Authority has ways of finding out if your initiative has weaknesses. Use this strategy to stay ahead of them and guard your initiative.

58 ✓ **Reflect on the purpose of the initiative**

35 ✓ **Take responsibility for your mess**

80 ✓ **Always be willing to learn**

78 ✓ **If your purpose is worthwhile, prepare to push forward against authority**

22 ✓ **Create some distance:**
Limit your interactions, since it may be difficult to distance yourself from the system's authority.

39 ✓ **Plan and deliberate**

49 ✓ **Winning in confrontations demands self-discipline**

69 ✓ **Use patience, silence, and inaction wisely and strategically**

82 ✓ **Never fight fire with fire**

56 ✓ **Don't burn the bridges between you and your opponents**

88 ✓ **Expose and discredit your opponents; don't blame them:**
You should only resort to this strategy if your initiative is attempting to remove authority (e.g. authority is corrupt).

62 ✓ **Involve relevant authorities**

AUTHORITY: MALEVOLENT

When you introduce an intervention that shakes the system in a way that affects authority's survival and growth, your authority is going to fight back. If they have resorted to this intensity, it is unlikely that you will continue in the system, because they will be out to crush you. Most of the times, at this intensity, the only way you can escape their wrath is to leave the system altogether.

They have the power to ruin your life. They can ensure they have reasons to punish or hurt you (e.g. planting evidence, giving you impossible tasks). They have the power to close down future opportunities, using their own support network to rob you of resources, and they can make it hard for you to advance your career — if it even exists at this point (e.g. they might try to ensure that you never find a new job, or they may tarnish your reputation as an employee, etc.).

At this point, you will have to make a decision: do you want to target authority, directly or indirectly? If you do, you will need to make sure you are ready to face one of the most intense malevolent opponents. Anything a malevolent resister in another subcategory can do is now multiplied by the power difference between you and authority.

In this situation, you are battling a giant, and you need to make sure you know how to deal with them, because otherwise they will crush you under their immense weight.

RECOMMENDED STRATEGIES/PRINCIPLES

(7) ✓ **Over-communicate your interest in listening to their point of view:**
Even at this intensity you should still reiterate to authority that you want to hear their point of view.

(23) ✓ **Mentally and technically prepare yourself; it will get (VERY) messy**

(47) ✓ **Don't be faint-hearted or indecisive**

(59) ✓ **Be wary around people who have nothing to lose**

(54) ✓ **Success depends on doing the right thing, at the right time, and in the right way**

(68) ✓ **As with a game of chess, think about your moves ahead of time and plan your strategy**

(66) ✓ **Work to minimize the damage**

(11) ✓ **Keep the fire contained**

(12) ✓ **Don't provoke them**

(83) ✓ **Protect your reputation:**
At this intensity, this is quite important, as your reputation may be one of the things which keeps your supporters from abandoning you.

(16) ✓ **Create and nourish your support network**

(64) ✓ **Take care of your supporters**

(32) ✓ **Ask for help**

31 ✓ **Vigilantly monitor the system:**
There are no boundaries at this intensity and, given their power, it's essential that you keep on top of their countermeasures and the changes in the system.

61 ✓ **Investigate to see if there is more to their resistance than meets the eye:**
Authority does not have to report to you, and your interactions may be limited. Make sure you know what they have in store for you so that you can prepare and possibly preempt it.

77 ✓ **Build a relationship with higher authority:**
In this scenario, it is important to maintain your relationship with higher authority. Stay close to them, keep them informed, and heed their warnings, otherwise your opponents may get ahead of you and turn these authorities against you.

71 ✓ **Never provoke authority**

76 ✓ **Be careful not to give authority a reason to "punish" you:**
As soon as you are vulnerable, your authority's resistance will rain down on you. They will do everything in their power to make sure you fail or suffer. However, at this intensity, you also need to be wary of attempts to trap you in situations where they have a legal right to punish you.

60 ✓ **Show your strength, but without provocation**

25 ✓ **Be ready to compromise**

13 ✓ **Consider involving mediators**

41 ✓ **Let them negotiate for you**

55 ✓ **Know when to accept temporary defeat**

84 ✓ **Consider tactically putting your initiative on hold**

36 ✓ **Double-check the sanity of the initiative**

33 ✓ **Debug the initiative**

58 ✓ **Reflect on the purpose of the initiative**

35 ✓ **Take responsibility for your mess**

80 ✓ **Always be willing to learn**

78 ✓ **If your purpose is worthwhile, prepare to push forward against authority**

39 ✓ **Plan and deliberate**

49 ✓ **Winning in confrontations demands self-discipline**

69 ✓ **Use patience, silence, and inaction wisely and strategically**

82 ✓ **Never fight fire with fire**

56 ✓ **Don't burn the bridges between you and your opponents**

88 ✓ **Expose and discredit your opponents; don't blame them**

62 ✓ **Involve relevant authorities**

COMPETITION SCENARIOS

You and your competitors are both competing for the same resources (e.g. clients, market share, votes) and going after the same opportunities, with each one of you working to ensure your own survival and growth. Resistance from them is natural and expected. It is not personal, but really is "just business". In fact, by definition, if they are your competition, then both of you are expected to go head-to-head within the same system. If you are not chasing the same opportunities and fighting over the same resources, you cannot count one another as the competition.

You don't hold power over your competitors. Since you are independent entities, each moving in their individual orbits, neither one of you has authority over the other. Because you are competing with one another, by definition, you don't work together. They are a unique subcategory and, unlike your authority, colleagues, constituents, and subordinates, you don't need the help or permission of your competitors. You can launch an initiative and do whatever you want to do, irrespective of what they think.

Competition can impact your initiative and its success, but not in the same way other roles can (e.g. your competition cannot withdraw their support because they do not support you to start with). However, you still need to know how to deal with them and the potential obstacles they may cause so that you can fulfill the purpose of your initiative.

Competitors can sabotage your work, attack you personally, hurt your reputation, spy on you and steal your work, monopolize the market and push you out of the system, etc. There are many things that they can do, so it would be naïve to ignore them if you wish to succeed.

COMPETITION: PASSIVE

In this case, competition is considered passive when they are competitors in principle, but not in practice. This usually happens when they are either not interested in your domain or they are stagnant.

In the first case, it may be that you are expanding to other domains, while your competitor is sticking to your original, shared domain. For instance, imagine that you are both shoe shop owners and target the same clientele. However, you have decided to expand to stock both adult and children footwear, while they are sticking to adult footwear. Although your initiative has brought in more customers, they are not interested in expanding their business.

The other scenario is you are still in the same business, but you have constantly been creating and innovating, while they have remained stagnant. For instance, imagine that you are both hotel owners. You have been keeping up to date with technological advancements, while your competitor has not changed anything for a while.

In either scenario, you don't need to worry about them, at least for the time being. However, you should still consider them as resistance, because they give your customers a choice which may draw them away from your organization. In addition to this, as long as your competitors still exist, they have the potential to improve, and then they may become a threat. Since they are still part of the same system and they are working in it, all they have to do is change their thinking, decide to catch up with you, and return to the same playing field. This may increase their resistance and mean that they pose a greater threat to you and the initiative.

RECOMMENDED STRATEGIES/PRINCIPLES

(48) ✓ **Don't focus on winning — it is about fulfilling the purpose of the initiative**

(53) ✓ **Do what is best for the system**

(81) ✓ **Constantly innovate and create exceptional value**

(73) ✓ **Make sure authority is on board**

(74) ✓ **Stay close to authority and always keep them informed:**
It is your initiative, and authority may hold you responsible for overseeing it. However, they will expect you to keep them posted on every development, otherwise they will not be able to help you deal with your opponents.

(75) ✓ **Attend to authority's warnings**

(76) ✓ **Be careful not to give authority a reason to "punish" you**

(83) ✓ **Protect your reputation**

(64) ✓ **Take care of your supporters**

(68) ✓ **As with a game of chess, think about your moves ahead of time and plan your strategy**

(45) ✓ **Be unpredictable**

(57) ✓ **Choose clarity or ambiguity, depending on the situation**

(15) ✓ **Maintain the momentum of your progress**

(34) ✓ **Create, score, and celebrate a stream of small victories:**
This strategy should have an effect on your constituents. You and your competition are offering the best you have, so if you can prove your initiative works, you will be more popular with your constituents. You should always work towards getting your shared constituency on your side.

(38) ✓ **Involve the members of the system in the initiative:**
This applies to members of your own organization or group.

(80) ✓ **Always be willing to learn:**
Your competition may have a better way of carrying out a similar initiative to yours. Don't discount this valuable opportunity to learn.

(69) ✓ **Use patience, silence, and inaction wisely and strategically**

(61) ✓ **Investigate to see if there is more to their resistance than meets the eye**

(42) ✓ **Don't let conflicts and diversions distract you:**
Your competition may make a public announcement with the intention of diverting your attention. Make sure you stay focus on what you are doing, so that you don't fall for such traps.

(44) ✓ **Use your opponents' mistakes:**
At times you may be on equal footing with your competitor. It is not until they make a mistake that you have a chance to get ahead. Don't miss even the slightest of opportunities.

87 ✓ **Never criticize or blame your passive or passive-aggressive resisters**

56 ✓ **Don't burn the bridges between you and your opponents:**
You may one day work with one another, so you don't want to create unnecessary divisions.

COMPETITION: PASSIVE-AGGRESSIVE

At this stage, your competition, is one step closer to becoming active and posing a threat to your initiative.

You should not ignore them. It isn't difficult for your competition to disguise their actions as simple competitiveness, but they be biding their time before adopting a more active approach. Many competitors may seem passive-aggressive, until they suddenly reveal a game-changing innovation that alters the entire nature of the industry or domain. This has the potential to push you out of the system, or at least push you back to second place. Therefore, it is crucial that you do not ignore them.

It is also important that you do not compare your progress to theirs. Even if they are behind in the game, you should always be looking for ways to offer your constituents exceptional value, and you should not compromise on that value regardless of how your competitors are doing.

RECOMMENDED STRATEGIES/PRINCIPLES

48   ✓   **Don't focus on winning — it is about fulfilling the purpose of the initiative**

15   ✓   **Maintain the momentum of your progress**

81   ✓   **Constantly innovate and create exceptional value**

73   ✓   **Make sure authority is on board**

(74) ✓ **Stay close to authority and always keep them informed**

(38) ✓ **Involve the members of the system in the initiative**

(64) ✓ **Take care of your supporters**

(54) ✓ **Success depends on doing the right thing, at the right time, and in the right way**

(75) ✓ **Attend to authority's warnings**

(27) ✓ **Mobilize with enthusiasm:**
This is again focused on your constituents. Make sure they feel the enthusiasm and excitement you have for your initiative.

(28) ✓ **Sell the benefits of the initiative (to your constituents)**

(34) ✓ **Create, score, and celebrate a stream of small victories (for your constituents)**

(31) ✓ **Vigilantly monitor the system**

(42) ✓ **Don't let conflicts and diversions distract you.**

(39) ✓ **Plan and deliberate:**
If you must confront your competitors make sure you have a plan in place.

(49) ✓ **Winning in confrontations demands self-discipline**

(69) ✓ **Use patience, silence, and inaction wisely and strategically**

(87) ✓ **Never criticize or blame your passive or passive-aggressive resisters**

(57) ✓ **Choose clarity or ambiguity, depending on the situation:**
There are times when you may wish to make your strategies known to your competition. However, you should only do this if it benefits your initiative. Otherwise, opt for ambiguity.

(68) ✓ **As with a game of chess, think about your moves ahead of time and plan your strategy**

(80) ✓ **Always be willing to learn**

(82) ✓ **Never fight fire with fire**

(45) ✓ **Be unpredictable**

(83) ✓ **Protect your reputation:**
At this intensity your competition may not opt to ruin your reputation, but remember that they might be concealing more intense resistance, so be careful.

COMPETITION: ACTIVE

In some cases, the first level of the competition's resistance starts here: active resistance. At this intensity, they are part of your reality. When you introduce a game-changing initiative, one that possibly threatens their position in the system, they will start to resist you actively, lobbying against you and trying to get ahead of you in the game. They will attempt to grab the opportunities you are after, and may try to neutralize the changes you are trying to implement.

They will utilize advertising and aggressive competitive tactics, but they will not go out of their way to stop what you are doing. Instead, they will focus on how they can surpass you by offering more value. In essence, this is the boundary between what can be considered aggressive competition and resistance. Once they intensify their resistance, they may go out of their way to target the initiative. This means that you need to make sure that you keep the competitive atmosphere alive, and do not provoke them further, if possible.

It may be difficult to avoid getting caught up in trying to prove yourself superior to the competition, but this carries the danger that you will forget what your main purpose is. No doubt you have heard about office rivalries or even taken part in a few of them. There is nothing wrong with having some fun or teasing the competition; it is part of the culture. However, make sure you do not partake in such activities at the expense of your purpose. Don't allow your competition's opposition to distract you from offering your uniqueness to the system. After all, they may try to bait you into a rivalry to distract you. This might open up a way for them to get ahead in the game.

RECOMMENDED STRATEGIES/PRINCIPLES

(48) ✓ **Don't focus on winning — it is about fulfilling the purpose of the initiative**

(53) ✓ **Do what is best for the system**

(15) ✓ **Maintain the momentum of your progress**

(81) ✓ **Constantly innovate and create exceptional value**

(38) ✓ **Involve the members of the system in the initiative:**
You need more support at this stage, since your competition is now actively working to resist you. Focus on gathering support by involving members of your organization in the initiative.

(73) ✓ **Make sure authority is on board**

(74) ✓ **Stay close to authority and always keep them informed**

(68) ✓ **As with a game of chess, think about your moves ahead of time and plan your strategy**

(54) ✓ **Success depends on doing the right thing, at the right time, and in the right way**

(83) ✓ **Protect your reputation:**
Your opponents will target your reputation to try to get your supporters (particularly constituents) to abandon you. Your organization may also be targeted. Make sure that you are protected, and that there is nothing that can be used to tarnish your reputation.

64 ✓ **Take care of your supporters**

27 ✓ **Mobilize with enthusiasm (for your constituents)**

28 ✓ **Sell the benefits of the initiative (to your constituents)**

34 ✓ **Create, score, and celebrate a stream of small victories (for your constituents)**

31 ✓ **Vigilantly monitor the system**

42 ✓ **Don't let conflicts and diversions distract you**

45 ✓ **Be unpredictable**

69 ✓ **Use patience, silence, and inaction wisely and strategically**

57 ✓ **Choose clarity or ambiguity, depending on the situation**

82 ✓ **Never fight fire with fire:**
Doing so will alienate your constituents.

47 ✓ **Don't be faint-hearted or indecisive**

39 ✓ **Plan and deliberate**

75 ✓ **Attend to authority's warnings**

49 ✓ **Winning in confrontations demands self-discipline**

44 ✓ **Use your opponents' mistakes:**
Remember not to use these mistakes to hurt your opponents or humiliate them. Instead, use them solely to get them to reduce their resistance.

58 ✓ **Reflect on the purpose of the initiative**

80 ✓ **Always be willing to learn**

55 ✓ **Know when to accept temporary defeat:**
If your competition undoubtedly has the better innovation, intervention, or service, slow down and
use the time to tailor a more beneficial initiative for
your shared constituency and the system.

56 ✓ **Don't burn the bridges between you and your
opponents**

COMPETITION: ACTIVE-AGGRESSIVE

If your initiative is causing a ruckus in the system, your competition will be keen to try and counter what you are doing. If you are: creating new and valuable innovations that put you ahead of the game; proposing policies that benefit your constituents and increase your market share; making valuable changes to the system and gaining more votes and support, etc., your competition will increase their resistance. They will be passionate about getting ahead of you, rendering your initiative useless, and trying to make you irrelevant (e.g. changing the market).

At this intensity, they will have crossed the boundary, moving from competitors to rivals. They will create ad campaigns aimed at sullying your organization's public image. They will try to persuade your shared constituency that they are more fitting for the job, that their products and services are superior, or that your organization does not have their best interest at heart. They will study what you are doing, and offer up similar but "better" policies, practices, products, or services. Basically, they will dedicate considerable amounts of time, resources, and energy to making sure that you fail. They will want to change the game in a way that makes you irrelevant.

It is important that you focus on offering your constituents your unique and beneficial initiative. If you compromise on this, you will lose them, and you will put your survival at stake.

RECOMMENDED STRATEGIES/PRINCIPLES

48 ✓ **Don't focus on winning — it is about fulfilling the purpose of the initiative**

58 ✓ **Reflect on the purpose of the initiative**

53 ✓ **Do what is best for the system**

23 ✓ **Mentally and technically prepare yourself for the worst; it will get messy**

47 ✓ **Don't be faint-hearted or indecisive**

73 ✓ **Make sure authority is on board**

74 ✓ **Stay close to authority and always keep them informed**

15 ✓ **Maintain the momentum of your progress**

81 ✓ **Constantly innovate and create exceptional value**

64 ✓ **Take care of your supporters**

31 ✓ **Vigilantly monitor the system**

42 ✓ **Don't let conflicts and diversions distract you**

38 ✓ **Involve the members of the system in the initiative**

54 ✓ **Success depends on doing the right thing, at the right time, and in the right way**

82 ✓ **Never fight fire with fire**

27 ✓ Mobilize with enthusiasm (for your constituents)

28 ✓ Sell the benefits of the initiative (to your constituents)

34 ✓ Create, score, and celebrate a stream of small victories (for your constituents)

69 ✓ Use patience, silence, and inaction wisely and strategically

75 ✓ Attend to authority's warnings

68 ✓ As with a game of chess, think about your moves ahead of time and plan your strategy

80 ✓ Always be willing to learn

45 ✓ Be unpredictable

57 ✓ Choose clarity or ambiguity, depending on the situation

39 ✓ Plan and deliberate

44 ✓ Use your opponents' mistakes

49 ✓ Winning in confrontations demands self-discipline

24 ✓ Fight with full force

55 ✓ Know when to accept temporary defeat

56 ✓ Don't burn the bridges between you and your opponents

88 ✓ **Expose and discredit your opponents; don't blame them:**

This usually entails showing your constituency that your opponents are either spreading false information, or they are doing something untoward behind the scenes. It is important that you use this not as ploy to get ahead, but because you want to expose the truth. Be careful not to get drawn in by the need to get ahead.

COMPETITION: MALEVOLENT

There will be times when the competition plays dirty. They will be ready to use their resources and all their knowledge to get on top. They will hurt you and damage your reputation; they may also be willing to break the law if it gets the job done.

This will not surprise you if you are familiar with corporate espionage. One common strategy is for companies to spy on their competition, either to keep track of what they are doing, to steal their ideas, or to sabotage their progress. This is one example of the many tactics your competition may use to try to either surpass you (e.g. by bringing you down, or delaying you, giving themselves time to rise), or get you out of the game completely.

They may target you personally, hiring private investigators, digging up stories of past failures, and using anything that will give them an edge and ruin your reputation. They might also fabricate information and spread it to your constituency. Since your competition may hold the same status in the eyes of some of your shared constituency, it can be difficult to control damage that you haven't foreseen and planned for. At this intensity, any strategy will be seen as fair by your competitors. That is why you need to protect yourself, your personal relationships, and your supporters.

The intensity of this might put so much pressure on you that you are tempted to compromise on what you have to offer. It is important that you don't allow them to bring you down, no matter how hard this is. You don't want your constituency losing out on exceptional value, or believing your competitors' false claims.

RECOMMENDED STRATEGIES/PRINCIPLES

(48) ✓ **Don't focus on winning — it is about fulfilling the purpose of the initiative**

(58) ✓ **Reflect on the purpose of the initiative**

(23) ✓ **Mentally and technically prepare yourself for the worst; it will get (VERY) messy:**
Your opponents will pull out all the stops, so make sure that you are ready for them. Consult your authority and get all the resources you need. Let everyone know what might happen so that they can prepare themselves for what is to come.

(47) ✓ **Don't be faint-hearted or indecisive**

(83) ✓ **Protect your reputation:**
Your competition will come after your reputation. If they damage it, your constituents will doubt you and may decide to take their money (or equivalent) to your competition. You need to be proactive and protect your reputation by being closer to your constituents.

(73) ✓ **Make sure authority is on board**

(74) ✓ **Stay close to authority and always keep them informed**

(64) ✓ **Take care of your supporters**

(62) ✓ **Involve the relevant authorities:**
Do this to protect your constituents, yourself, and your interests.

38 ✓ **Involve the members of the system in the initiative**

53 ✓ **Do what is best for the system**

75 ✓ **Attend to authority's warnings:**
This refers to the authority in your organization and will only happen if your authority feels things are getting out of hand.

15 ✓ **Maintain the momentum of your progress**

81 ✓ **Constantly innovate and create exceptional value**

68 ✓ **As with a game of chess, think about your moves ahead of time and plan your strategy**

54 ✓ **Success depends on doing the right thing, at the right time, and in the right way**

80 ✓ **Always be willing to learn**

27 ✓ **Mobilize with enthusiasm (for your constituents)**

28 ✓ **Sell the benefits of the initiative (to your constituents)**

34 ✓ **Create, score, and celebrate a stream of small victories (for your constituents)**

31 ✓ **Vigilantly monitor the system**

42 ✓ **Don't let conflicts and diversions distract you**

45 ✓ **Be unpredictable**

69 ✓ **Use patience, silence, and inaction wisely and strategically**

(57) ✓ **Choose clarity or ambiguity, depending on the situation**

(39) ✓ **Plan and deliberate**

(44) ✓ **Use your opponents' mistakes**

(24) ✓ **Fight with full force:**
Make sure that you don't alienate your constituents with this strategy.

(49) ✓ **Winning in confrontations demands self-discipline**

(84) ✓ **Consider tactically putting your initiative on hold**

(55) ✓ **Know when to accept temporary defeat**

(88) ✓ **Expose and discredit your opponents; don't blame them**

(56) ✓ **Don't burn the bridges between you and your opponents**

(82) ✓ **Never fight fire with fire**

CONSTITUENTS SCENARIOS

Every system is made up of individuals or entities. As the person exercising leadership, you will have people you serve, whose interests are usually high up on your list of priorities. The system's survival and growth are contingent on their support, and a big part of that support is dependent on preserving their interests. Ideally, changes that benefit the system will benefit its constituents. Sometimes, however, you will need to introduce changes that will not be in line with some of your constituents' interests. When this happens, your constituents will begin to question their loyalties to you and the system.

In essence, leadership is for your constituents. Without them, there is no one to serve, and there would be no need for an initiative. They are the end users, and you are working to make sure their lives are elevated. There is little chance of success if your constituents are not on board. Their support really affects your survival in the system. If they don't support your innovation or intervention, it will probably not have the intended effect and will fail.

Of course, not every single one of your constituents will be on board. There will be people who will resist. Does this mean that you should abandon your initiative? Not necessarily. When it comes to your constituents, you need to consider the number of people resisting. If the majority of your constituents are resisting the proposed initiative, you will need to approach their resistance differently than if the minority of your constituents are resisting.

If the majority are resisting, you might consider whether they need more time, a more detailed explanation, or to see tangible results before they can understand the benefits of the initiative, its necessity, and its importance. You will have to move forward carefully, and eventually they will (hopefully) understand. If you find that over time their resistance has not wavered, or worse has intensified, you will have to ask yourself what is wrong with the initiative, or with your approach. You will need to put things on hold and go back to the drawing board. It could be that:

- **They are not ready.** It is too soon for you to propose such an initiative, and you may need to ease people into it.

- **You misinterpreted the current reality.** It is possible that change is not necessary, or that you are introducing the wrong initiative for the current situation.

- **You are missing something.** You might have the right idea, but have missed something when formulating the initiative. It is incomplete, and you will need to see what it is that you missed.

- **Your approach or the way you are communicating it needs to change.** It could be that you chose the wrong approach, or that you were not able to properly relay all the details.

If the minority of your constituents are resisting you, you might not be so alarmed. This is a different situation altogether and has its own strategies, but you still shouldn't forget about them. They are part of your constituents, for whom the initiative is intended, and there is a possibility that their concerns are legitimate. They also have the potential to increase their numbers and become a majority.

This is a delicate situation, because without your constituents, your initiative cannot serve its purpose. Losing them is out of the question, but they are resisting you and you need to seriously check the direction of your initiative, from the approach all the way to the change it is trying to implement.

Your constituents are your major critics, and their reviews of you and your initiative can either tarnish or enhance your reputation. If they cast you in a negative light, your reputation will suffer, and eventually you might be ruined, losing all your credibility.

Furthermore, any form of resistance from your constituents can fuel resistance from other roles. When your opponents, in other roles, see that your constituents are resisting you, they will take advantage of the situation and increase their own resistance. They will jump in and try to mobilize your constituents against you. That is why when dealing with your constituents, especially on the more intense side of spectrum, you need to be careful, swift, and vigilant, so that you can deal with their resistance, and avoid giving your other opponents a deadly weapon.

Finally, there is one other possible scenario. Your constituents may be manipulated by populists. If one of your opponents claims to be one of them, that they understand them and that they are best suited for the role — basically they have a populist's agenda — then they can easily manipulate the masses. You need to be wary of such attempts to take advantage of your constituents and manipulate them.

CONSTITUENTS: PASSIVE

Even passive resistance from your constituents is a negative sign, because ideally you want them to be on board with your initiative, enthusiastically supporting it. Of course, you need to consider if the majority or minority of your constituents are opposing you, because each situation requires you to have a different mindset and a different approach.

Your constituents may experience discomfort because of your initiative, and they may not be willing to buy in completely. Unlike the other roles, your passive constituents may be vocal about their concerns. They may let you know that they are not fully on board with this new change. They may say that they are not sure if they want to invest their time and/or money in the initiative.

It is not unusual for them to not see the benefits of the initiative as fast as its creator. However, they may be willing to be patient till the initiative has borne some fruit. Their loyalties towards you and/or your organization or party will keep them from intensifying their resistance and will afford you some leeway.

If you face passive resistance from the minority, it's not necessarily bad news. Change often causes resistance, and you must accept that not everyone will be on board. If you face it from the majority, however, then the situation becomes more urgent, and you will need to consider how best to deal with their concerns, avoiding an increase in the intensity of their resistance.

RECOMMENDED STRATEGIES/PRINCIPLES

2 ✓ **Respect the history of the relationship:**
Your system needs constituents to function, so it is of paramount importance that you let them know how much you value their support, and that you are willing to do what is necessary to maintain your relationship (especially if those opposing you are the majority).

7 ✓ **Over-communicate your interest in listening to their point of view**

1 ✓ **Ensure any negativity doesn't become contagious**

3 ✓ **Limit the conflict to the relevant issues:**
When it comes to this subcategory, make sure they do not bring up your past failures or other unrelated issues. This will create tension that you don't want.

11 ✓ **Keep the fire contained**

12 ✓ **Don't provoke them**

73 ✓ **Make sure that authority is on board:**
Even at this intensity, if authority does not approve of what you are doing, you risk their resistance as well.

68 ✓ **As with a game of chess, think about your moves ahead of time and plan your strategy**

27 ✓ **Mobilize with enthusiasm**

87 ✓ **Never criticize or blame your passive or passive-aggressive resisters**

(28) ✓ **Sell the benefits of the initiative**

(74) ✓ **Stay close to authority and always keep them informed:**
Authority can help smooth things over with your opponents. When you keep authority in the loop, make sure your opponents don't know authority is with you. Otherwise, authority good relationship with them will be at risk, and you may lose authority's support.

(75) ✓ **Attend to authority's warnings**

(15) ✓ **Maintain the momentum of your progress**

(16) ✓ **Create and nourish your support network:**
Try to use this strategy to get as many of your constituents on your side as possible. If only a small percentage of your constituency is opposing your initiative, you increase the chances of it succeeding.

(64) ✓ **Take care of your supporters**

(38) ✓ **Involve the members of the system in the initiative:**
This is a little different when dealing with your constituents, but try to involve them in the initiative. For instance, you might start issuing competitions, surveys, etc., to help them feel engaged.

(53) ✓ **Do what is best for the system:**
This is synonymous with doing what is best for your constituents. Consider whether what you are doing truly benefits them, and act accordingly.

(54) ✓ **Success depends on doing the right thing, at the right time, and in the right way**

81 ✓ **Constantly innovate and create exceptional value**

34 ✓ **Create, score, and celebrate a stream of small victories**

31 ✓ **Vigilantly monitor the system**

42 ✓ **Don't let conflicts and diversions distract you**

61 ✓ **Investigate to see if there is more to their resistance than meets the eye**

36 ✓ **Double-check the sanity of the initiative**

33 ✓ **Debug the initiative**

58 ✓ **Reflect on the purpose of the initiative**

80 ✓ **Always be willing to learn**

83 ✓ **Protect your reputation**

69 ✓ **Use patience, silence, and inaction wisely and strategically**

CONSTITUENTS: PASSIVE-AGGRESSIVE

At this intensity, some of your constituents may give you the benefit of the doubt, but many of them may begin to shift their loyalties and withdraw their interests. They will ignore your phone calls, mock your promises, bring up past failures, and generally begin to doubt your commitment to their well-being. All of these behaviors are dangerous, because your constituents are one step closer to withdrawing their interests entirely and distancing themselves from anything related to your initiative.

You need to handle this situation delicately and intelligently. If the majority of your constituents are resisting you, you will need to consider all the paths open to you to get them back on your side. If you cannot, you will need to work on lessening their numbers, or at least making them passive or neutral. If you have to halt your initiative so that you can quell their resistance, then do it and handle their concerns in the best way possible. The good news is that because they are not active yet, you still have a chance of salvaging the situation with little to no harm incurred.

Losing a lot of constituents will have an enormously negative impact on your initiative. Passive-aggressive resistance is not to be ignored or taken lightly. You constituents may not openly lobby against you, but their inaction and passive-aggressive behavior will create controversy around your initiative, and that alone can bring in more doubting constituents. If you lose them, you will lose your chance of making a beneficial impact on the system.

RECOMMENDED STRATEGIES/PRINCIPLES

(2) ✓ **Respect the history of the relationship**

(7) ✓ **Over-communicate your interest in listening to their point of view**

(1) ✓ **Ensure any negativity doesn't become contagious**

(3) ✓ **Limit the conflict to the relevant issues**

(11) ✓ **Keep the fire contained**

(83) ✓ **Protect your reputation:**
If word gets out that some of your constituents are upset, it can ruin your reputation with other members of your constituency. Make sure you take measures to protect your reputation against any backlash.

(73) ✓ **Make sure authority is on board**

(74) ✓ **Stay close to authority and always keep them informed**

(75) ✓ **Attend to authority's warnings**

(15) ✓ **Maintain the momentum of your progress**

(38) ✓ **Involve the members of the system in the initiative**

(16) ✓ **Create and nourish your support network**

(64) ✓ **Take care of your supporters**

(81) ✓ **Constantly innovate and create exceptional value**

(27) ✓ **Mobilize with enthusiasm**

(28) ✓ **Sell the benefits of the initiative**

(34) ✓ **Create, score, and celebrate a stream of small victories**

(54) ✓ **Success depends on doing the right thing, at the right time, and in the right way**

(53) ✓ **Do what is best for the system**

(68) ✓ **As with a game of chess, think about your moves ahead of time and plan your strategy**

(87) ✓ **Never criticize or blame your passive or passive-aggressive resisters**

(36) ✓ **Double-check the sanity of the initiative**

(84) ✓ **Consider tactically putting your initiative on hold:**
From this intensity onward, if the majority of your constituency is opposing you then you will need to strongly reconsider what you are doing and possibly put your initiative on hold, maybe indefinitely.

(33) ✓ **Debug the initiative**

(58) ✓ **Reflect on the purpose of the initiative**

(80) ✓ **Always be willing to learn**

(31) ✓ **Vigilantly monitor the system**

(61) ✓ **Investigate to see if there is more to their resistance than meets the eye**

69 ✓ **Use patience, silence, and inaction wisely and strategically**

42 ✓ **Don't let conflicts and diversions distract you**

CONSTITUENTS: ACTIVE

At this intensity, some of your constituents feel that they need to withdraw their interests. They cannot give their support to an initiative that they do not believe will benefit them. Unless they are dependent on your organization or the initiative, you constituents will not stick around when they are not getting anything out of your initiative.

Although their interests and commitments usually grant you some leeway, at this intensity, they will have given them up. They will oppose you by withdrawing all their interests from anything related to the initiative, or from the organization overall. They will boycott your projects, products, and services. In turn, anyone in their personal or professional circles may decide to join them, and further decrease your support.

If it is the minority of your constituents, you may still have a chance to salvage the situation. You will need to work with them and resolve their issues. If you fail to do so, they may intensify their resistance, and also influence others to oppose you.

If the majority of your constituents are actively opposing you, your initiative has almost met its end. It will be hard to get them back, and anything short of a miracle will not do the trick. You need to think hard about what has gone wrong and why. You should not experience this form of resistance if your initiative was the right move to address the current reality. You should also bear in mind that your constituents rarely start at this intensity, so you should have been paying attention and addressing their concerns before they reached this level.

You need your constituents to get behind what you are doing. If your clients boycott your new products, sales will go down, and you may have to scrap the whole project. If your voters decide to withdraw their vote, you will be unable to secure a successful election. If your benefactors don't agree to fund your initiative, you will have to stop it and look for other funds. Without your constituents' support, your initiative will be of no use, since your constituents — who the initiative is for — are not interested in it.

RECOMMENDED STRATEGIES/PRINCIPLES

2 ✓ **Respect the history of the relationship**

7 ✓ **Over-communicate your interest in listening to their point of view**

58 ✓ **Reflect on the purpose of the initiative**

1 ✓ **Ensure any negativity doesn't become contagious**

3 ✓ **Limit the conflict to the relevant issues**

11 ✓ **Keep the fire contained**

83 ✓ **Protect your reputation:**
This may prove difficult if the majority of your constituency are opposing you. However, you should do your best to keep your reputation from being tarnished.

73 ✓ **Make sure authority is on board**

74 ✓ **Stay close to authority and always keep them informed**

75 ✓ **Attend to authority's warnings**

16 ✓ **Create and nourish your support network**

64 ✓ **Take care of your supporters**

(80) ✓ **Always be willing to learn**

(81) ✓ **Constantly innovate and create exceptional value**

(27) ✓ **Mobilize with enthusiasm**

(28) ✓ **Sell the benefits of the initiative**

(34) ✓ **Create, score, and celebrate a stream of small victories:**
If you face resistance from this level onward, you need to work vigorously to show some results if you genuinely think your initiative is beneficial. Otherwise, you will need to give it up, especially if the majority of your constituency is resisting you.

(38) ✓ **Involve the members of the system in the initiative**

(31) ✓ **Vigilantly monitor the system**

(61) ✓ **Investigate to see if there is more to their resistance than meets the eye**

(68) ✓ **As with a game of chess, think about your moves ahead of time and plan your strategy**

(53) ✓ **Do what is best for the system**

(54) ✓ **Success depends on doing the right thing, at the right time, and in the right way**

(36) ✓ **Double-check the sanity of the initiative**

(33) ✓ **Debug the initiative**

(69) ✓ **Use patience, silence, and inaction wisely and strategically**

(84) ✓   **Consider tactically putting your initiative on hold**

(15) ✓   **Maintain the momentum of your progress**

(89) ✓   **Avoid conflict and head-on collisions when possible, but do what it takes to protect yourself and the initiative:**
If you are dealing with a small number of opposing constituents, you may consider engaging them in a head-on collision to protect yourself. If the majority are opposing you then don't consider this tactic.

(48) ✓   **Don't focus on winning — it is about fulfilling the purpose of the initiative**

(39) ✓   **Plan and deliberate**

(42) ✓   **Don't let conflicts and diversions distract you**

(45) ✓   **Be unpredictable**

CONSTITUENTS: ACTIVE-AGGRESSIVE

In general, if your constituents have either started their resistance at this intensity or have reached this intensity, they will no longer be part of your constituency. They will have given up their loyalties and moved on to your competitors or other alternatives.

They may not only stop supporting you and encourage others to boycott you, but they may also start counter-initiatives against your organization or party. From a political standpoint, they might stage protests and mobilize others to vote against you or to not vote at all, thereby affecting your chances of winning an election.

If the minority of your constituents are at this intensity, you may be able to salvage the situation. However, you should not allow even a minority to reach this level. You will need to address their resistance as soon as you can, and try to win some of them back. If your constituents pull their support, it could put a strain on your survival and that of the initiative. This becomes more urgent if your constituents succeed in lobbying others to join them in their resistance, turning them from the minority to the majority.

If the majority are at this intensity, you are going to have a hard time bouncing back. You may have to consider dropping the initiative, not only for their sake, but for yours. If you keep at it, their opposition will push you out of the system. For instance, your organization may wish to distance itself from you and the initiative, and may even consider letting you go. In the end, without its constituents, the organization will suffer significantly, so they may decide to push you out for the sake of their continued survival. They may use this as a show of good faith to their constituents.

You cannot leave your constituents' resistance unchecked at any level, but at this intensity you must look for ways to show them some positive results, or else you will suffer major consequences, including your continued existence in the organization.

RECOMMENDED STRATEGIES/PRINCIPLES

58 ✓ **Reflect on the purpose of the initiative**

2 ✓ **Respect the history of the relationship**

7 ✓ **Over-communicate your interest in listening to their point of view**

53 ✓ **Do what is best for the system**

48 ✓ **Don't focus on winning — it is about fulfilling the purpose of the initiative**

1 ✓ **Ensure any negativity doesn't become contagious**

3 ✓ **Limit the conflict to the relevant issues**

11 ✓ **Keep the fire contained**

83 ✓ **Protect your reputation**

73 ✓ **Make sure authority is on board**

74 ✓ **Stay close to authority and always keep them informed**

75 ✓ **Attend to authority's warnings**

16 ✓ **Create and nourish your support network**

64 ✓ **Take care of your supporters**

38 ✓ **Involve the members of the system in the initiative**

81 ✓ **Constantly innovate and create exceptional value**

27 ✓ **Mobilize with enthusiasm**

34 ✓ **Create, score, and celebrate a stream of small victories**

28 ✓ **Sell the benefits of the initiative**

68 ✓ **As with a game of chess, think about your moves ahead of time and plan your strategy**

45 ✓ **Be unpredictable**

31 ✓ **Vigilantly monitor the system**

61 ✓ **Investigate to see if there is more to their resistance than meets the eye**

42 ✓ **Don't let conflicts and diversions distract you**

36 ✓ **Double-check the sanity of the initiative**

33 ✓ **Debug the initiative**

54 ✓ **Success depends on doing the right thing, at the right time, and in the right way**

69 ✓ **Use patience, silence, and inaction wisely and strategically**

80 ✓ **Always be willing to learn**

39 ✓ **Plan and deliberate**

84 ✓ **Consider tactically putting your initiative on hold**

89 ✓ **Avoid conflict and head-on collisions when possible, but do what it takes to protect yourself and the initiative**

88 ✓ **Expose and discredit your opponents; don't blame them:**
If the majority of your constituents are resisting you because of false information, you will want to expose the source of misinformation and discredit them. This may help you back into the good graces of your constituency.

CONSTITUENTS: MALEVOLENT

As with your subordinates, any of your constituency who are harboring this level of intensity have withdrawn their support completely. However, unlike your subordinates, your constituents may have power over your fate. They may believe you have betrayed their loyalty.

They will try to sabotage and halt your progress. They may hire private investigators to pry into your personal life and gather information they can use to get their "revenge". They will make it about you and will target you personally. They may organize mass protests, and at this intensity the animosity they harbor for you may lead to chaotic, potentially dangerous, behavior. Since they are part of a group, they may fall prey to mob mentality, where the inhibition of personal responsibility fades away, and they may break the law to hurt you (e.g. vandalize your house, burn down the company factory). You will need to protect yourself.

There is something wrong with having your voters, consumers, or clientele harboring such intense resistance towards you. It rarely reaches this stage. It is only after you have refused to quit, listen to them, change your initiative or approach, or address their concerns altogether, that people may decide they need to resort to extreme measure to gain your attention, end your initiative, or both. Don't let it reach this stage, even with the minority of your constituents.

RECOMMENDED STRATEGIES/PRINCIPLES

58 ✓ **Reflect on the purpose of the initiative**

23 ✓ **Mentally and technically prepare yourself for the worst; it will get messy**

47 ✓ **Don't be faint-hearted or indecisive**

48 ✓ **Don't focus on winning — it is about fulfilling the purpose of the initiative**

83 ✓ **Protect your reputation**

73 ✓ **Make sure authority is on board**

74 ✓ **Stay close to authority and always keep them informed**

75 ✓ **Attend to authority's warnings**

76 ✓ **Be careful not to give authority a reason to "punish" you:**
If you lose your consistency, the organization will suffer, not just your purpose. This will be reason enough for your authority to punish you. Be careful.

16 ✓ **Create and nourish your support network:**
It is possible you will lose your support because your constituency may go to great lengths to harm you and anyone who supports you. To avoid such harm your support network may dissolve.

64 ✓ **Take care of your supporters:**
You need your supporters more than ever so make sure you take great care of them. They will help to protect you, since your survival may be at stake.

(66) ✓ **Work to minimize the damage**

(32) ✓ **Ask for help:**
You may consider asking some of your constituents to vouch for you and to try and get their malevolent cohorts to calm down. They may buy you enough time to show some positive results.

(7) ✓ **Over-communicate your interest in listening to their point of view**

(13) ✓ **Consider involving mediators**

(69) ✓ **Use patience, silence, and inaction wisely and strategically**

(41) ✓ **Let them negotiate for you**

(11) ✓ **Keep the fire contained**

(12) ✓ **Don't provoke them**

(54) ✓ **Success depends on doing the right thing, at the right time, and in the right way**

(53) ✓ **Do what is best for the system**

(84) ✓ **Consider tactically putting your initiative on hold**

(27) ✓ **Mobilize with enthusiasm**

(28) ✓ **Sell the benefits of the initiative**

(31) ✓ **Vigilantly monitor the system**

(61) ✓ **Investigate to see if there is more to their resistance than meets the eye**

(42) ✓ **Don't let conflicts and diversions distract you**

(59) ✓ **Be wary around people who have nothing to lose**

(1) ✓ **Ensure that any negativity doesn't become contagious**

(36) ✓ **Double-check the sanity of the initiative**

(33) ✓ **Debug the initiative**

(35) ✓ **Take responsibility for your mess**

(39) ✓ **Plan and deliberate**

(40) ✓ **Know when to confront**

(60) ✓ **Show your strength, but without provocation**

(24) ✓ **Fight with full force:**
If you are not facing the majority of your constituency, you may consider bringing in all your tools and tactics to the table when you confront them.

(44) ✓ **Use your opponents' mistakes**

(49) ✓ **Winning in confrontations demands self-discipline**

(55) ✓ **Know when to accept temporary defeat**

(62) ✓ **Involve relevant authorities**

(57) ✓ **Choose clarity or ambiguity, depending on the situation**

(68) ✓ **As with a game of chess, think about your moves ahead of time and plan your strategy**

(45) ✓ **Be unpredictable**

(80) ✓ **Always be willing to learn**

(89) ✓ **Avoid conflict and head-on collisions when possible, but do what it takes to protect yourself and the initiative**

(82) ✓ **Never fight fire with fire**

(88) ✓ **Expose and discredit your opponents; don't blame them**

ARCHENEMY SCENARIOS

This is going to be a short chapter, because it is simple and straightforward. This level of resistance has been separated out from the roles because of its extremity, and because similar strategies apply to dealing with this sort of opponent regardless of what role they play in your life.

I want to take this moment to express something important. Despite the existence of archenemies, you should not wear yourself out with paranoid thoughts and ideas. Most people who have an issue with you would not think of going to such extreme lengths to hurt you. In other words, it is rare (if ever) that you will find yourself facing such opposition, but it does happen, especially if you want to create major changes. Don't discount it, but don't obsess over it.

Your archenemy represents the most intense form of resistance, the most extreme form of animosity. In general, this is as personal as it is going to get. There is no legal, moral, or ethical boundary they will not cross. If they want to prevent your initiative, they will target all aspects of your life. At this level, the role only differs in how close the relationship is to you.

You must protect all the people who are tied to the initiative or to you. Your archenemies will target anything and anyone if it means that they can threaten you into submission. You need to protect your family, your personal circle, your supporters, and yourself. You must also do what is necessary to protect your initiative from their actions, otherwise it may come crashing down.

Take all the necessary precautions: 1) inform whoever is involved of the danger you are facing, and 2) inform the appropriate authorities, presenting evidence to support your claims.

Assume the worst, and multiple it many-fold. Anything you can think of, they might do, and more. There is no limit to the lengths they are willing to go. If you have skeletons in the closet and they know about them, they will come out. Never assume that your archenemies will operate within the boundaries of what you think is rational. Never say that they would not do something, or that going to such lengths would hurt them too. People at this intensity are willing to hurt themselves if it means that they can take you down with them.

In the movie *The Fog of War*, Robert McNamara, the secretary of defense during the *Cuban Missile Crisis* (1962), said that he later asked Fidel Castro if he would have gone as far as ordering a nuclear strike against the United States had the crisis escalated. Castro's reply was that he had already ordered a full nuclear attack on the US early in the crisis, and his instructions were to launch when the missiles were ready. McNamara was dumbstruck to hear that Castro had done this, knowing that it would have started a global nuclear war, and that American retaliation could wipe out Cuba.

History is full of examples where leaders have made major miscalculations when predicting what the "enemy" might do, because they try to apply common sense and rational thinking to their opponents. These miscalculations often resulted in defeats, catastrophes, and sometimes had fatal consequences.

Do whatever is necessary to defend yourself and your people, because it is a legitimate, legal, and moral right to do so. It can be difficult to deal with archenemies, but there are steps you can and should take to mitigate the damage they can do.

RECOMMENDED STRATEGIES/PRINCIPLES

47 ✓ **Don't be faint-hearted or indecisive:**
This will test every fiber of your resolve. If you are not prepared to deal with this intensity, you should immediately give up your initiative.

23 ✓ **Mentally and technically prepare yourself for the worst; it will get messy:**
Individuals at this intensity will be absolutely obsessed with bringing you down however they can. This is the messiest it is going to get. Prepare yourself mentally, emotionally, and physically.

16 ✓ **Create and nourish your support network:**
Make sure they are aware of the danger. Individuals at this intensity will target them too if it means bringing you down.

64 ✓ **Take care of your supporters:**
They are your responsibility. If you have supporters, you must do what you can to guard them.

53 ✓ **Do what is best for the system:**
If the resistance you are facing will bring too much harm to the system, you need to consider alternative routes, including abandoning the initiative.

54 ✓ **Success depends on doing the right thing, at the right time, and in the right way**

68 ✓ **As with a game of chess, think about your moves ahead of time and plan your strategy**

66 ✓ **Work to minimize the damage**

84 ✓ **Consider tactically putting your initiative on hold**

59 ✓ **Be wary around people who have nothing to lose**

31 ✓ **Vigilantly monitor the system:**
Both you and your supporters need to remain aware of everything that is going on around you, including your archenemy. They may not always be acting openly or in plain sight.

32 ✓ **Ask for help:**
Do not hesitate to ask anyone you believe can help you. There is too much at stake for you to shy away from help.

62 ✓ **Involve relevant authorities**

82 ✓ **Never fight fire with fire**

69 ✓ **Use patience, silence, and inaction wisely and strategically**

41 ✓ **Let them negotiate for you:**
In the rare event that you can get your archenemy to negotiate, you will want to let others handle it. It is too risky for you to negotiate with someone who wants to harm you personally.

15 ✓ **Maintain the momentum of your progress**

(83) ✓ **Protect your reputation:**
At this intensity individuals may go to extreme lengths to spread rumors and even to provide false evidence that will ruin your reputation.

(22) ✓ **Create some distance:**
In fact, you want to stay as far away as you can.

(39) ✓ **Plan and deliberate**

(40) ✓ **Know when to confront**

(44) ✓ **Use your opponents' mistakes:**
These mistakes will act as evidence that you may pass on to the relevant authorities.

(24) ✓ **Fight with full force:**
Don't hesitate to fight back but only if you are sure you can win. Don't attempt to fight them if there is even a small chance you will fail.

(35) ✓ **Take responsibility for your mess:**
If it has reached this stage of resistance because of a mistake on your part, you need to have the courage to admit you have done something damaging.

(55) ✓ **Know when to accept temporary defeat:**
If the resistance is too much, you will need to consider this strategy. Your initiative may not be worth potentially risking your survival over it.

(45) ✓ **Be unpredictable:**
This always applies at this intensity. Your archenemy must not know anything you are planning.

This constitutes the most intense form of resistance. You are now dealing with your enemy. However, this does not mean that you need to treat them any different than other opponents. Your interactions with them do change, of course, because you need to protect yourself, your supporters, and your initiative, but they are still human.

There are strategies/principles that are still considered fundamental to your interaction with your enemies. Given that this is a special case, I have outlined the 33 strategies and principles that remain fundamental in this most intense form of resistance. Please take them into consideration when you are formulating your plans to deal with your enemies.

Archenemy
Fundamental Strategies/Principles

4 Always be kind and courteous	**14** Stay focused on your purpose
9 Objectively diagnose the root of their resistance	**5** Always be compassionate and empathetic
18 Don't make it personal or take it personally	**67** Actively and authentically listen to all parties involved
52 Never humiliate your opponents	**43** Don't be provoked
6 Over-communicate	**19** Think creatively
63 Take care of yourself physically, mentally, emotionally, and spiritually	**21** Keep ego out of it
10 Be conscious of the cultural codes of conduct and protocols	**51** Never underestimate your opponents
17 Stay close to your support network	**86** Give credit to your supporters

Archenemy
Fundamental Strategies/Principles

65	Tailor your approach to your target audience	97	Don't allow your initiative to become an extension of yourself
95	Make smart use of your relationship network	20	Stay calm
96	Learn to live with the heat without internalizing it	90	Do favors
94	Adapt the tactics when necessary	93	Don't always revert to your default thinking
91	When mobilizing, target the mind and the heart	46	Expand your repertoire of options
92	Battles should be won before they are fought	103	Frequently review your map of existing and potential supporters, opponents, and authority
101	Make an accurate interpretation of the situation and the resistance	99	Stay close to your opponents
72	Use authority to gauge the system overall	100	Accept causalities publicly
50	Don't assume that you can always predict the moves of your opponents		

THE FIRST OPPONENT (YOU) SCENARIOS

The greatest resistance you face will probably come from within. It can keep you stuck, unable to move forward and grow, and it will weigh against any effort you make to let go of the current reality and create a better one for yourself. You need to shed this resistance, win this battle, and lead yourself to elevate your life.

It is normal for everyone to sometimes face resistance from within. We fear pain, failure, loss. Many of us are afraid to try something new because we might lose something in the process, or we might fail. Even if we know it is good for us, we freeze and postpone — we resist. We also experience bouts of self-doubt or low self-esteem. Sometimes we feel worthless. At other times, we might feel like we don't have enough energy to do anything. We may even feel that life has no meaning. It is in these moments that we may face negative thoughts (e.g. "I am not good enough", "no one could like me"), and sometimes more serious obstacles (e.g. self-sabotage, self-harm).

Although these feelings are normal, you will need to deal with your resistance. If you don't, you will remain stuck and stagnant, and you may even risk becoming worse, escalating your self-resistance, and forcing yourself to regress instead of grow.

How do you avoid self-resistance? It all starts with self-appreciation, self-respect, and self-love. You need to appreciate that you deserve to be happier and live a more fulfilled life. You need to respect yourself enough to work on improving your life, and you need to keep moving forward. Finally, you need to love who you are and grow from within, not for the sake of an external source, but for yourself. After all, if you don't think you deserve better, it will be difficult to strive for better. If you resist yourself, no one can push you to change until you deal with your own resistance.

Denying that you deserve better stems from not realizing your uniqueness, not realizing that you are loved, feeling powerless, or thinking that you are unable to handle your reality. All this is an illusion because in fact you are unique, you are loved, you are powerful, and you are capable of handling whatever life throws at you.

When it comes to your uniqueness, you have something special to offer and share with others. It is true that you might not be "better" than others, but that doesn't mean you are not unique. It doesn't matter what you are offering to others. It could be as simple as a beautiful smile. The point is that you need to believe there is no other person like you, and that within you lies a treasure that will improve the life of at least one other person.

If someone has ever thanked you for something you have done, then you have something to offer. Your life has meaning, and it is worthwhile. Your action(s) helped make this person's life easier.

When you consider whether you are loved, don't confuse it with being popular or the center of attention. This is often simply a shallow form of admiration, not love. To know that you are loved — which is an undeniable fact — you need only look at that one person in your life, be it a friend, sibling, parent, or soulmate, who has a deep admiration for you. It is in their eyes that you will see you are loved.

What about the challenges you have faced in life? Life may have thrown you curve ball after curve ball. How can you find the energy to keep growing if life will not let you? Nothing you go through now, or will go through in the future, should ever leave you stumped. There will be no situation you cannot handle, because our ability to overcome even the most difficult circumstances is strong beyond your imagination.

Throughout history, people have suffered unimaginable atrocities and calamities (e.g. wars, terrorism, slavery, natural disasters), yet they have been able to push through despite it being easier for them to give up. You might say that they were different, they were stronger than you. That would be premature. There is no doubt that it was their strength, conviction, relationships, and determination that got them through these horrors. However, the reality is that anything others can do, you can do too if you are determined. As long as it is humanly possible, you can rise to the occasion and handle whatever life throws your way.

Even after the inferno of forest fires seemingly decimates all life forms, life will always return after the first rain

Don't let these obstacles stand in your way. All those negative feelings — which bring you down, make you doubt yourself, or lead you away from the belief that your life is special — are just obstacles that you can overcome. It is an illusion to believe in those feelings and thoughts. Your mind is using psychological "warfare" to faze you. No matter how tough it may seem, remember that you can handle it.

The flames of the fire are full of energy, because they keep the fire alive

We are designed to grow, to explore, to understand, to solve problems, to be creative, to adapt, to forget, and to overcome suffering. All we need to do is remove the artificial obstacles, the psychological games our minds play, and let the force of life within us — that can only be positive — take over. Think of it like gravity setting the path for water to flow and form streams, rivers, and waterfalls. Water does not have to do anything except allow gravity to act. The moment that you remove the obstacles impeding the flow, gravity will draw the course and water will follow and find its path. The same happens with you. The moment you remove the obstacles preventing your progress, you will flow naturally towards growth.

If billions of people have managed to build a life and survive through unimaginable horrors, yet still find the ability to smile, you can do it too. Don't think any less of yourself, just strip away the obstacles standing in your way and let the gravity of your growth take hold as you continue in your journey.

Service to others is another way you can see your true potential. The more you serve, the more you share. The more you share, the more you give. The more you give, the more you help others. The more you help others, the more you will feel that you can also help yourself.

None of this will work if you don't take full responsibility for your life. While others can help you, you need to help yourself first, and this starts with you believing that you can do that. Remember the positive moments in your life, the moments where you helped others, the challenges and fears you have overcome, your inner strength, and how humanity throughout time has come overcome multiple crises, disasters, and atrocities. You need to reflect on your true potential in overcoming the internal resistance.

People will tell you that you deserve a better life, but listening to them without believing it yourself will not encourage you to take the actions that will help you grow. You need a deep, deep conviction that you deserve to be happy. It is only this depth of self-appreciation, self-respect, and self-love that will empower you to change, to let go of whatever is holding you back, such as:

- Bad, damaging habits.

- Negative thinking — thoughts that are demeaning, self-deprecating, and undermining.

- Defeatist mindsets and worldviews.

Only when you let go of anything that is keeping you stuck, or moving you backwards, can you begin to replace the negatives with positives. When you believe in yourself and your capabilities, you can begin to adopt empowering thoughts, mindsets, and world-views, which can then drive you to strengthen your good habits. In short, this can help you find the strength to overcome any form of resistance that stands in your way, even if the source of that resistance is within you.

We want to change, and work for it, but the fear of the loss we might incur keeps us from trying

When you are convinced that you deserve better, dealing with the resistance within you — the scared, self-doubting version of yourself — becomes easier. Taking the first steps towards elevating your life and changing your reality becomes easier.

Once you have decided that you want more, and that you deserve to enjoy life, your conviction and self-belief will keep you moving forward even when you doubt yourself (which will happen). They will remind you that you do deserve better and that you are willing to work for it. Even if you are not sure you will succeed, you will still find it easier to try. This mindset will drive your journey forward: you deserve to live a full life. This is the main motivator, and the most powerful one at that.

You need to know how to deal with yourself as the enemy so that you can successfully deal with other forms of resistance. When you are facing resistance from external forces, the stress and tension of that conflict will make you doubt yourself and may bring out your demons and insecurities.

Sometimes you might fail to deal with external resistance, not because you cannot handle it, but because you are doubtful, scared, insecure, and self-critical. This will paralyze you and prevent you from bringing forward the better version of yourself, the one that is capable of dealing with external resistance. You cannot win over others with a defeated spirit. If your opponents are able to rile you up and, even for a moment, make you doubt yourself, they may win.

It is also important to remember that, in all situations, your self-resistance will not only affect your life but the lives of others around you. Whatever state you are in, it will be contagious. If you are brimming with positivity, those around you will catch on and feel it too. If you are exuding negativity, those around you will follow suit. You should avoid being the source of negativity for the people around you.

If you allow your negative mindset, worldviews, insecurities, and fears to dictate your life, then you are not the only one that will suffer. Your friends, family, colleagues, etc., will also suffer, especially if they depend on you. The moment you stop yourself from moving forward is the moment you decide either to halt the progress of those around you or to let them go on their own journey. In both cases, you will suffer.

Remember that we are all fighting the same battles, each one of us trying to live a well-deserved, fulfilled, peaceful, and joyful life. Change the way in which you see yourself, believe that you deserve to be better. This will help you overcome internal resistance, and by extension, external resistance.

It is time that you trump the enemy within, the obstacles standing in the way of your growth, so that the best of you can surface and conquer. Only through self-leadership can you hope to lead others, for you cannot mobilize others towards growth if you are unable to do the same for yourself. It is your right and duty to develop and live a happy life so that you can be the voice of positivity, and a contagious positive presence for those around you and those who are connected to you.

This is a special role, and as such requires its own strategies. The strategies in this category aim to help you develop and overcome internal resistance. Take your time and read through them carefully.

Remember that you cannot bring about significant change and lead others if you cannot lead yourself. You owe it to yourself to live the best life you can.

FIRST OPPONENT (YOU) STRATEGIES/PRINCIPLES

(A) Focus on purpose

The first, most obvious, step you can take is to clarify your purpose. With a clear understanding of what makes you tick, you will not only be able to guide yourself towards progress, but you will also enjoy the journey of self-leadership.

Try to make a list of the activities, skills, talents, etc. that you have, and the things you enjoy. These may not be clear from the start, because clarifying your purpose can be a difficult journey. Listing your skills may help you to dig deeper and remember what you are passionate about, or what used to make you happy.

It will allow you to start trying things out. If you find that you are good at something (e.g. you are an inspirational communicator) and that you love to do it, you are a step close to clarifying your purpose. This will help the uncertainty fade away, and you will inspire and lead yourself forward. The next thing you have to consider is what you have to offer and how it could benefit others. Remember, purpose is **putting your uniqueness in the service of others.** If people benefit from your uniqueness (e.g. people's lives are improved by hearing your inspirational video blogs), this will be the key to finding your purpose. It will also give your life motivation and meaning.

It may help to ask yourself:

- What is it that you want from life?

- Where do you want to live? With whom?

- What do you want to do?

- How do you want to live?

- What can you do for others?

When you find the answers to these questions, make sure you start acting accordingly, in ways that transform your answers into your reality.

(B) Decide on your identity

Who are you? How do you see yourself? Spend some time reflecting on how you define yourself in different moods and at different moments. You may sometimes see yourself as a good person, and at other times you might focus only on your flaws. Those are transitional and contextual. The key here is not to focus on the context, but to take an overall mindset. Truly look at yourself and consider this simple yet complex question: who are YOU?

You may say that you are compassionate, kind, caring, strict, assertive, self-conscious, confident, etc. You may focus on your worldviews and values. You might believe in "karmic justice", "all people deserve to be treated equally," "relationships are essential for a happy life," or "family always comes first." It doesn't matter what you focus on, whether it's your worldviews, values, traits, attributes, flaws, habits, etc. It is important that you truly examine yourself, be fair to yourself, and be truthful with yourself. This way you can examine not only who you are, but who you potentially could be.

Your friends and family can help highlight the blind spots you have about yourself. Your most trusted and loved companions may exaggerate your virtues, but even the exaggeration has an element of truth. Take their words in whatever way you wish, but do not dismiss them. Instead, register them in your mind and reflect on them. This will help you to make a fair judgment about your identity.

Love who you are and who you could be. Put yourself in the shoes of the best version you can be at any moment. With that perspective, describe who you are. It is this perspective that you need to consider, not one that brings even a hint of self-doubt.

Take all this information and make an honest, truthful, compassionate, and loving decision about how you wish to define your identity, flaws and all.

(C) Surround yourself with people who push you forward

Sometimes, no matter how hard you try, you just cannot find your motivation. In this case, you should look to those around you to help nudge you forward. If you are surrounded by people who constantly bring you down, you will find yourself stuck and demoralized, which won't help your purpose.

In order to avoid that, you will want to make sure you choose a group of individuals who not only focus on their own progress, but who also motivate and help you to do the same. If you are surrounded by people who are successful in their work, you will be encouraged to work harder yourself.

Some of you may say that seeing those around us succeed may actually make us feel worse, perhaps inadequate. This could be true, but if you find friends who care enough to look out for you, they will also nudge you forward. In addition, research has shown that simply observing other people donating to good causes or helping others out can motivate us to follow suit. Sometimes just hearing about other people's success stories helps to push us forward. Therefore, surrounding yourself with positive, encouraging, and supportive individuals will help give you the push that you need to overcome your own internal resistance.

(D) You need to decide if you are happy enough, or if you deserve a more fulfilling life

Take some time to consider what you are doing in life:

- Are you unhappy with your life?

- Would you like to change the path your life is currently taking?

- Do you believe you deserve to live a more fulfilling life?

If you say yes to any of these, you are taking the first step towards realizing you need to change your lifestyle. Remember that change cannot happen successfully if you are not willing to give it your all.

Unfortunately, sometimes we lose sight of what we truly deserve, which is to live a more fulfilling life. Keeping the above questions in mind will stop you from falling into a routine that is comfortable but not really fulfilling. They will also help you wake up if you are leading a dysfunctional life.

At this moment, make a decision about whether or not you believe you deserve to be happy. Even if the world thinks you do, it is only you that can make the decision that moves you in the direction of fulfillment and happiness.

(E) Accept that it is your right to be happy

Living a happy life is your unconditional right. You don't need to earn it. Therefore, it is your right to fight for your happiness

Living a happy life doesn't mean being perfect, not making mistakes, or having a spotless record. It doesn't mean that you never feel fear or sadness, that you are never discouraged, that you never regret things or miscalculate. The deeper meaning of being happy comes from accepting your humanity with all its moments of brilliance and vulnerability. You have to accept that being human — which means being imperfect — is not a crime, sin, weakness, or something to feel ashamed of. In spite of this imperfection and because of it, it is your legal, moral, spiritual, and divine right to be happy.

Consider what the *Decleration of Independance* of the United States says about happiness: "the pursuit of happiness" is considered to be an "unalienable right".

Furthermore, look at all major religions. When they broach the subject of happiness, they don't talk about temporary happiness, but eternal happiness. This is usually represented in the concept of a transcendental, higher place, such as Heaven or Nirvana.

Therefore, know that you deserve to be happy, and more importantly accept that it is your divine right to be. This conviction will help fuel your growth and aid you in the battle against the resistance within.

Defeat all forms of resistance and remove all obstacles and negativity that would undermine this right, whether these are people or circumstances

(F)   ## Read books and listen to stories about people who inspire you

---

Inspiration is not limited to the physical. It comes from virtual sources too. If there is someone or some group out there whom you know has an inspiring effect on you, take an in-depth look at their lives. If possible, read books about them, watch documentaries about them, look up news articles and footage. Whatever medium you choose, if they are a true inspiration to you, tap into that resource and be inspired.

People can have a profound effect on us. If they are someone you hold in high regard, their positive actions may have a tremendous lasting effect on you. They will motivate you to lead yourself towards the reality you know deep down that you deserve.

(G) Take care of your body: eat, sleep, and move

"My body is my temple". You may have heard that before from a friend, family member, colleague, or the actor/actress up on screen. It is important that you take care of your body. If you do not, you will limit your functionality. You know that you must eat, but remember to eat healthily. You know you must sleep, but try to maintain a healthy sleep schedule. You know you must move, because exercise helps stimulate the mind and may increase your life-span, so implement and stick to an exercise routine that works for you.

You may have bad habits (e.g. smoking) that are harming your body. You may be the type of person who loves to binge eat, or you might enjoy being a couch potato. Everyone has their own lifestyle, but if you do not find a balance that helps nurture your body, you may face major complications down the line. You will also affect your brain if you don't take good care of yourself. Focus on the essentials for life (sleep, eat, move), not only because you need to survive, but also so that you can function at your optimal level, and work towards a better reality.

(H) Pray, play, meditate, and spend more time in nature

Meditation has been scientifically shown to have many physical and psychological benefits. It boosts your immunity, reduces stress, enhances memory, increases emotional regulation, allows you to gain a better understanding of yourself, and more. Meditating may help increase positive emotions while decreasing negative emotions. It may also help you better understand who you are, and gain control over your thoughts, feelings, and actions.

Consider engaging in fun activities. Whether you like sports, board games, or group play activities, you will experience enjoyment and positive emotions, and you will also reap social, physical, and psychological benefits. When you play with others and enjoy their company, you:

- Increase your chances of meeting and connecting with people.

- Laugh, which helps to decrease stress and blood pressure.

- Increase your creative abilities.

- Increase your levels of productivity.

Fun provides benefits in all facets of your life. Google provides its employees with facilities where they can play and have fun. This actually increases their creativity and cooperation, which increases their productivity and leads to more innovations, ultimately helping the company grow, and keeping its employees satisfied.

When you are experiencing internal resistance, use the above strategies to try and deal with it. Have fun with others, engage in meditation, prayer, or spend some more time in nature — this will help your mental and physical health, lower stress, and enhance your performance and creative problem-solving capabilities. You will be able to pinpoint what is resisting you and deal with it, easing your journey and increasing the chance of leading yourself towards a better reality.

I Watch motivational videos and speeches

Watch videos, documentaries, and speeches where people relate their life stories, and explain how they courageously overcame horrible situations. At the time, they may have felt like nothing short of a miracle could get them out of the situation, but they tackled those obstacles and removed them from their lives. If they were able to do it, you can too; it just takes courage and self-belief.

Don't blame yourself for feeling pessimistic, especially if you have gone through a difficult time. While it's important to deal with your own resistance, you must address it positively and be kind to yourself. Remember that watching other people succeed can motivate us to follow in their footsteps and use their techniques to improve our own lives.

J Ask close friends and family for help

It takes courage to admit that you need help. Many of us would rather deal with our issues on our own in case others think we are weak or fail to understand us.

However, sometimes you need to approach others because you cannot motivate yourself.

The help supporters can offer comes in many different forms, such as advice, compliments, pointing out the positive aspects in your life, recalling happy, shared memories, listing all your skills and achievements, taking you to workshops, talks or seminars, or just listening while you talk. Any of these or a combination of them might be the boost you need. Utilizing your support network can work wonders in terms of getting you back on track.

If you find just one person who believes in you and your potential, that may be enough to help you see that you are capable of more than you think, that you are strong, resilient, loved, and unique.

(K) Consider hiring a Life Coach

If you find that you are unable to get unstuck on your own, you might want to consider hiring a life coach (a neutral party), who will work with you to get you where you want to be in life.

The advantage of having a neutral party in this situation is that you do not need to talk to friends or family if you are finding this difficult, and you will get a fresh perspective, rather than the one your immediate group can offer. Some of us may feel hesitant about asking a stranger for help, but when you're struggling, it's important to use all the tools at your disposal. Instead of letting your resistance control your life, find someone who can help you break it down. A Life Coach can do that, tailoring their approach to specifically fit your needs, requests, and resistance.

(L) Attend self-development seminars

It could be that you are stuck because there is some skill, mindset, or habit that you need to either learn or get rid of. Sometimes all you need is some help from people who have already succeeded in a certain area.

Consider joining a self-development course or attending a self-development seminar. This will move you into a new space and context, which might help you progress with your life. You can work on improving your skill set or shedding negative habits and worldviews. These seminars are geared towards helping you develop and achieve your goals.

In addition, when you watch speakers and lecturers share their expertise, their stories, or their conundrums with the rest of you, you may feel more motivated to overcome your own difficulties and get to where you want to go.

(M) Make a list of your positive contributions

It helps at times to remind yourself of what you have done for others. Sit down with yourself, or others who know you well, and make a list of the positive contributions you have made in other people's lives. No matter how small or insignificant you think they are, add them to the list. You may be surprised to find how small positive contributions eventually add up.

Think of a time when someone expressed gratitude for something positive you did for them. Consider the moment you heard the words "Thank you" (or something similar). These moments signify an action on your part that enhanced the life of another person, even if only for a moment.

Your ability and willingness to help another person by saying or doing something positive for them is a testament to your capabilities. Remember how you felt after they thanked you, hold on to that feeling, and use it to traverse current and future obstacles.

(N) Volunteer for a cause you care about

Try to extend beyond yourself and help others. When you act in the service of others, you will not only benefit them, but you will benefit yourself too. When you do something to improve the life of another individual, it will give you feelings of satisfaction, pride, and it will also highlight your uniqueness and capabilities. Added to this, you will likely feel gratitude from the individual. Focus on those moments and you will see that if you can help others, you can help yourself.

Stepping outside of your normal routine and distancing yourself from your own concerns can be a good way to overcome internal resistance. Studies have shown that helping other people or doing volunteer work helps to improve our physical and mental health, increase our sense of well-being and self-esteem, and gives us a general feeling of satisfaction. Therefore, when you are feeling stuck, try putting your focus on helping others; this may give you a good boost, both physically and mentally.

Remember, service is a large part of purpose, so this may even help you clarify your purpose.

Seek professional help (e.g. therapy, counseling)

There is no shame in considering professional help. The term "professional help" tends to have a negative connotation, but remember that it is natural to depend on others, and many great individuals had to hit rock bottom before they got their lives back on track. However, don't wait for that to happen. Instead, ask for help. If you feel that you need some assistance getting back on your feet, or shedding those negative thoughts and resisting obstacles, then seek some professional help in the form of therapy, group counseling, etc.

A therapist may be able to help you:

1. *Reconcile with friends and family.* It is possible that as you are going through your dilemma, you push your close friends and family away, sometimes to the point of ruining the relationship. With the help of your therapist/counselor, you may be able to convince your lost friends and family to give you another chance. The people closest to you may actually encourage you to continue with your therapist, joining in on your sessions and offering you support.

2. *Guide you out of the fog of resistance.* Therapists, counselors, and other professionals can act as your guide through the thick fog of resistance. Unfortunately, there will be times when resistance will blur your vision, and so you will not know which path you need to take. However, with the help of a professional you can figure out how to get your life back on track.

3.   *Open new doors for future opportunities.* When you get your life sorted out, you will be more prepared to take on new things, such as: seeking new job opportunities, following your dreams, checking a couple of things off your bucket list, etc. With a fresh state of mind and with guided assistance, you can do whatever you want to do, and start aspiring to new goals.

4.   *Clarify and revitalize your purpose.* With less issues to worry about, you can turn your focus back onto your purpose. In fact, your therapist or counselor may encourage you in the journey of revitalizing your purpose. They will help you find meaning in life, and will aid you in tapping into your uniqueness. Ultimately, professional help may breathe life into you and allow you to reach your full potential both physically and mentally.

(P) Double-check your interpretations

Your thoughts, feelings, and actions depend on your interpretation of any given situation. If your interpretation is negative, this will lead to negative thoughts, which lead to negative feelings, and eventually you will act in a negative way. You might start turning down new opportunities and/or ruining your relationships with others. If you have a positive interpretation, this will lead to positive thoughts, which lead to positive feelings, and then to positive actions. Everything stems from how you interpret the situation.

Interpretations are prone to blind spots and errors. All our life experiences, lessons, values, worldviews, old pains, etc., tend to work as filters for the information coming from our environments, and this leads to specific interpretations. It is a subjective process, so you should try and be aware of what filters you are putting on situations.

Start by studying where your interpretation comes from. Is it a demeaning or self-defeating belief? If it is, try to take a step back and see if your interpretation is based on reality, or whether your mind is playing tricks on you. It may help to ask yourself these questions:

- What are the facts? What do they say?

- What does the past say? Are there similar events in my history?

- Does the evidence, considered from an objective view, corroborate my interpretation?

Make sure you are honest and truthful with your answers. The enemy is the negative interpretation that comes from low self-worth, self-confidence, and self-esteem. You need to challenge it, and consider alternative interpretations: what are the other possible readings of this scenario?

Ask yourself to what extent your interpretation will move you forward. To what extent will it make you a whole, joyful person? If it is useful and realistic, keep it. If it isn't, forget about it.

Another thing you can do to double-check your interpretation is to ask somebody who knows you well to review it, to act as a second pair of eyes and offer you another perspective. They can work with you and help you analyze the situation and the accuracy of your interpretation.

Always question and analyze your version of things, because your true internal resistance lies in there. It is the dysfunctional mindset that is the enemy. When you question your filters, you have an opportunity to check the facts and see if they support that interpretation. If they don't, you need to find another interpretation, but if they do, you can address the situation and deal with it accordingly.

(Q) Do what you love

Try to do what you love and see how happy that makes you feel. When you are doing something that you know you enjoy, something that lifts and lightens your heart, it will seem like the obstacles fade away, at least momentarily. However, it is not enough to lose yourself in something you love without solving the root of the issue.

The good news is that doing what you love will highlight the positivity within you, and all those negative obstacles that are fueling your internal resistance will seem easier to tackle. Use that positivity to overcome the obstacles, so that you can continue moving towards growth.

(R) Be patient with yourself

Try to hold steady and be patient. Sometimes, all it takes is to wait a difficult situation out, stand your ground, and be ready to push forward when the chance presents itself.

"Patience is a virtue" for a reason. When you wait, you will allow the initial stress and panic to calm a little, after which you can actually take a step back and look at the resistance you are facing, study it, and eventually ascertain exactly how to overcome it.

When you feel like things are never going to get better, don't give in to despair. Instead, hold steady, be patient, and you will figure out a way to rise above your difficulties, no matter how hard this seems at first.

(S) Face your fears

Try to face your fears and see how easily they become a thing of the past. Remember all your childhood fears, and how terrifying they felt at the time. Think of how you managed to progress through them, and how you eventually grew up to be the person you are at this moment.

If you were able to overcome terrifying fears when you were just a vulnerable and fragile child, you can definitely handle life's obstacles now that you have grown up. You are now stronger, wiser, and more experienced, so don't stop when you start to feel scared. Instead, gather up some of that strength, wisdom, and experience to overcome your internal resistance and move past whatever terrifying event you may be going through.

Take things one small step at a time, but confront your fears as you have done in the past. Start out in shallow waters, where there is little risk of drowning, and take baby steps toward the deeper end.

When you can swim and float, it will not matter how deep the water beneath you is

(T) Stand up and assert your right to a good life

You have the right to a good life. Make sure that right is known to the people around you through:

- **Your Words.** Make it clear to those standing in your way that you will not accept anything less than what is within your rights.

- **Your Actions.** Do whatever you can to make sure that your actions bring you happiness. Don't do something that will push you further away from the life you deserve, but work towards making it a reality.

- **Your Decisions.** Make the decision to remove all the obstacles that stand in your way. Take the decision to move forward and create an elevated, fulfilled life.

(U) Recall the times you triumphed over challenges

Reflect on the strength that got you to where you are today, despite all the challenges that you have had to overcome. If you stick to the facts and remain objective, you will see that you are capable of more than you give yourself credit for.

Life rarely deals you a perfect hand. There will have been some moments in your life when you thought, "Why is this happening to me?" "How in the world am I going to get past this?" or "This is too hard; should I just give up?" Despite that, you will still have overcome many of those challenges.

If you look back at them, you might find that, in retrospect, some of them appear so easy that you laugh about your past worries and stress. These moments are the records of your strength, the tally of your triumph. Looking at them can reinforce your belief that you can deal with all present and future obstacles.

(V) Take care of a pet or garden

Sometimes it can help to take care of another living being, so considering buying or adopting a pet. Pets have been shown to decrease stress, encourage exercise, boost cardiovascular health, help build strong social relationships, improve resilience and self-confidence, and they also serve as excellent companions — you avoid feeling lonely. All in all, they can increase your physical and mental health, allowing you to feel better about yourself and helping you overcome whatever obstacles and challenges lie ahead.

If you are not an animal-lover, consider tending to a garden. Being outside exposes you to Vitamin D, which is an essential nutrient for humans. Spending more time in nature can decrease your stress levels and boosts your overall mood, increase healthy eating, and can be a good way to build relationships with neighbors. Therefore, it can improve your physical and mental health, and make it easier for you to overcome your internal resistance.

(W) Keep a daily journal of any positive thoughts or actions

It might help to keep a physical record of the good things in your life. This means that you don't have to rely on your mind to recall the positive aspects in your life, which is good if it has the tendency to play tricks on you, especially when you are going through a rough patch. Consider keeping a daily journal, where you can catalogue all the positive events you have experienced, thoughts you have had, and actions you have taken.

You can carry it around, and jot down every positive occurrence. Alternatively, you can reflect on the day when the memories are still fresh, and write down any relevant positive information. If you didn't experience anything noteworthy, sit and think about your life overall. For instance, if at the moment you believe you are a caring person, jot that down — it counts as a positive thought.

When you are feeling down, or you are going through bouts of self-doubt, you can refer back to your journal and see the positivity in your life. You can see your accomplishments, your true beliefs, your attributes and traits, or your benevolent actions.

(X) Don't isolate yourself

Try as hard as you can not to isolate yourself from others. Healthy relationships are key to maintaining a healthy lifestyle. If you truly wish to triumph over your resistance, do what you can to be around people.

In addition, try to avoid feeling alone when you are in a crowded place. If you visit a communal place, whether it's a workplace, school, spiritual establishment, restaurant, café, bar, etc., don't spend time alone. If you can, try to talk to and interact with others around you. If you are too shy to do so, look at what other people are doing. You never know when you will see something that will make you smile or laugh.

Human connections can increase your chances of a longer life by 50%, boost your immune system, make you more understanding, empathetic, cooperative, etc.

(Y) Do things you have always wanted to do, even if you don't feel like it

Is there something you always wished you could do? Do you have a bucket list? If so, it might be time to consider checking something off that list. It could be anything, like traveling, going for a hike, adopting a pet, running a marathon, starting a book club, or opening a restaurant. If you feel you don't have the time or energy, choose something that won't overwhelm you.

Give something new a try, especially when you don't feel like it. Procrastination can be the subtlest form of resistance. Don't try to convince yourself that you have no time, or that you will do it later. If you fail to follow through, those negative feelings of regret will pour in, and your failure will just add to the list of internal resisters. Instead, think about what you want to do and do it. The sense of accomplishment will boost your morale and serve as one more testament to your capabilities.

(Z) Travel to and visit as many new places as you can

Consider planning a trip to a new country, or even just a new region. Try to explore places whenever you get a chance. It will refresh your mind and your soul. It will temporarily distract you from your issues, allowing you to take a break from your current environment, and letting your mind reboot. Clear and refreshed, you may be better equipped to deal with your internal resistance.

When you experience new places, cultures, communities, etc., you will stimulate your curiosity, learning, and trying new things. This overall sense of "newness" will give you a broader perspective on life, one that will help you tackle those inner demons and insecurities.

You will also get a chance to meet new people, and possibly build relationships with future friends. You may see things that inspire you. You may hear other people's stories, and learn about how they have overcome hardships in life. Their histories might give you a new perspective that helps you deal with your own issues.

You might even fall in love with the new place and decide to move there, getting a fresh start to revitalize yourself. Traveling can rejuvenate you.

Remember that traveling is not an excuse to run away from your problems. This is the type of resistance that comes from within, and so you must address it, not run from it.

YOU: PASSIVE

At this intensity, you are just "average". You are not enthusiastic, but you are also not negative or hurtful. You are quite flat. On the graph of your life, you would be considered on the border between betterment and growth, and negative thinking and self-deprecation. You are not excited, but you are not apathetic or lethargic.

If we were to consider you being in the ocean, at this stage of resistance you would not be swimming forward, but you would be staying afloat. You would be drifting with the waves, having a great time one day, and a bad time another day. Overall, you would be moving back and forth around the same spot.

Somewhere down the line, you might feel that you want more out of life, but you might also feel that there is no incentive to move forward. It can be difficult to get out of a routine and abandon many of your habits for the sake of moving forward.

The good news is that this is the easiest form of self-resistance to handle. All you need is to give yourself a small push. Start by finding something that captures your heart, something you are passionate about. This will automatically give you a boost, a sort of renewing and refreshing energy.

RECOMMENDED STRATEGIES/PRINCIPLES

(A) ✓ **Focus on purpose**

(D) ✓ **You need to decide if you are happy enough, or if you deserve a more fulfilling life**

(E) ✓ **Accept that it is your right to be happy**

(Q) ✓ **Do what you love**

(G) ✓ **Take care of your body: eat, sleep, and move**

(H) ✓ **Pray, play, meditate, and spend more time in nature**

(T) ✓ **Stand up and assert your right to a good life**

(M) ✓ **Make a list of your positive contributions**

(F) ✓ **Read books and listen to stories about people who inspire you**

(I) ✓ **Watch motivational videos and speeches**

(L) ✓ **Attend self-development seminars**

(N) ✓ **Volunteer for a cause you care about**

(Y) ✓ **Do things you have always wanted to do, even if you don't feel like it**

(Z) ✓ **Travel to and visit as many new places as you can**

YOU: PASSIVE-AGGRESSIVE

Have you ever been the pessimist in your group? Have you ever done something fully believing that you would not succeed? There will be times when your hesitation is accompanied by negative worldviews such as "life is unfair" or "I am always dealt a bad hand". There is no doubt that you may have faced some difficult challenges in your lifetime, possibly some so difficult that they changed your outlook on life.

Your values and habits have adapted to your negative world-view, and, as a result, you are skeptical and cynical about yourself; you are having self-doubts. These can be so serious that even when you do partake in a new activity or opportunity, you tell yourself you are doomed to fail. This mentality will then affect how your approach the opportunity or activity and you probably will fail. Then you will use that as evidence that you knew this would happen from the start. In fact, there is a psychological term to describe this exact situation: *self-fulfilling prophecy.*

If we consider the graph of your life, you would be in the negative quadrant now. You are doubting yourself, your abilities, and whether or not you deserve to live a purposeful, fulfilled life. As such, it will be harder to deal with this type of resistance, especially if you consider that your skepticism is coming from embedded, self-defeating beliefs. The roots of your resistance are more deeply entrenched than in the passive intensity.

Let's return to our ocean analogy. At this intensity, you may want to swim or float, but a part of you is weighing you down, so much so that you are barely floating.

If you find yourself resisting in this way, you should recognize that resistance and try to stop it from escalating to anything worse. Remember, you need to figure out how to convince yourself that you deserve better, because only then can you pull the roots of resistance out and move forward.

RECOMMENDED STRATEGIES/PRINCIPLES

(A) ✓ **Focus on purpose**

(B) ✓ **Decide on your identity**

(D) ✓ **You need to decide if you are happy enough, or if you deserve a more fulfilling life**

(E) ✓ **Accept that it is your right to be happy**

(T) ✓ **Stand up and assert your right to a good life**

(G) ✓ **Take care of your body: eat, sleep, and move**

(H) ✓ **Pray, play, meditate, and spend more time in nature**

(Q) ✓ **Do what you love**

(P) ✓ **Double-check your interpretations**

(R) ✓ **Be patient with yourself**

(S) ✓ **Face your fears**

(U) ✓ **Recall the times you triumphed over challenges**

(M) ✓ **Make a list of your positive contributions**

(C) ✓ **Surround yourself with people who push you forward**

(F) ✓ **Read books and listen to stories about people who inspire you**

(I) ✓ **Watch motivational videos and speeches**

(L) ✓ **Attend self-development seminars**

(N) ✓ **Volunteer for a cause you care about**

(W) ✓ **Keep a daily journal of any positive thoughts or actions**

(Y) ✓ **Do things you have always wanted to do, even if you don't feel like it**

(V) ✓ **Take care of a pet or garden**

(Z) ✓ **Travel to and visit as many new places as you can**

YOU: ACTIVE

Was there a moment in your life when you shot down opportunities you knew were good for you? At that moment, did you say to yourself that you were not good enough? Were you ever self-deprecating (e.g. "I suck" or "Nobody likes me")?

It is possible that your life experiences have dealt you a bad hand and this has come to dominate your thoughts and feelings. This will work against you, preventing you from seeking opportunities, shooting them down before you have a chance to test yourself. If you are not willing to give new opportunities a try, you will never be able to prove to yourself that you are in fact good enough.

This form of internal resistance can be quite damaging to your journey of survival and growth. At this intensity, you are stuck with dysfunctional habits. Your self-doubting and self-deprecating beliefs are now deeply entrenched, and the roots of your resistance are beginning to spread. You risk ending up in a cycle that could easily spiral towards deeper doubts, self-pity, lack of confidence, etc., and this will intensify your resistance even further.

This is dangerous because you are actively engaging in practices that are harmful. Added to this, your negative thinking has spun into exaggerated statements, which will further fuel your dysfunctional patterns. You need to understand that at this stage, you might be making choices that are not only resisting your progress but are actually hurting you. In short, you are actively making matters worse for yourself.

For instance, someone who eats immense quantities of unhealthy food, smokes, and spend hours as a couch potato is actively hurting themselves. If they don't decide to change, no one will be able to convince them otherwise.

At this intensity, the weights on your shoulder are quite heavy, and you are not only fighting to stay afloat, but actually gasping for air. As you push up, your lack of self-belief and your negative actions are pushing you down hard. You sink, hold your breath, and then finally you get to break the surface. Make sure you shed some of those weights as soon as you can; you at least deserve to float.

Unfortunately, there may be moments in your life where you feel you cannot do it alone. The thoughts have taken hold and you are finding it difficult to get rid of them. You will need to be willing to ask for help and agree to put in the necessary work on your end. Otherwise, you will find it difficult to get your life back on track. Therefore, let others help pull you out so you can then lead yourself towards fulfilling your purpose. Only then can you deal with your internal resistance, but it will need patience, effort, and the willingness to change and ask for help.

RECOMMENDED STRATEGIES/PRINCIPLES

(A) ✓ **Focus on purpose**

(B) ✓ **Decide on your identity**

(E) ✓ **Accept that it is your right to be happy**

(C) ✓ **Surround yourself with people who push you forward**

(J) ✓ **Ask close friends and family for help**

(P) ✓ **Double-check your interpretations**

(T) ✓ **Stand up and assert your right to a good life**

(G) ✓ **Take care of your body: eat, sleep, and move**

(H) ✓ **Pray, play, meditate, and spend more time in nature**

(Q) ✓ **Do what you love**

(R) ✓ **Be patient with yourself**

(S) ✓ **Face your fears**

(U) ✓ **Recall the times you triumphed over challenges**

(M) ✓ **Make a list of your positive contributions**

(F) ✓ **Read books and listen to stories about people who inspire you**

(I) ✓ **Watch motivational videos and speeches**

(K) ✓ **Consider hiring a Life Coach**

(L) ✓ **Attend self-development seminars**

(N) ✓ **Volunteer for a cause you care about**

(V) ✓ **Take care of a pet or garden**

(W) ✓ **Keep a daily journal of any positive thoughts or actions**

(Y) ✓ **Do things you have always wanted to do, even if you don't feel like it:**
You may not be able to do this alone, so consider asking your family and friends to do these activities with you. They may encourage you when you need it most.

(Z) ✓ **Travel to and visit as many new places as you can**

YOU: ACTIVE-AGGRESSIVE

What happens when your resistance gets aggressive? When you begin to deliberately hurt yourself? Or you intentionally abuse your bad habits? Did you ever enthusiastically sabotage yourself, your career, or other aspects of your life? Was there a point in your life when it seemed like you had hit rock bottom? The emotional toll such an event takes on you is heavy to say the least. If you find that you are refusing one opportunity after another and indulging in your bad habits solely to escape what you are feeling, it may be hard to turn things around and start responding positively.

The roots of your resistance are so deeply entrenched that you cannot pull them out with your own two hands. In the ocean analogy, you are actively adding more weights to your shoulders, not bothering to swim, swallowing water, and only pushing upwards when you need to breathe.

When you active-aggressively work against yourself, it is less like you are falling towards rock bottom, and more like you are racing towards it, without any intention of bouncing back.

Indeed, some people hit rock bottom and never bounce back. When everything looks so down and dark, people tend to believe that there is no opportunity they deserve, that even if they tried, there is no coming back from this stage. It is crucial that you realize the darkness is just your internal resistance to change. No matter how impossible it might seem from the bottom, you can still climb back up. You need to reflect on the good times, not spend too long regretting your mistakes, and focus on the realization that you can have a better life.

The choice is in your hands. If you believe you deserve better, you are more likely to look for ways to improve your situation. At this point, when you look within, you will be able to see what it is that is stopping you. If it is your bad habits, you will need to try to replace them, and remember to ask for help when you need it. If it is a negative worldview, you need to dig deep and look for a positive memory which contradicts it. Whatever is stopping you from moving forward, remember that you don't have to fight it alone. Ask your friends and family to help, and don't be ashamed of seeking professional help either.

RECOMMENDED STRATEGIES/PRINCIPLES

(A) ✓ **Focus on purpose**

(B) ✓ **Decide on your identity**

(C) ✓ **Surround yourself with people who push you forward**

(E) ✓ **Accept that it is your right to be happy**

(X) ✓ **Don't isolate yourself**

(J) ✓ **Ask close friends and family for help:**
You don't have to climb up from rock bottom on your own. Make use of this strategy. These individuals want to help you, so give them a chance to do that.

(O) ✓ **Seek professional help (e.g. therapy, counseling)**

(P) ✓ **Double-check your interpretations:**
At this stage, your mindset and thoughts are working against you. This strategy will help you get the objective truth about yourself.

(T) ✓ **Stand up and assert your right to a good life**

(G) ✓ **Take care of your body: eat, sleep, and move**

(H) ✓ **Pray, play, meditate, and spend more time in nature**

(U) ✓ **Recall the times you triumphed over challenges**

(R) ✓ **Be patient with yourself:**
It can be difficult not to fall deeper down the hole at this stage, but you need to be patient. With time, things will improve. You just need to put in the effort and ask for help.

(S) ✓ **Face your fears**

(Q) ✓ **Do what you love**

(I) ✓ **Watch motivational videos and speeches**

(F) ✓ **Read books and listen to stories about people who inspire you**

(K) ✓ **Consider hiring a Life Coach**

(L) ✓ **Attend self-development seminars**

(M) ✓ **Make a list of your positive contributions**

(N) ✓ **Volunteer for a cause you care about**

(V) ✓ **Take care of a pet or garden**

(W) ✓ **Keep a daily journal of any positive thoughts or actions**

(Y) ✓ **Do things you have always wanted to do, even if you don't feel like it**

(Z) ✓ **Travel to and visit as many new places as you can**

YOU: MALEVOLENT

What happens beyond rock bottom? The answer to that is severe self-sabotage. You may resist your own growth, not solely by escaping your issues, but by engaging in dangerous and destructive behaviors (e.g. abusing drugs, engaging in self-hurting practices, breaking the law). This sabotages not only your growth but also your survival. This is considered reckless. Life may have dealt you a really bad hand and you simply do not see the possibility of a fulfilled life. Your worldviews at this stage may be self-destructive, and you may not even believe that there is a point to life. You may reach a stage where you don't care if you lose your life, and you might start to actively seek out danger.

At this stage, you may not only deny yourself opportunities, but you may sabotage all facets of your life. You may ruin your relationships, ranging from the professional setting (e.g. clients, coworkers, subordinates, bosses, etc.) all the way to your closest family members and friends. At this stage, you may find it difficult to pick yourself up. Deep, deep inside, you might wish that you could move on, but it can feel like it is impossible to do that. You may have given up and decided not to even try to find your way back. At this intensity, the roots of your resistance have gone too deep down into the soil.

In the ocean analogy, the weight is immense, but you don't fight it. Sometimes, you let go of yourself, coming close to the point of drowning. At times, resisting your body's request for air. You may contemplate not making your way up to the surface, and only push yourself up enough to snatch a breath and repeat.

You should not allow yourself to reach this stage. If you feel yourself resisting on other intensities, then work towards floating, and then swimming forward. It takes time, will, and believing that you don't deserve to resist yourself at this, or lesser intensities. Remember that if you are convinced you deserve a fulfilled life, others can help you through your difficulties. When those around you offer their help, don't deny them. Also, decide to feed that deep,

deep urge to get your life back on track. Of course, there are times when you will need professional help, give it a shot and try. Make a decision to change, and then seek out guidance from trusted and capable others so they may help you navigate through these challenging, self-defeating times. You just need to find the light of motivation, which at this stage may be a glimmer in the darkness, but focus on it and walk towards it. With help and guidance you can work to uproot the resistance and then take measures to live the life you deserve.

It will be tiring, and may seem nearly impossible, to overcome this resistance, but even the most deeply rooted tree can be dug up.

"Happiness can be found, even in the darkest of times, if one only remembers to turn on the light"

– J. K. Rowling

RECOMMENDED STRATEGIES/PRINCIPLES

(A) ✓ **Focus on purpose**

(X) ✓ **Don't isolate yourself:**
When you find yourself doing so, seek out a person you know will listen or understand. At times, this would be a neutral party such as a counselor or therapist. It may not be your intention to push people away — you may not wish to be alone — but your actions might isolate you. Be careful.

(C) ✓ **Surround yourself with people who push you forward**

(J) ✓ **Ask close friends and family for help**

(O) ✓ **Seek professional help (e.g. therapy, counseling)**

(P) ✓ **Double-check your interpretations**

(B) ✓ **Decide on your identity**

(E) ✓ **Accept that it is your right to be happy**

(R) ✓ **Be patient with yourself**

(U) ✓ **Recall the times you triumphed over challenges**

(S) ✓ **Face your fears**

(M) ✓ **Make a list of your positive contributions**

(T) ✓ **Stand up and assert your right to a good life**

(G) ✓ **Take care of your body: eat, sleep, and move:** Give this strategy the time it deserves. In this scenario, you will be actively working against this strategy, so make sure you focus on getting your life back on track, one step at a time.

(H) ✓ **Pray, play, meditate, and spend more time in nature**

(V) ✓ **Take care of a pet or garden**

(K) ✓ **Consider hiring a Life Coach**

(F) ✓ **Read books and listen to stories about people who inspire you**

(I) ✓ **Watch motivational videos and speeches**

(L) ✓ **Attend self-development seminars**

(W) ✓ **Keep a daily journal of any positive thoughts or actions**

CONCLUSION

"Enemy" is a loaded word, and for a good reason. It is a word that instills thoughts of tension, conflict, danger, threat, etc. Enemies can take an emotional toll on us, ranging from slight discomfort all the way to intense fear and anger.

When we hear the word, many of us may be taken back to a professional or personal incident, while others may be in denial about having enemies. I hope that after reading this book, you have formed a clearer idea about who could possibly be an opponent or an enemy, but I also hope that you have widened your definition of an opponent. Remember that an opponent, in the broadest sense of the term, includes your rivals, competitors, antagonists, adversaries, etc., with major differences and nuances between each term.

"Every single being, even those who are hostile to us, is just as afraid of suffering as we are, and seeks happiness in the same way we do. Every person has the same right as we do to be happy and not to suffer. So let's take care of others wholeheartedly, of both our friends and our enemies. That is the basis of true compassion."

– Dalai Lama XIV

I hope this book has helped you better understand how to deal with opponents. Remember that being unable to properly maneuver your resistance can mean not only the end of your initiative, but it can also threaten your survival in the system. It takes careful employment of strategies, principles, and techniques to minimize resistance and achieve success for your initiative. A one-size-fits-all strategy does not exist, and you need to tailor your strategies to suit whatever role and intensity you are dealing with. I hope that the categorization of your enemies/opponents by role and intensity will help you choose how best to introduce positive leadership acts, and how to deal with your opponents' resistance in the most compassionate way possible.

Remember that your opponents are rarely trying to harm you personally. They are resisting your intervention because it is threatening their dimensions [9-Ds] (loyalties, values, world views, insecurities, hopes and dreams, commitments, agendas, hungers, and experiences). Don't forget that your opponent is also human, and has the right to resist what you are doing if they feel they are not benefiting, or if they are negatively affected, regardless of the other benefits your initiative may bring.

Sometimes you will need to compromise or negotiate, sometimes you will need to think creatively, understand your opponent's perspective, and over-communicate so you find mutually beneficial solutions. Remember that you want to push the system towards survival and growth. Keep the head-on confrontations and conflicts as last resorts, and only use them when there is no other way. The ultimate strategy remains trying to turn your opponents and enemies into your supporters, remembering to approach them with compassion and empathy.

I sincerely hope that you have read this book thoroughly, and that you will consider it your go-to consultant when you think about exercising leadership and introducing a purposeful and beneficial change.

Perhaps the key goal of this book has been to convey the importance of a fulfilling journey towards survival and growth for yourself and for your system. Remember that an act of leadership requires a purpose that serves others, allowing them to live a fulfilled and happy life.

"It is easy enough to be friendly to one's friends. But to befriend the one who regards himself your enemy is the quintessence of true religion. The other is mere business"

– *Mahatma Gandhi*

NOTES

PART ONE

Introduction

Britannica, The Editors of Encyclopaedia. "Nelson Mandela." *Encyclopædia Britannica*, Encyclopædia Britannica, Inc., 15 Aug. 2018, www.britannica.com/biography/Nelson-Mandela.

Ewenstein, Boris, et al. "Changing Change Management." *McKinsey & Company*, July 2015, www.mckinsey.com/featured-insights/leadership/changing-change-management.

Global, CPP. "Workplace Conflict and How Businesses Can Harness It To Thrive." *CPP Conflict Report*, July 2008, http://img.en25.com/Web/CPP/Conflict_report.pdf.

History.com Staff. "Martin Luther King, Jr." *History.com*, A&E Television Networks, 2009, www.history.com/topics/black-history/martin-luther-king-jr.

History.com Staff. "Rosa Parks." *History.com*, A&E Television Networks, 2009, www.history.com/topics/black-history/rosa-parks.

Ilgaz, Zeynep. "Conflict Resolution: When Should Leaders Step In?" *Forbes*, Forbes Magazine, 15 May 2014, www.forbes.com/sites/85broads/2014/05/15/conflict-resolution-when-should-leaders-step-in/#d13a45933576.

Nanda, B.R. "Mahatma Gandhi." *Encyclopædia Britannica*, Encyclopædia Britannica, Inc., 10 May 2018, www.britannica.com/biography/Mahatma-Gandhi.

"The Bus Boycott Sparks a Movement." *Last Days & Legacy | The Martin Luther King Jr. Center for Nonviolent Social Change*, www.thekingcenter.org/bus-boycott-sparks-movement.

Vaidya, Chunibhai. "Assassination of Mahatma Gandhi: The Facts Behind." *Students' Projects: The Story of Gandhi,* www.mkgandhi.org/assassin.htm.

Chapter 1:

Kouly, Michael. *Wide Open: The Tens Eyes of Leadership*. 1st ed., Michael Kouly, 2018.

Chapter 2:

Collin, Catherine, et al. *The Psychology Book: Big Ideas Simply Explained*. DK Publishers, 2012.

Duignan, Brian. "Gun Control in the U.S." *Encyclopædia Britannica*, Encyclopædia Britannica, Inc., www.britannica.com/story/gun-control-in-the-us.

"Observational Learning" in Petri, Herbert L., and Charles N. Cofer. "Motivation." *Encyclopædia Britannica*, Encyclopædia Britannica, Inc., 28 Sept. 2017, www.britannica.com/topic/motivation/Behavioristic-approaches-to-motivation#ref362905.

Schuler, A. J. (2003). "Overcoming resistance to change: Top ten reasons for change resistance." www.SchulerSolutions.com

Chapter 3:

Aesop. *The Oak Tree and The Reed. Aesop's Fables.* A new translation by Laura Gibbs, Oxford University Press, 2008.

Bureau, Our. "Mahatma's Sons Opposed Death Penalty for Godse, Apte. I Belong to That School of Thought: Gopal Gandhi." *@Businessline*, Business Line, 18 July 2017, www.thehindubusinessline.com/news/mahatmas-sons-opposed-death-penalty-for-godse-apte-i-belong-to-that-school-of-thought-gopal-gandhi/article9774957.ece.

Brandon, Rick, and Marty Seldman. *Survival of the Savvy: High-Integrity Political Tactics for Career and Company Success.* Free Press, 2004.

"Emotional Intelligence." *Psychology Today*, Sussex Publishers, www.psychologytoday.com/us/basics/emotional-intelligence.

Gawande, Atul. *The Checklist Manifesto: How To Get Things Right.* Penguin Random House, 2014.

"Get up and WOOP." *WOOP My Life*, woopmylife.org/new-page-3.

History.com Staff. "Selma to Montgomery March." *History.com*, A&E Television Networks, 2010, www.history.com/topics/black-history/selma-montgomery-march.

Kavanagh, Kevin T., et al. "Estimating Hospital-Related Deaths Due to Medical Error." *Journal of Patient Safety*, vol. 13, no. 1, Mar. 2017, pp. 1–5., doi:10.1097/pts.0000000000000364.

Klein, Gary. "Performing a Project Premortem." *Harvard Business Review*, 1 Aug. 2014, hbr.org/2007/09/performing-a-project-premortem.

Oettingen, Gabriele. *Rethinking Positive Thinking: inside the New Science of Motivation.* Current, 2015.

Russell-Jones, Neil. *The Managing Change Pocketbook.* Management Pocketbooks, 1995.

Shepardson, David. "2017 Safest Year on Record for Commercial Passenger Air Travel: Groups." *Reuters*, Thomson Reuters, 1 Jan. 2018, www. reuters.com/article/us-aviation-safety/2017-safest-year-on-record-for-commercial-passenger-air-travel-groups-idUSKBN1EQ17L.

Shilling, Dianne. "10 Steps To Effective Listening." *Forbes*, Forbes Magazine, July 2014, www.forbes.com/sites/womensmedia/2012/11/09/10-steps-to-effective-listening/.

Syed, Matthew. *Black Box Thinking: Why Most People Never Learn from Their Mistakes--but Some Do.* Portfolio Penguin, 2016.

Zenko, Micah. *Red Team How to Succeed by Thinking like the Enemy.* Basic Books, a Member of the Perseus Books Group, 2015.

Chapter 4:

Zacharek, Stephanie, et al. "TIME Person of the Year 2017: The Silence Breakers." *TIME*, TIME, time.com/time-person-of-the-year-2017-silence-breakers/.

PART TWO

Axelrod, Alan, and James Holtje. *201 Ways to Deal with Difficult People.* McGraw-Hill,   1997

Axelrod, Alan. *Profiles in Audacity: Great Decisions and How They Were Made.* Sterling Pub. Co., 2006.

Bloom, Linda, and Charlie Bloom. "Honoring the Rule of Reciprocation." *Psychology Today*, Sussex Publishers, 10 Oct. 2015, www.psychologytoday.com/us/blog/stronger-the-broken-places/201510/honoring-the-rule-reciprocation.

Brinkman, Rick, and Rick Kirschner. *Dealing with People You Can't Stand: How to Bring out the Best in People at Their Worst.* McGraw-Hill, 2002.

Kanter, Rosabeth Moss. "Ten Reasons People Resist Change." *Harvard Business Review*, 25 Sept. 2012, hbr.org/2012/09/ten-reasons-people-resist-chang.

Krause, Donald G. *Sun Tzu The Art of War for Executives*. Nicholas Brealey Publishing, 1995.

Stevenson, Richard W. "British Air Tells Virgin Air It's Sorry and Pays $945,000." *The New York Times*, The New York Times, 12 Jan. 1993, www.nytimes.com/1993/01/12/business/british-air-tells-virgin-air-it-s-sorry-and-pays-945000.html.

Brandon, Rick, and Marty Seldman. *Survival of the Savvy: High-Integrity Political Tactics for Career and Company Success*. Free Press, 2004.

PART THREE

Chapter 2:

"Amsterdam Fire Chief Leen Schaap 'Had Death Threats from Staff' - BBC News." *BBC*, BBC, 17 July 2018, www.bbc.co.uk/news/world-europe-44858538.

Chapter 6:

Douglas, Karen M. "Deindividuation." *Encyclopædia Britannica*, Encyclopædia Britannica, Inc., 3 Aug. 2017, www.britannica.com//topic/deindividuation.

Chapter 7:

Morris, Errol, director. *The Fog of War: Eleven Lessons from the Life of Robert S. McNamara*. Sony Pictures Classics, 2003.

Chapter 8:

"20 Scientific Reasons to Start Meditating Today." *Psychology Today,* Sussex Publishers, www.psychologytoday.com/us/blog/feeling-it/201309/20-scientific-reasons-start-meditating-today.

Chillag, Amy. "Why Adults Should Play, Too." *CNN*, Cable News Network, 2 Nov. 2017, edition.cnn.com/2017/11/02/health/why-adults-should-play-too/index.html.

Hayes, Kim. "5 Health Benefits of Gardening and Planting." *AARP,* 14 June 2017, www.aarp.org/health/healthy-living/info-2017/health-benefits-of-gardening-fd.html.

Holland, Emily. "7 Health Benefits of Owning a Pet." *The Chopra Center*, 13 Feb. 2017, chopra.com/articles/7-health-benefits-of-owning-a-pet.

Lazarus, Clifford N. "How to Stop Self-Fulfilling Prophecies of Failure." *Psychology Today*, Sussex Publishers, 29 Mar. 2018, www.psychologytoday.com/us/blog/think-well/201803/how-stop-self-fulfilling-prophecies-failure.

Loria, Kevin. "Being Outside Can Improve Memory, Fight Depression, and Lower Blood Pressure - Here Are 12 Science-Backed Reasons to Spend More Time Outdoors." *Business Insider,* Business Insider, 22 Apr. 2018, www.businessinsider.com/why-spending-more-time-outside-is-healthy-2017-7#walking-in-nature-could-improve-your-short-term-memory-1.

Naprawa, Amanda Z. "Benefits of Gardening, How Community Gardens Improve Nutrition." *@Berkeleywellness*, 23 Aug. 2016, www.berkeleywellness.com/healthy-eating/nutrition/article/community-gardens-growing-good-health.

Schnall, Simone, et al. "Elevation Leads to Altruistic Behavior." *Psychological Science,* vol. 21, no. 3, 2010, pp. 315–320., doi:10.1177/0956797609359882.

Seppälä, Emma. "Connectedness & Health: The Science of Social Connection." *The Center for Compassion and Altruism Research and Education,* 27 June 2017, ccare.stanford.edu/uncategorized/connectedness-health-the-science-of-social-connection-infographic/.

Smith, Jen. "The Benefits of Hiring a Life Coach." *The Huffington Post*, TheHuffingtonPost.com, 6 Dec. 2017, www.huffingtonpost.com/jen-smith/the-benefits-of-hiring-a_b_10022676.html.

The Editors of Encyclopaedia Britannica. "Declaration of Independence." *Encyclopædia Britannica*, Encyclopædia Britannica, Inc., 25 Apr. 2018, www.britannica.com/topic/Declaration-of-Independence.

Yeung, Jerf W. K., et al. "Volunteering and Health Benefits in General Adults: Cumulative Effects and Forms." *BMC Public Health*, vol. 18, no. 1, Nov. 2017, doi:10.1186/s12889-017-4561-8.

ABOUT THE AUTHOR

Michael Kouly began his career as a Reuters war journalist. He covered armed conflicts that involved, Israel, Lebanon, Syria, Iran, Hezbullah, Islamic extremists, terrorism, the United States, Kuwait, Iraq and others... He also covered musical concerts, fashion shows and car racing.

Writing about wars, geopolitics, international diplomacy, and global events offered Michael unique opportunities to witness, analyze and write about leadership at the highest levels: where bad leadership meant the loss of thousands of lives and good leadership led to avoiding wars, saving lives, and rebuilding shattered countries.

Michael also exercised corporate leadership over a period of 30 years as he led the growth of regional and international businesses. He is a three-time CEO and president at organizations like Reuters, Orbit, and Cambridge Institute for Global Leadership, managing people in more than 20 countries.

Over the span of his career, Michael made some good decisions that generated remarkable success and also some not so good decisions that offered valuable lessons on what works and what doesn't when exercising leadership — emphasizing the mindset of "you either win or learn".

From as far back as he can remember, Michael has been fascinated by leadership. He has spent his life learning about leadership, purpose, and strategy by practicing them, watching others lead, and by conducting extensive research on the art and science of mobilizing people and organizations towards growth and noble purposes.

Michael is a World Bank Fellow, author, and keynote speaker about leadership, strategy, purpose, and international politics. He is the founder of the Kouly Institute and the creator of unique Executive Leadership Programs, that have been delivered to thousands of top business executives, NGOs, and government leaders worldwide.

He also dedicates time to various non-profit organizations such as the Middle East Leadership Academy (MELA), Central Eurasia Leadership Academy (CELA), South East Asia Leadership Academy (SEALA) and Leaders Across Boarders (LAB).

His calling is to help people, organizations and countries lead purpose driven lives.

Michael studied at Harvard and Princeton Universities, and is an advisor to state leaders.

OTHER BOOKS BY THE AUTHOR

WIDE OPEN

Leadership is a dangerous enterprise, but the rewards are valuable. This book is designed to be your companion in your thrilling journey of remarkable survival and outstanding growth.

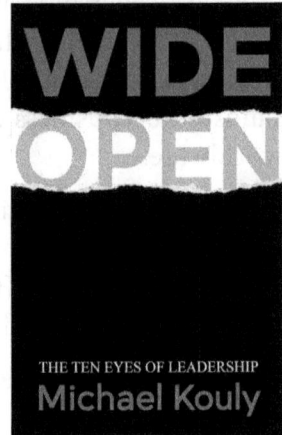

THE TEN EYES OF LEADERSHIP
Michael Kouly

THIS UNIQUE AND ILLUMINATING BOOK WILL OPEN YOUR EYES WIDE, SO YOU LEARN MORE ABOUT:

- **Authority:** You are surrounded by authority figures such as parents, bosses, CEOs, presidents, or governments. As you already know, not understanding how to deal with authority is risky.

- **Enemies:** Enemies are a fact of life. They could be passive or aggressive. Enemies want to undermine you and your acts of leadership. Not understanding how to deal with enemies is dangerous.

- **Understanding Yourself and Others:** It is hard to survive and grow and to lead yourself without understanding what drives your thoughts, feelings, words, actions, behaviors, dreams, and ambitions. It is impossible to lead others without understanding them first.

- **Understanding Systems:** We live and work in systems. A system can be a family, team, company, community, city, country or the world. Systems have their unique psychology and rules. Not understanding systems will put your existence and progress at risk, as you may be excluded or isolated from the group that you belong to.

BOOK 1 OF THE
SELF-LEADERSHIP BOOK SERIES

FINDING YOUR HUMMUS

This book will provide you, your colleagues, family and friends with insights about life and business to unleash your personal and organizational power.

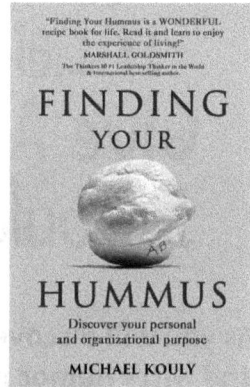

"Finding Your Hummus is a WONDERFUL recipe book for life. Read it and learn to enjoy the experience of living!"
MARSHALL GOLDSMITH
The Thinkers 50 #1 Leadership Thinker in the World & International best-selling author.

FINDING
YOUR

HUMMUS
Discover your personal
and organizational purpose

MICHAEL KOULY

• Shift happens in life and business, are you ready?

• What is the prime philosophy behind starting a business of growth and sustainable success?

• Do you, your people and business have a guiding purpose? This book is about finding your calling.

• Do you have a personal and organizational strategy to fulfill your purpose? This book is about self-awareness, self-motivation and self-leadership that together can achieve self-fulfillment.

• How do you deal with competition, conflict and confusion? This book is rich with empowering inspirational quotes that generate strength and lead to self-actualization.

• What is the mindset to lead a life of resilience, abundance and significance? This book is about finding your passion and discovering your way of living a purpose driven life.

BOOK 2 OF THE
SELF-LEADERSHIP BOOK SERIES

If I didn't
Give A ....
I would...

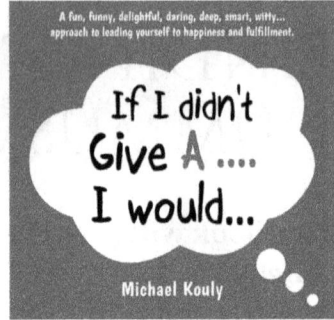

A fun, funny, delightful, daring, deep, smart, witty...
approach to leading yourself to happiness and fulfillment.

If I didn't
Give A ....
I would...

Michael Kouly

As you will discover,this entertaining book of insightful and witty humor is not like other self leadership books.

WHILE ENJOYING THE EXPERIENCE OF THIS BOOK, YOU'LL ALSO:

- **Blow off steam:** We all have personal issues, challenges, and obstacles that accumulate stress that must be released to keep us in a state of peak motivation.

- **Know yourself:** Sometimes an entire life is spent being stuck at the expense of personal, business, social and relational opportunities for success. Self-discovery is the first step to the healing, actualization, and optimization of your life.

- **Reflect:** Recognizing your priorities, what you really want and what matters most to you is the key to your growth in all aspects of your life.

- **Decide:** To solve problems and catch opportunities, decisions are needed. This book will help you decide and act to expand your potential in a fun, playful, smart and effective way.

- **Lead:** True leadership starts with the self where smart and effective strategy, action and execution are the keys to the growth of our capacity.

BOOK 3 OF THE
SELF-LEADERSHIP BOOK SERIES

MUTE

It doesn't matter who you are or what you do. You carry voices in your head, voices that are always talking to you. Some of the voices whisper, others shout. Some make logical arguments, others create dramas.

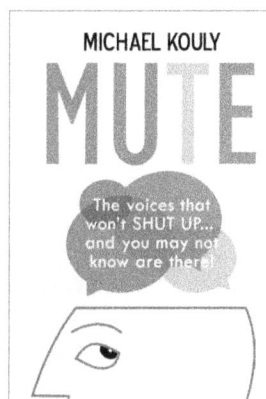

Do you know the voices in your head? Do you know where they've come from and how they are controlling you?

As soon as you meet a person, you begin to carry their voice with you. This starts with your parents, loved ones, hated ones, bosses, spouses, heroes, and everyone who is or was significant in your life.

What do these voices want? They want you to live life their way.

What about your freedom? Well, this book is about exactly that: exercising your freedom.

We will look at how you can willingly listen to the encouraging voices and mute the negative ones.

We want to give you the tools to live a happy, successful and fulfilling life that is aligned with your personal purpose and best self.

Life is a blink. There is no time to waste living under the influence of negative voices. Read this book, share it with others, and learn how to lead a life of freedom and meaning so you can become a beautiful voice in the heads of those around you.

In The Making...
New Titles
by Michael Kouly

FORGET
HAPPINESS

**Read this book and fill
your life with joy.**

You deserve it.

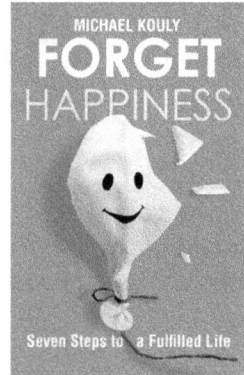

This unique book offers a practical, clear, and realistic roadmap for reaching fulfillment. It is a pleasant and easy read that will lift your spirits, encourage you, and help you discover and love your beautiful self so that you may live a life of purpose, meaning, beauty, and joy.

We live in the most comfortable and exciting time in history, and yet stress, anxiety, depression, suffering, and inner emptiness are greater than ever before, even among the rich and successful. Happiness has become a tired buzzword. An increasing number of self-help books idealize and promise it, yet it remains frustratingly elusive.

This book asks you to stop looking for happiness because happiness cannot be found on its own. Happiness is an outcome, a result, a consequence of living a life of fulfillment. When you align your life with your true self and feel fulfilled, deep happiness, joy, and inner peace will become part of your natural state.

BEYOND STRATEGY

WHY "BEYOND STRATEGY"?

Many people find strategy intimidating, complex, or abstract, but it doesn't have to be.

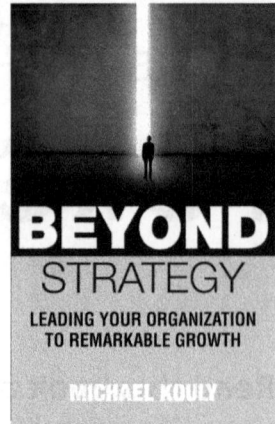

BEYOND STRATEGY
LEADING YOUR ORGANIZATION
TO REMARKABLE GROWTH
MICHAEL KOULY

This book presents a new way of thinking about strategy that is uniquely based upon the Purpose-Driven Growth Model (PDG), in which your organization's purpose and profitability is key to guiding its growth.

- It explores strategy concisely and thoughtfully, examining what the concept encompasses and how strategies can be constructed in a fast-changing and uncertain world.

- It illustrates the differences between strategies that flourish and strategies that languish, and delves into the reasons driving each outcome.

- It offers comprehensive thinking, and tools which view strategy holistically, emphasizing how to lead organizations towards sustainable growth and exceptional performance.

The PDG Model sketches out a practical hybrid of strategy and leadership, that must be unified to fulfill organzational purpose, create growth, and deliver profits. Leadership without strategy is futile, and strategy without leadership is doomed. The two must synchronize to produce results.